JOURNAL FOR THE STUDY OF THE OLD TESTAMENT
SUPPLEMENT SERIES
102

JSOT Press
Sheffield

THE PRAYERS OF DAVID

(Psalms 51–72)

Studies in the Psalter, II

Michael Goulder

Journal for the Study of the Old Testament
Supplement Series 102

Published by JSOT Press
JSOT Press is an imprint of
Sheffield Academic Press Ltd
The University of Sheffield
343 Fulwood Road
Sheffield S10 3BP
England

Typeset by Sheffield Academic Press
and
Printed in Great Britain
by Billing & Sons Ltd
Worcester

British Library Cataloguing in Publication Data

Goulder, M.D. (Michael Douglas)
The prayers of David (Psalms 51–72).
1. Bible. O.T. Psalms. Selections—Critical studies
I. Title II. Series
223.206

ISSN 0309-0787
ISBN 1-85075-258-3

CONTENTS

PREFACE

My fascination with the Prayers of David goes back nearly half a century to my education at Eton. It was the War, and morning service in College Chapel was enlivened once or twice a year by a visit from the King and Queen when residing at Windsor Castle. It was in some way known to the School authorities that Her Majesty's favourite psalm was no. 68, an ancient Hebrew war song of great power and obscurity; and whenever the royal party attended we sang Psalm 68 *con animo*, to the majestic organ-playing of Dr. Ley. The scene is still evocative, with overtones both tragic and comic. There between the soaring perpendicular pillars, raised in the Wars of the Roses between the two battles of St. Alban's, were lifted the voices of those who were to hazard their lives at Anzio and Arnhem: the same time-honoured words were chanted forth, in the frail confidence that the God of battles would stand by the righteous, that is, the singers. But even then I owned to some doubts. 'Though ye have lien among the pots', we sang, 'yet shall ye be as the wings of a dove, That is covered with silver wings, and her feathers like gold. When the Almighty scattered kings for their sake, Then were they as white as snow in Zalmon'. I did not know what these words meant, though I had every expectation that their meaning was known to the School chaplains; I was also unclear what we were doing in singing them, though I felt that in some opaque way they were doing harm to the Germans.

In time I became the Rector of St Christopher's, Withington, in the diocese of Manchester, and there, following the Prayer Book, we sang Psalm 68 at Evensong on Whitsunday. Here again it was rendered *fortissimo*, with a three-figure congregation; but now the moral noose was tighter, for I still did not know the meaning of the words, nor why we were singing them. However, I still had confidence that there were Old Testament scholars in the University of Manchester who could explain them. It was not until I became a University Lecturer myself that I began to realise that no one could explain them. Then, one morning in 1970, I thought I saw what lay behind them.

In the years since 1970 I have developed a new general theory of the Psalms—different from, though indebted to, the old Davidic theory, the historical theory of the 19th century, and the *Gattung*-theories of our own century—that of Gunkel with mainly personal psalms, and that of Mowinckel with mainly national psalms. Its distinctiveness rests in its attempt to honour critically the old biblical traditions of interpretation—the collections in which the psalms are gathered (as Book IV, or the Psalms of Asaph); the order in which they stand; and the technical, topographical, musical and historical notes which are given in the Headings or body (Selah) of each piece. The men who wrote these Headings, or who set the psalms in this order, may have misunderstood the intention of the original authors; but they may also know more than we do, and we are surely unwise to neglect the sole stream of commentary which links the psalmists to the learned commentators of the Jewish academies and the Church. I reached the common conclusion that most of the historical notes were late and worthless for the psalms' original meaning; but I also reached the uncommon conclusion that the collections and the order of the psalms in them were the keys of interpretation, *sine quibus non*.

I have accordingly set my hand to a series of commentaries based on this principle. The JSOT published the first, *The Psalms of the Sons of Korah*, in 1982: a proposal that the Korah psalms (42–49, 84–85, 87–88) were composed for use at the autumn festival at Dan, and provided a serial psalmody to cover the week's celebrations. The Korah psalms were (in my view) older than most of those in Book I, and also fewer, clearer and more interesting. I delayed writing a second volume, partly in order to assimilate any criticisms, and partly so as to finish a major work on St Luke's Gospel. This is the second volume now, *The Prayers of David*, covering almost all the remaining psalms in Book II, 51–72. I hope to write a third, shorter book on the Psalms of Asaph (50, 73–83), and will then have covered almost all the Second and Third Books: I will not look further ahead than that, though the general theory provides for the whole Psalter. I have given the book a subtitle, *Studies in the Psalter*, to mark my debt to Mowinckel, and also to mark the distinction; for his illuminating writings remain substantially Studies in the Psalms, without any significant relation to their ordering or grouping.

It is this present volume which promises to be at once the most absorbing and the most scandalous of my *Studies*: for its conclusion is that the Prayers were indeed written 'for David', in his lifetime, by one of his closest attendants, a priest; that they cover the last years of his life serially from the death of Uriah to the succession of Solomon; and that the Selahs in the text provided opportunities for the recitation of sections of the earliest form of the 'Succession Narrative'. Such a result is far too interesting to be acceptable; even those who do not suspect me of fundamentalist biblicism, or of seeking cheap publicity, must wonder why I should labour to resurrect a theory nearly two hundred years dead. But the answer to such wise scepsis can only be that I have found the evidence overwhelming, and I trust that my reader will find the same.

We know the rich panorama of our own world by direct apprehension; that of even a century ago we see through a glass. As the distance increases, so does the distortion of the pane of our ignorance and our false presuppositions. Before the Tudors, how many people can we claim to know? For historical knowledge in the personal sense three things are needful: enough archaeological discovery to give us confidence of the background; a serial account of the events of the time, written within a generation; and somebody's first-hand, red-blooded, uncamouflaged response to those events. A moment's reflection will show how rare is such a shaft of personal light: the mediaeval chronicles and the Paston Letters, the Acts of the Apostles and the Letters of Paul. Even letters may be written for the eyes of an Emperor, or the public; even autobiographies may be concerned with the quest for more territory, or for God. But here, from all but three millennia ago, comes such a shaft of light. We have excavations enough to know something of the physical basis of life in David's reign over Israel in the tenth century BC. We have an account of the events between Absalom's rising in 2 Sam. 15.7 and David's return to Jerusalem in 2 Sam. 20.3, written soon after David's death by one of his 'recorders', and incorporated a generation later into the 'Succession Narrative'. In Pss. 51–72 we have the contemporary personal response to these events, written by a participant, sometimes in the king's name, sometimes in his own; and these are *t^epillôṯ*, Prayers, in which his heart is opened to God with all the devotion, hatred, loyalty, fear, desperation and triumph of which he is capable. What a treasure have we overlooked! Blessed are our eyes, for they see what many scholars and righteous men desired to see, and saw not.

My warm thanks are due to the many classes to whom I have taught the psalms, and not least to the Benedictine nuns at Stanbrook Abbey; to the School of Theology, Claremont, which invited me to give the chapter on the 68th Psalm as the Knopf-Hill Lecture in 1987; and especially to my colleague and friend John Eaton, who has kindly read the text, and made invaluable suggestions. The translation of the psalms printed before each section of the commentary is from RV mg (1881): variations are signalled, normally by the Hebrew in parenthesis.

August, 1989 Michael Goulder

Chapter 1

THE PRAYERS OF DAVID AND THE SUCCESSION NARRATIVE

Of the 150 psalms in the Hebrew Psalter, seventy-three bear in their headings the name of David (*l^eḏāwiḏ*); but these seventy-three are not spread randomly. There is only one David psalm (86) in Book III (73–89), two (101, 103) in Book IV (90–106), and a scatter in Book V (107–150). But the first two books both contain what appear to be collections of David psalms. All the psalms in Book I (1–41) carry David's name except for 1, 2, 10 and 33. Book II opens with a series of psalms 'of the sons of Korah' (42, 44–49) with 'a psalm of Asaph' as Psalm 50; but the rest of the book (51–72) consists mainly of David psalms (51–65, 68–70), and 72 bears Solomon's name (*liŠ^elōmōh*). At the end of 72, and so at the end of Book II, there is a short rubric, 'The Prayers of David the son of Jesse are ended' (72.20).

Franz Delitzsch (I, 19f.) thought that 'the Prayers of David' extended over the whole span from 3 to 72:[1] but this would involve an insertion of Korah and Asaph psalms into the Prayers, and also the ignoring of the Books division at 41. The latter is not trivial, because Book I shows an overwhelming preference for Yahweh over Elohim for God (272 times to 15), whereas the second David collection prefers Elohim (122 times to 23). Most more recent commentators therefore restrict 'the prayers of David' to the second collection, 51–72, and it is these psalms which are the subject of the present book. The description *t^epillôṯ* is suited to them: Hans-Joachim Kraus defines the word as 'a term for lamentation- and petitionary prayer' (I, xxiiif.), and many of them, especially 51–64, are psalms of this kind. It is clear that the rubricist understood 72 to be of the prayers of David despite the Solomon superscription (which might be later). It is not clear whether 66, 67 and 71, which do not bear David's name, were in the collection that he knew; that has to be determined from internal evidence, and I will so far anticipate my discussion of them as to say that they seem to me to belong in the collection from the beginning. There is Greek evidence for a David superscription to 67 and 71, and many Hebrew manuscripts take 71 as a continuation of 70. My understanding is that 'The Prayers of David' was a title for the collection 51–72.

We have no idea, if we are frank, of the age of the tradition associating 51–72 with David, or of its reliability; and its normal dismissal as 'secondary' rests upon the flimsiest basis. Hebrew psalmody goes back at least to the days of Deborah, and early tradition plausibly attributes occasional poems to David—the laments for Saul and Jonathan (2 Sam. 1.19-27) and for Abner (2 Sam. 3.33f.), and the Last Words (2 Sam. 23.1-7)—and a musical gift (1 Sam. 18.10; Amos 6.5). Psalm 18 has an especial link with David in that a closely similar version is given as his Song in 2 Sam. 22, and Davidic authorship in whole or in part, by the king or by his retinue, is still widely considered possible (Artur Weiser; John Eaton; Louis Jacquet; cf. Jacquet, I, p. 434). The D-historian attributes to David the institution of music in the Temple worship from the begining (2 Sam. 6.5), and Nehemiah saw himself as restoring Davidic musical worship at the Return (Neh. 12.36; cf. 12.24, 45f.). Twelve psalms mention the king (2, 18, 20, 21, 28, 45, 61, 63, 72, 84, 89, 110), and many more are argued for today; so some of the Psalter, especially of the first two books, goes back at least to the time of the monarchy. The Davidic tradition is pervasive and unchallenged, being received with enthusiasm by the Chronicler (1 Chron. 15–16 especially) and on into Talmudic times (b. Pes. 117a; b. Bab. Bath. 14b; Cant. R.4; Eccl. R.7.19). Naturally, such a tradition cannot be accepted uncritically; but it might have been expected that the Psalter would have been treated in the same way as the prophecies of Isaiah, Jeremiah and Ezekiel. In each of their books critics have isolated a core of oracles which can be attributed to the prophet himself, while noting signs of later expansions by his successors. The analogy would suggest, it might be thought, that a similar procedure had been followed with the psalms: that somewhere in the Psalter there is a core of Davidic psalms, and that the sons of Korah, Asaph and others have added to these and perhaps amended them.

Why then has this analogy not been followed, or indeed, in modern times, considered? It arises from the greater ambiguity of the material, and from the accident of the development of psalms scholarship. The Prophets may mention the Assyrians or the

Chaldaeans, king Jehoiakim or the River Chebar; the psalmists speak more easily of their enemies and evil-doers unspecified. Until the beginning of the nineteenth century the Davidic tradition was accepted universally in Christian as in Jewish scholarship: indeed, not just the seventy-three David-psalms but the entire Psalter was commonly ascribed to him. The collapse of this consensus came with the commentary of W.M.L. de Wette in 1811.

Before de Wette it was already seen, for instance by Johann Eichhorn, that some psalms contained references to the fall of Jerusalem or the Exile, and that others contained 'Chaldaisms': hence the theory that all the psalms were written by David was wrong, and sometimes the Headings were in error, where such psalms were attributed to either David or his musicians. What de Wette did was to doubt the Davidic tradition even when there were no reasons of this kind: with his critical principles all the other David psalms became 'problematisch' (p. 20). He pointed out quite reasonably that the prefix *l*^{e}- did not have to mean 'by David', but might mean 'for' or 'about'. But his critical principles were to observe the 'uniformity' of so many of the psalms, especially of the laments, and to maintain that 'no poet repeats himself who can write an elegy like that on Saul and Jonathan'. The criterion is thus an aesthetic one. The Israelites had much *Unglück* in their history, especially in the exile, and they comforted themselves by producing imitations of the Davidic originals (p. 24). Thus a psalm like 69 is an imitation of 22, and 70 is of 40.13-17: in fact it is virtually a reproduction of it, and the 'worst cases' were such copies as 108, which has a Davidic Heading. The criteria are extended a little in taking any artificial psalm (like the alphabetical psalms) or one with flowing expressions as late; while roughness of style and difficulty of content imply antiquity. But in his treatment of the Prayers, the fact that a psalm is a lament is enough to discount the Davidic tradition (as with 52 and 54). 51 is not Davidic because the last verses (on building the walls of Jerusalem) 'can only have been written in exile' (p. 341). 55 does not fit the normal view that the false friend was Ahitophel because speaker and friend are spoken of as living in the same city (p. 348). 53 is a copy of 14.

The modern reader will not perhaps be impressed by de Wette's aesthetic criteria; and if he is impressed by de Wette's logic over 51 and 55, I shall hope soon to disabuse him. But a scholar may have deeper convictions than those which he puts in his Introduction, and de Wette, who was thirty-one when the first edition of his *Commentar* was published, was not writing his first book. He had already in 1806-1807 produced his two-volume *Beiträge zur Einleitung in das Alte Testament*, in which he had shown that Chronicles was a late book, dependent on Samuel–Kings, and that the Pentateuch is a late compilation, and not written by Moses. These amazing innovations justify John Rogerson's admiration for him in *Old Testament Criticism in the Nineteenth Century*; and de Wette would not have been human if he had not felt that tradition was a shackle on the ankle of truth, and that the Davidic tradition had been as inhibiting to the true interpretation of the psalms as the Mosaic tradition had been for the Pentateuch. Subsequent generations have cheered the two moves equally; but I should not need to stress that there is a difference between the good reasons offered for dispensing with the Mosaic authorship of the Pentateuch and the rather subjective reasons for which he dismissed the Davidic connection with most of the Prayers.

De Wette opened a gate out of the over-cropped eighteenth century field of interpretation into the boundless pastures of possibility; and nineteenth-century critics followed him. Where he had been wisely agnostic about alternative historical settings, they were prepared to use their imaginations; and at times the joy of freedom came to resemble a stampede for the Maccabaean lake. Poor David was soon left behind. We may watch the progress of the movement to abandon him in the great mid-nineteenth century commentators: H. Ewald (1839/40), F. Hitzig (1835/36, 1863/65), J. Olshausen (1853), and H. Hupfeld (1855/62). Ewald and Hitzig still wished to retain a rump of Davidic psalms, seventeen in the case of Ewald, fourteen in Hitzig's second book, *Die Psalmen*, all of which were in Books I and II, while the whole of the last Books belonged in the Maccabaean period. But their reasons for such a judgment seemed to their successors no less subjective than de Wette's: Ewald appealed to 'the peculiarly powerful spirit and uniquely exalted stance' (Pt. 2, p. 1) of his selected group, which forbade ascription to anyone but David, and Hitzig preferred to abide with tradition where he could.

Justus Olshausen saw that these reasons were nothing but prejudices; and his was the first major commentary to dispense with the Davidic tradition completely. Unlike the other critics, he was not himself a theologian, and he thought that this exempted him from their presuppositions (p. I), perhaps with some justice; though the speed with which he justifies the corporate 'I' = Israel, or dismisses the evidence of the Prologue of ben Sira as an obstacle to his Maccabaean theory (p. 12), shows that he too could make prejudgments. Here are his comments on the Davidic tradition.

> 'However, it has long since been impossible for a more accurate, relatively unprejudiced treatment to escape the conclusion that this tradition, notwithstanding its age, is in almost all cases not to be held as trustworthy, in that by far the greatest part of those [seventy-three] psalms cannot possibly, from their content, stem from the times indicated by the tradition. But this means that the weight [of the Davidic Headings] is not merely weakened in general, but totally undermined, and their statements worthless for criticism, even for those psalms whose composition it is not completely impossible to date at the time indicated, and which could be partially understood from conditions at the time' (pp. 4f.).

The only scientific approach, according to Olshausen, was to match the conditions given in the psalm's text with those of a known period of Israelite history, and that meant in most cases the second century. Hupfeld was more sceptical about post-exilic conjectures, but he thought that not a single psalm could be ascribed to David with anything like certainty: since some of the Headings had proved unreliable, we should not trust any of them. Thus in fact neither Olshausen nor Hupfeld offers any argument against the Davidic tradition as such. They both discredit it by discrediting (some of) the historical notes, and by reversing the *onus probandi*; Ewald and Hitzig accepted the tradition unless it was proved wrong, they allowed no weight to a source so often found wanting. But their scepsis is as illogical as their predecessors' sentimentality: the presence of a number of forged Vermeers does not 'totally undermine' the tradition that there are genuine Vermeers.

The tide of the nineteenth century was with the radicals. Among major critics of the mid-century, only E.W. Hengstenberg (1842-47) and F. Delitzsch (1867) retained the Davidic authorship as often as they felt that it was possible. As the century wore on, late dating became more and more *de rigueur*; with T.K. Cheyne (1891) the major concern is the peril from North Arabia in the post-exilic period; with Bernhard Duhm (1899) it can be declared forthrightly that no unprejudiced critic could regard any psalm as pre-exilic, and he dated most after 170. Conservatives like A.F. Kirkpatrick were increasingly on the defensive.

The movement to reject the Davidic tradition rested on three general considerations. First, the Headings were not part of the psalms but secondary; and in a climate of opinion in which so much had been achieved by scepsis of tradition, it seemed good to regard the Davidic connection as due to no more than Jewish piety. In some cases the name of David (108, 139) or of his musician Asaph (79, 83) were attached to psalms obviously much later; and the attempts of those like Delitzsch and Kirkpatrick to follow the historical notes where possible seemed like a rearguard action, a casting about for some way to retain the tradition by unconvincing conjectures. Secondly, a better method seemed to be to hand: to look for links between the psalm text and Israel's history; so each critic could find his preferred setting with Hezekiah or Josiah, the returning exiles or the Antiochene oppression. Then, thirdly, there was the recurrent mention, or implying, of the Temple. Hardly any of the David psalms clearly imply the fall of Jerusalem or the exile, but the Temple is certainly often there; and the Temple was built by Solomon. This argument comes in almost every commentary, to this day, as a means of giving the David tradition the *coup de grâce*.

It may be suitable to examine this surprising argument at once. The biblical tradition does indeed say that David was forbidden by God to build a temple (2 Sam. 7), that David bought the site of the future temple from a farmer, whose threshing floor it had been (1 Chron. 21), and that Solomon built it after his death; but then we should hardly expect the D-historians to tell us that it was built as a replacement for, and on the site of, a Canaanite shrine to a heathen god. Even so, they seem to tell us that by accident, for in 2 Sam. 12.20 David washed and changed and 'came into the house of the LORD and worshipped'.[2] It is indeed difficult to believe that an independent city like Jebus with its own priesthood could have lacked some such building, when the Elid priesthood had the temple of the LORD in Shiloh, and the priesthood of Jonathan ben-Gershom served the ephod in a house at Dan, and even the wretched Micah built a house of gods to be served by his priest. Furthermore, since David took the Jebusite priest Zadok and his family over with the city, we can hardly think that he did not take the local shrine over also. No doubt David wished to replace the building with something more in keeping with his empire, and this will be the fact behind the D-history; but Rupprecht has argued a very plausible case in his book, and the likelihood must be that David took over a Jebusite shrine just as the Turks turned Aghia Sophia in Constantinople into a mosque.

Konrad Rupprecht[3] argues that the former Jebusite shrine was taken over by David and incorporated into the Solomonic Temple: Solomon extended the building and refurnished it, but did not demolish it. The D-historians were silent about the site: they turned the old shrine into a tent which he made for the Ark, and composed as a false trail the legend that Yahweh had forbidden him to build the Temple. But the truth is implied by Psalm 132: David sought and found a *māqôm/miškānôṯ* for the Ark, *viz.* the Jebusite shrine. The foundation legend of this shrine had been that it had begun with a theophany to Araunah, a Jebusite, who had erected an altar as in stories in Genesis and Judges; this tale was adapted to Israelite use, and survives as the legend of the Temple site in Chronicles. But it was suppressed by the D-history, which wished to ascribe all the Temple to Solomon *de novo*; and has only been included in the latest stages of 2 Samuel's composition, with the census story. Rupprecht regards the widespread practice of taking over the holy places of earlier cultures as no more than lending general probability to his case. His argument sometimes verges on the speculative, but as things stand he has offered the most likely hypothesis.

With the twentieth century came Hermann Gunkel, and concern with Davidic and other historical settings was soon made to seem outmoded and absurd. From his *Ausgewählte Psalmen* in 1904 to his commentary, *Die Psalmen* (1929), and its posthumously issued *Einleitung* (1933), his influence steadily increased in his lifetime, and it has remained dominant to this day, especially through subsequent commentators like H.-J. Kraus, whose *Biblischer Kommentar* (3 vols., five edns from 1961) has been the standard commentary for three decades. Gunkel took up the principle of classifying the psalms into *Gattungen*, which had already been laid down by de Wette;[4] but he developed a penetrating analysis which revealed a regular sequence of features for each group, a recurring form for each *Gattung*. This analysis, especially of the hymns and national laments, seemed obviously to go with the grain of the text; and it was combined with profound Hebraic learning, a soaring but controlled imagination, and a sympathy for 'der heissblütige Hebräer', which carried all before it. The old debates between conservative supporters of a Davidic setting and liberal advocates of the periods of Josiah or the Maccabees seemed increasingly unrealistic: these had been guesses based on prejudices, childish things to be put away with the arrival of a mature, scientific approach. The real debate turned out to be with Sigmund Mowinckel and his (mainly Scandinavian) followers, who wished to carry Gunkel's hypotheses further. From p. 1 of the first of his six-volume *Psalmenstudien* (1921-4) Mowinckel claimed that Gunkel had only lifted the tip of the veil in his study of the laments. The urge to extend Gunkel's cultic settings became increasingly acute with Harris Birkeland's *Die Feinde des Individuums in der israelitischen Psalmenliteratur* (1933). Birkeland persuaded his teacher Mowinckel to abandon his theory of sorcerers behind many of the 'I'-laments, and to see the speaker as the king or other national leader in a cultic prayer.

The central debate thus moved away from the tedious problems of date and place in the national history, to the more interesting and soluble questions of speaker, setting in life, enemies, poverty and wealth, etc. However, the need to settle the historical setting did not go away, for all that it could be treated in a final paragraph. Many psalms might give little clue to their time of origin; but others, like 60 and 68 in the Prayers, give rather a lot of clues, and the exegete cannot always be above such matters. Gunkel himself was often on marshy ground in such discussions. He thought the speaker of the 'I'-laments was a pious Israelite oppressed by wealthy and ungodly enemies: these psalms were the backbone of the Psalter, and belonged in the post-exilic period. But then, as Mowinckel pointed out (*Ps.st.* I, p. 111), our evidence is that those in power in Israel after the exile were in general in favour of strict religious observance; it is not till Maccabaean times that we hear of pious laity in tension with godless authority. So the Maccabaean date favoured by Hitzig, Duhm and Emil Balla[5] is the natural setting, on Gunkel's hypothesis, for these laments; but Gunkel's clear head told him that so late a date was impracticable. Further, a number of the 'I'-laments mentioned the nations, peoples, etc., and these had to be sited in the Diaspora.

From Gunkel's time on, serious discussion of the Davidic tradition was quietly dropped from professional study. Its perseverance in Catholic and fundamentalist Protestant circles did nothing to commend it either. The Papal Biblical Commission had declared David to be the 'praecipuus Psalterii carminum auctor'—and much more—on 1st May, 1910.[6] Two learned Catholic commentaries appeared in 1936, by Jean Calès and Heinrich Herkenne, both of whom print the Commission's findings in whole or part, and espouse them with enthusiasm. 'Heterodox critics' (Calès, I, p. 518) objected to Davidic authorship of 51 that the king could hardly say 'Against thee *only* have I sinned', if he had had Uriah murdered after sleeping with his wife. Calès replied confidently that sin is an offence against God to the point that one can say, in some sort, that it is against God alone (p. 516); Herkenne found *l*^{e}*ḇadd*^{e}*ḵā* a clear textual error for *liḇdōq*, to test, (pp. 188f.). The critics did not accept the reference to Doeg in the Heading of 52, as giving the true context of the psalm, because there is no mention in 52 of the priests whom Doeg murdered. This is, says Calès, because David is writing a *maskil*, a general instruction against the crimes of the perverse tongue;[7] Herkenne[8] says the psalm fits Doeg well, and there was no need to mention the massacre. Both authors credit 54 to David among the Ziphites, as the Heading says, and avoid the problem posed by the 'strangers' by reading *zēḏîm* for *zārîm*. *Non tali auxilio nec defensoribus istis*.

Such apologetics brought limited credit to the Church, and in 1943 Divino Afflante Spiritu gave Catholic exegetes a new freedom, to attend to modern critical tendencies, and in particular the genres of the biblical writings. So the way was opened to recognize Gunkel alongside St Benedict and St Bernard[9], and David was soon eased out, uncomfortably, by the Catholic commentators of the 50s. Robert Tournay could say,

> [David] remains none the less the initiator of the psalm genre and the organizer of Israelite liturgy. So he should be called the principal author of the Psalter, that is, the most notable and the most eminent. But it is unfortunately impossible to know even approximately how many of the psalms have the poet king as author.[10]

Edward Kissane takes a more Irish solution. He says, 'if there is nothing in the body of the Psalm which is inconsistent with the Title which ascribes it to David, the safest course is to accept the testimony of tradition'.[11] But David is often not mentioned in the commentary, e.g. on 56, 57, 58 and 59, despite their Davidic title, and he is usually rejected when he is, e.g. on 51, 55.

So was the tradition of two and a half millennia and more abandoned by nineteenth- and twentieth- century scholarship. Sometimes an individual psalm, like 18 or 51, might still be ascribed to David,[12] but the respectable distanced themselves from any idea of a Davidic collection like 51–72; only the occasional evangelical, like Derek Kidner, would maintain such a position, on lines similar to

Calès and Herkenne. It was not that good reasons had been brought against the tradition, except where the historical notes were insisted on. It was that the tide of learned discussion had left the Davidic question marooned. But to the unlearned, the great army of Bible readers, Sunday School teachers, independent church ministers and third-world Christians, David was still king. They put not their trust in commentators, nor in any professor of Hebrew: for there was no help in them.

The Prayers of David

Perhaps, then, the reasons for rejecting the David tradition have not been very overwhelming: but the question remains what reasons there might be for giving it any credence. This book attempts a detailed examination of the texts, and its conclusion is to justify the Davidic connection; but it may be helpful to consider one or two general points first.

Whoever added at the end of 72, 'The Prayers of David the son of Jesse are ended', thought that the preceding psalms belonged together in a collection with a common author; and I have suggested provisionally that this collection comprised Psalms 51–72. We may therefore enquire how far 51–72 appear to have any common features, in the way that Psalms 120–134, the songs of Ascents, share common features—brevity, a courageous optimism, concern for Jerusalem, Aramaisms, etc. Some things are immediately striking, like the high proportion of 'individual laments'. Gunkel (*Einl.*, p. 172) lists forty psalms of this type preserved in the Psalter, of which 51, 54, 55, 56, 57, 59, 61, 63, 64, 69, 70 and 71 are from the Prayers, more than half of the collection; and in the commentary he associates 52, 58 and 62 with the group, despite their slightly freer form. Within this group critics often observe a family likeness besides. Duhm, writing on 59, notes common features of 55–59 and suggests the same author; or 61–63 have been linked together as a triptych (cf. Jacquet, II, 289).

One psalm, 64, may suffice for the moment as an example of features which recur within the Prayers. The psalmist's enemies (who come in every Prayer except 51 and 65) are here said to have whet their tongue like a sword, and to have aimed their arrows, even bitter words, at the perfect one. Such ideas recur in many of the Prayers. The mighty man of 52.2 has a *tongue* sharpened like a knife with devouring and deceitful *words*. The false friend of 55.21 has *words* softer than oil, and yet they are drawn swords. The 'lions' of 57.4 have teeth which are spears and *arrows*, and *their tongue* a sharp *sword*. The young lion of 58.7 *aims* his *arrows* too—the verb is in common with 64.3, the surprising *dārᵉḵû*, which might have been expected more easily of 'treading' a bow. The 'dogs' of 59.7 have *swords* in their lips. There are many references to deceit (52.2, 4; 55.23; cf. 12ff.), lying or treason (52.3; 58.3; 59.12; 63.11), covenant-breaking (55.20), reproach (57.3; 69.9, 10ff., 19f.), or gloating enemies crying 'Aha' (70.3).

Psalms 64 and 59 share a common structure as well as the swords/ lips/lies. Both psalms open with a petition to preserve the speaker's life from *enemies*, *evil-doers* who are seeking to kill in secret (59.1-3; 64.1-3), although he is without fault (59.4)/perfect (64.4). They plot evil and belch out with their mouth, for who doth hear? (59.7); like the secret council of the wicked who plan trouble, saying, *Who* will see them? (64.5). God is to consume them for the sin of their mouth, and men will know that God rules in Jacob (59.12f.); God will shoot down the wicked of 64, their own tongue being against them (v. 8), and all men will nod their heads (v. 9). Evil *speaking* (*sippēr*) is their basic fault (59.12; 64.5). These correspondences are considerably closer than the general parallels of form isolated by Gunkel.

We shall find that the Prayers are in fact linked to each other by a web of common language and ideas, and even occasionally of structure; such links are noted below in the discussion of the individual psalms. Naturally some of these features recur on occasion outside the Prayers. In 7 the wicked are lions after the speaker's soul, digging a pit for him etc.; in 14, 35 and 40 there are parallels to the Prayers so close that there must be a literary relationship. But the links of vocabulary, thought and atmosphere in the Prayers are such as to distinguish them from the similar psalms in Book I; and these matters can link the 'I'-laments with the other psalms in the Prayers, as in the names used for God.

I have already noted that the psalmists of Books II and III feel most at ease addressing God as *ᵉlōhîm*, while not being averse from Yahweh and other names. In Psalms 42–84 *ᵉlōhîm* occurs 200 times (ignoring expressions like 'my God'), while Yahweh comes forty-four times; and this dramatic contrast to Books I, IV and V, which together have *ᵉlōhîm* twenty-two times and Yahweh 611 times (figures from Kirkpatrick, I, p. lv; Kirkpatrick notes that the use of

ʾᵉlōhîm in the second group is often required by the sense, or copied in from a duplicate, as when it comes six times in 108). Gunkel and Kraus explained this difference by the idea that Yahweh was always original, and that an editor has gone through changing Yahweh to *ʾᵉlōhîm*. He does not seem to have been a very competent editor, since he missed Yahweh forty-four times! But there is also the problem of 108, which combines 57.7-11 with 60.5-12; as its six uses of *ʾᵉlōhîm* are so abnormal for Book V, it is generally thought that 108 is later, so *ʾᵉlōhîm* was in use for 57 and 60 by the time of 108's composition. The Chronicler similarly reproduces considerable parts of 105, 96 and 106 without any attempt to replace Yahweh with *ʾᵉlōhîm*. As no plausible reason for the substitution is offered, and as the visibly late psalms, like 137 or 119, use Yahweh, it seems proper to take the text seriously, and suppose that the present distribution of divine names is original. The suggestion that an 'Elohim-recension' was made from reverence for Yahweh's name[13] is not borne out by evidence from the Chronicler or the agreed late psalms.

The distribution of the names for God is as follows for the Prayers:

	ʾᵉlōhîm	*Yhwh*	*Yāh*	*ʾᵃḏōnāî*	*'ēl*	*Other*
51	5			1		
52	3				2	
53	7					
54	4	1		1		
55	5	2			1	
56	9	1				
57	6			1	1	1 (*'elyôn*)
58	2	1				
59	5	3		1		1 (*ṣᵉḇā'ôt*)
60	5					
61	3					
62	7			1		
63	2					
64	3	1				
65	2					
66	7			1		
67	5					
68	24	3	2	6	1	1 (*šaddaî*)
69	7	5		1		1 (*ṣᵉḇā'ôṯ*)
70	3	2				
71	6	3		2		
72	2	1				
	122	23	2	15	5	4

It will be seen that *ᵉlōhîm* has the preponderance in every psalm in the collection. This goes for 66, 67 and 71, which lack David's name in the heading; and is as true for 'national psalms' like 53, 60 and 68, 'harvest psalms' 65 and 67, and royal psalms like 72, as for the 'I'-laments. Furthermore the preponderance is greater than in the Korah and Asaph groups where, even excluding 85–89, *ᵉlōhîm* outweighs Yahweh by only 78 to 21. Yahweh and *ᵃḏōnāî* are often used for variety in parallel to *ᵉlōhîm*; e.g. '*Make haste*', O God, to deliver me; Make haste to help me, O LORD . . . Make haste unto me, O God, [ ], O LORD, make no tarrying' (70.1, 5). Both of these, the main alternative names, are to be found as much in the other psalms as in the 'I'-laments. The large number of names of God in 68, and their variety, arise from the psalm's length and exuberance. *'ēl* is sometimes used as a general term for 'a god', and may cause problems in counting: e.g. 68.20, '*hā'ēl* is unto us an *'ēl* of deliverances'.

Not only do the Prayers share a preference for *ᵉlōhîm*: they also tend to address God as such in the opening line of the psalm, often in the second word:

51	Be merciful unto me, O God
55	Give ear, O God, to my prayer
56	Be merciful unto me, O God
57	Be merciful unto me, O God
61	Hear, O God, my cry
62	Only unto God is my soul silent
64	Hear, O God, my voice
69	Save me, O God

cf.

71	In thee, O LORD, do I put my trust
68	He arises, does God

Psalm 71 is exceptional in having Yahweh in the opening line; but 71 may be a continuation of 70 (see p. 229). *ᵉlōhîm* comes in the opening line of the Prayers in other than second position:

53	The fool hath said in his heart, There is no God
54	O God, by thy name save me
59	Deliver me from mine enemies, O my God
60	O God, thou hast cast us off
63	O God, thou art my God
65	There shall be silence before thee *and* praise, O God

66	Make a joyful noise unto God, all the earth
67	God be merciful unto us
70	O God, to deliver me
72	Give the king thy judgements, O God

ᵉlōhîm thus comes in the first line of nineteen Prayers out of twenty-two; and we may contrast this with the Korah psalms, where this is the case only three times (43, 44, 46) out of twelve, or the Asaph psalms, where God is addressed in the first line of only 74, 75, 79 and 83 (out of twelve), although the word is normal in the first line. It may also be noted that 51 has the same opening as 56 and 57, with 67 closely similar; and 61 and 64 begin similarly. The two missing psalms, 52 and 58 also have a family resemblance in being (uniquely in the psalter) addressed to enemies:

52	Why boastest thou thyself in mischief, O mighty man?
58	Do ye indeed speak righteousness, O ye mighty ones (*'ēlîm*)?

It is not my intention to adduce further evidence here for the common authorship of 51–72; the detail would be unreadable, and is more easily assimilated in the study of the individual psalms below. I hope that I have indicated enough to raise the possibility that the Prayers belong together by genuinely common features. This conclusion must come as a surprise when psalms have for so long been grouped together by their *Gattungen*. But then a difference of *Gattung* is irrelevant to the question of common authorship: we do not deny that Constable painted portraits because we are used to admiring his Suffolk landscapes.

Hypothesis

Before the Psalter is fragmented, and psalms are treated as individual units, to be interpreted in the light of their membership of a supposed *Gattung*, we should first attempt to honour as much as we can of the tradition. I am proposing therefore to accept three features of the tradition which are commonly ignored or rejected. First, I accept the association with David. I do not think that David wrote the Prayers himself, but (as will be seen) that they were composed by a court poet, a priest, probably one of David's sons, 'for David': that is, they were written during his lifetime, in response to situations in which he found himself. Second, I accept the order of the Prayers as representing the chronological order of their writing, and in consequence as mirroring the sequence of events in the king's life to which they are a response. Thirdly, I accept the *idea* behind the historical notes in the Headings, *viz.* that a psalm can be understood only in the light of the circumstances for which it was composed. The *actual* historical notes I take to be late guesses, and mostly wrong: but the first and the last historical notes happen to be right, and to provide us with the key to the whole.

For the first of these interpretive principles, I have to concede an element of veering. Sometimes, as in 51, the psalmist speaks in the name of the king. Sometimes, as in 61.6; 63.11, he refers to the king in the third person; or as in 53.5; 55.22; 68.23, 28, addresses him in the second person. Often the text leaves us in two minds as to which is intended. But such veering is to be expected in a spokesman. We find the same in the Fourth Gospel, where the evangelist has Jesus speaking in 3.10ff., but lapsing into the community's first person plural at 3.11 (cf. 21.24). It is only in a modern society that the functions of a speech-writer and his or her political leader are clearly differentiated.

It will be seen that it is the second of these three positions which is novel, and determinative. We are used to collections of Christian hymns which are largely not ordered at all, or ordered alphabetically: it is expected that the minister will select those hymns best suited to the theme of his service. But earlier collections were not at the disposal of the minister. The Book of Common Prayer tells him that he is to read Psalms 50–52 on the tenth morning of each month, and the Collects, Epistles and Gospels are set for the successive Sundays and Saints' Days in cycle. This pattern is, as far as I know, universal: the Church provided lectionaries so that priests, monks and nuns would know what they should read or pray in a given order, right back to the first such collection that we possess, the Armenian Lectionary from the convent of St. James in Jerusalem[14] from the early fifth century. Before that the Torah was read in Jewish synagogues in given cycles, whether annual or triennial (b. Meg. 29b), a practice of unknown antiquity. In my *The Psalms of the Sons of Korah*,[15] I argued that the order of Psalms 42–49 was significant, being the order in which these psalms were sung, one each evening in sequence, at the autumn festival at Dan in the eighth century; and that the order of 84–85, 87–89 was significant also in a similar way. Where we have liturgical texts from other Near Eastern communities, like the Babylonian New Year (*akitu*) festival,[16] they are also prescriptive of rites, prayers, hymns, etc. which are to be performed in the order given. The presumption that the order of the psalms in our Psalter is not significant, is in every way extraordinary: the presumption that it is incomprehensible arises from the neglect of the tradition in the Headings—for the Prayers, from the rejection of the David tradition.

If then we are to reconsider the Prayers as the possible production of David's retinue, and as reflecting the events of his life in sequence, we shall need to know where this story is supposed to begin and to end. Here I must be content to state my hypothesis and its *prima facie* basis in the texts: in every case there are complications, objections and problems to be weighed, and these are expounded in the detailed exegesis in later chapters. I take 51 to be a psalm written to express David's penitence after the death of Uriah. This is what the Heading says, and despite objections, the text fits this situation well. The speaker has done something dreadful, the guilt of which is elaborated in terms unparalleled in the Psalter; in v. 14 it is described as blood-guilt. As the penalty for murder in Israel was death, and there is not the least suggestion that this is to follow, the speaker is in a privileged position. He looks forward to teaching God's ways to transgressors, and ultimately to offering sacrifice when the walls of Jerusalem have been built. As David administered justice and extended Jerusalem, as well as ordering Uriah's death, there are *prima facie* grounds for accepting the tradition for 51.

I take 72 to be a psalm composed for the accession of King Solomon, an event that took place during David's lifetime and shortly before his death. The Heading of the psalm is 'For Solomon', and this tradition again agrees well with the text. The psalm is a prayer for 'the king . . . the king's son', a phrase suitable for a newly enthroned monarch. The prayer is for three primary matters: that the king may administer justice well for the poor, that there may be much prosperity, and that kings of foreign nations near and far may come bearing tribute. In particular Sheba is mentioned twice, and its gold. Now these are the very blessings with which legend has credited Solomon. In 1 Kings 3 he prays for wisdom, and by divine wisdom judges between the two poor women; in 1 Kings 4 peace and prosperity reign; in 1 Kings 10 the Queen of Sheba comes with spices and very much gold. There is a *prima facie* suggestion that such tales are legendary developments of the prayers for Solomon's success at his accession. So the Prayers may begin with a response to the murder of Uriah, and end with a response to Solomon's coronation: in terms of our biblical account of David, the period covered would be from 2 Samuel 11 to 1 Kings 1.

Now it may well have already occurred to the reader that this is a familiar section of the Davidic story; for it approximates quite closely to the so-called Succession Narrative, which in the classic account of Leonhard Rost ran from 2 Samuel 9–20 with 1 Kings 1–2. Much has been written about the Succession Narrative since Rost, and I shall wish to review the question, and to propose my own elaboration of his solution, and a rather different central theme for the early period. But I am in agreement with Rost—and with Julius Wellhausen before him—in seeing a tenth-century, nearly contemporary tradition as presenting a continuous story from David's sin over Uriah to his abdication in Solomon's favour. That tradition excluded 2 Samuel 21–24; its main topic was the rebellion of Absalom, in which David fled to Mahanaim, but it included the further rebellion of Sheba (2 Sam. 20) and the attempted usurpation of Adonijah in 1 Kings 1.

Between 51 and 72 stands a fair number of 'laments', many of them rather general in character; but there are also two psalms with much detail, names, etc., Psalms 60 and 68, neither of which has achieved a very comfortable setting in Israelite history from the commentators. The speaker of 60 grieves that God has 'rent' the land. He appears to be involved in a civil war, for he means to divide Shechem, and to mete out the valley of Succoth: he does not speak from Jerusalem, it seems, but from the East Bank of Jordan, for Gilead and Manasseh, Moab and Edom are under his control. So we have a rare combination of circumstances, and one which answers well to the time of David's withdrawal to Mahanaim: had the East Bank garrisons not been loyal to the king, his cause must have been lost; and the Philistines who are bidden to shout for him could suitably be David's Cherethites, Pelethites and Gittites.

Psalm 68 celebrates a major victory. It is also in a civil war, for the enemy are twice referred to as rebels, *sôr^{a}rîm* (vv. 6, 19), though they have been assisted by 'kings of armies', 'calves of the peoples' from (it seems) the Egyptian frontier lands. The impression of rebellion is strengthened by the mention of only Benjamin, Judah, Zebulun and Naphtali as in the victory procession. The psalm is in part addressed to the king, to whom Yahweh had said 'I will bring back from Bashan . . . that thou mayest dip thy foot in blood': it appears again that he is returning in victory from the East Bank. So perhaps the victory is Joab's defeat of Absalom's rebellion 'in the forest of Ephraim' (2 Sam. 18.6). Psalm 68.14 says the Almighty scattered the enemy kings in a snowstorm in Zalmon; and Zalmon is in Judges 9 the wooded mountain by Shechem whence Abimelech and his army cut branches. We seem to be getting a coherent picture with Psalm 60, against a background of the Absalom story in 2 Samuel.

In this way it looks as if a case might be made out for regarding 51-60-68-72 as a sequence of responses to David's sin, his coming to Mahanaim, his army's victory over Absalom, and his son Solomon's anointing as king. In between come a series of less clearly marked psalms, whose theme is often the enemy's pursuit of the speaker, watching for his life; sometimes encamping against him and eating up his people (53); sometimes trying to ambush him ('they have digged a pit before me', 57); often shooting at him with words. But each psalm has its own specific detail, as when the psalmist of 55 reproaches his own comrade whom he had trusted—interpreted correctly in the Jewish tradition as Absalom, but incorrectly taking David as speaker. The exegesis of such details we may postpone. It must suffice to say that 52–59 make a plausible series of prayers for a priest sharing David's retreat from Jerusalem; that 61–67 make a suitable sequence of responses to the events of David's residence in Mahanaim; and that 69–71 can be seen as reactions to the risings of Sheba and Adonijah.

If all this were convincingly argued, we should have a collection of 'The Prayers of David the son of Jesse' from the Uriah incident to David's abdication in Solomon's favour, in order. But we should still need to posit a motive for the collection and preservation of the sequence; and the only plausible motive must be a liturgical one. I suggest that the Prayers were chanted liturgically in a procession one day in the autumn festival at Jerusalem. They would require, if they were to be understood, some association with a recited account of the events. This I take to be now embedded in our 2 Samuel–1 Kings story, and to have been taken serially at the points in the Psalms text marked Selah. I do not think that Wellhausen and Rost were right to think that the interest of this story was primarily political. Rather, it would seem to be religious. The community is reliving the experience of its founder-king. He had sinned against Yahweh, and had suffered the divine judgment that the sword should never depart from his house; but God had had mercy on him and delivered him from his enemies, and he had lived to see his favourite son enthroned amid expectations of a golden age. Like king, like people: each year brought its catalogue of troubles, no doubt in just punishment for national sin; but each New Year it was possible to hope, through the liturgy, that atonement had been made for the past, and that a time of peace, prosperity and hegemony lay ahead.

In this way there seems to be a prospect of both honouring the Davidic tradition within critical limits, and of making sense of the Prayers as a collection, both in their order and against an imaginable setting. To test it, two tasks lie ahead. First, some review will be required of the Succession Narrative question, and a soundly based solution proposed therefor, since I am suggesting that the Prayers can be understood only in the light of such a Narrative. I attempt this in Chapter 2. When the ground has been cleared so, the way will be open to examine each of the Prayers in detail, and this will occupy the remainder of the book in Chapters 3–9.

In two significant respects my Davidic hypothesis has the advantage over its competitors: I am defending the tradition of nearly three millennia, and my theory should be easily falsifiable. The second point is as weighty as the first. Sir Karl Popper[17] has repeatedly urged that scientific advance can only come from clear hypotheses (conjectures) which *exclude* some possible states of affairs, and are thus capable of being falsified (refuted). It is difficult to see how the views of either Gunkel or Mowinckel can attain the dignity of hypotheses under such a definition. They both fragment the evidence, so that every psalm is treated as a unit, and can be interpreted in the light of other psalms or not, as the expositor wishes. They both amend the text freely, and Gunkel especially is liable to suppose the combination of two or more original poems within one given psalm, extensive changes of order, etc. For him the enemies are normally wealthy, godless Israelites; if they are said to be foreigners, then the psalm was composed in the Diaspora. For the later Mowinckel the enemies are normally foreign armies; but now and again they are the sorcerers of *Ps.st. I* still.

This pliability does not mean that either Gunkel or Mowinckel is wrong. It means merely that their successors have no idea which, if either of them, is right—a situation which may be quickly confirmed from a passing perusal of modern commentaries. Their approaches are as quicksilver, and are in principle irrefutable; and this tends properly to bring the subject into disrepute. By contrast, mine is a genuine hypothesis, which should be falsifiable in a few minutes if it is wrong. I am offering to interpret twenty-two psalms sequentially, against a background of historical tradition partly preserved in the D-history. I need to provide a convincing answer to objections against the settings given for 51 and 72, such as 'Against thee only have I sinned' in 51.4. I have to give a plausible explanation for all the names and details of difficult psalms like 60 and 68, within my given historical sequence. I have to expound every line of the intervening, more general psalms, each of which however has its own specificities, which are often unexplained in the commentaries. In marked contrast to the latter, my way is a narrow linear track defined in advance, and hedged in with problems on all sides, from which I have foresworn escape by textual emendation, alterations of order, variations of hypothesis and the like. I hope that I may trust my reader to recognize special pleading if any is to be found.

Chapter 2

THE SUCCESSION NARRATIVE AND THE PASSION OF DAVID

The idea that behind our 2 Samuel–1 Kings lies an independent Succession Narrative is more than a century old.[1] So far as I know it is first found in Julius Wellhausen's revision of F. Bleek's *Einleitung in das Alte Testament*.[2] Three features appealed to Wellhausen as signs of 'eine sehr gute historische Quelle', old, though not as old as Judges 9. First there was a distinctive and specific style of writing, of 'sichtlicher Objektivität'; one notices by contrast with other matter 'das stoffliche Detail', with, for example, 'so viele historische Namen'. Second, the story, which Wellhausen identified provisionally as 2 Samuel 9–20, 1 Kings 1–2, seemed to mark out the steady progression by which Solomon became king. Thirdly, there is a brief note of some stylistic elements which these chapters have in common. Wellhausen was a little uncertain of the precise delimitation of the Narrative. It should contain 2 Samuel 9, David's kindness to Mephibosheth, because the latter is a character in the Narrative at 2 Sam. 16.1-4; 19.24-30. On the other hand 2 Sam. 9.1 is not at all a suitable opening for a Narrative, and Wellhausen thought the beginning had been lost. Nor did he feel any confidence in 2 Samuel 10–12, much of which he took to be later addition. But 2 Samuel 21–24 were an appendix to David's reign, clearly of a different stamp, and the core of the Narrative was 2 Samuel 9; 13–20 and 1 Kings 1–2.

It was the political plot which gave Wellhausen's proposal its plausibility. Amnon was David's firstborn son (2 Sam. 3.2) and natural heir, killed for his incestuous lust. Absalom was the eldest son of Maacah, David's third wife (3.3), killed for his rebellion. Adonijah was the eldest son of David's fourth wife, Haggith (3.4), set aside for his presumptuous aspiration to David's throne during his father's lifetime, and later killed for further presumption. Hence came the accession of the wise and wealthy Solomon, the eldest (surviving) son of David's last wife, Bathsheba. The source had a political motivation: it was the Narrative of the 'Thronnachfolge Davids'.

It was nearly fifty years till Wellhausen's suggestion received its full and classic exposition in Leonhard Rost's *Die Überlieferung von der Thronnachfolge Davids*.[3] Rost was contesting the standard position of his day, maintained by Karl Budde and many, that there were two continuous stories running from Genesis through the Histories, and he concentrated attention on two blocks of material, the Ark Narrative, which he took to comprise the greater part of 1 Samuel 4–6 and 2 Samuel 6, and the Succession Narrative. He excised a few verses from 2 Samuel 14 and 1 Kings 2 as later, but otherwise he retained Wellhausen's main outline of the latter in 2 Samuel 13–1 Kings 2. 2 Samuel 9-12 was also part of the Narrative, but included an already existing account of the Ammonite War: this provided the backdrop for the Bathsheba-Uriah story which was integral to the Narrative. Rost followed Wellhausen in including Nathan's parable and the death of the baby as punishment for David's sin, but in excluding the oracles that the sword should never depart from David's house, and that others should sleep with his wives in public. He amended Wellhausen by adding two preliminary passages: Michal's reproof of David in 2 Samuel 6, and her subsequent fate of childlessness; and a few fragments from Nathan's revelation that God would give David a house, a dynasty to rule after him. An ending at 1 Kings 2 provided Rost with a clear, strong close to his Narrative, but he was left, like Wellhausen, with the problem of a weak opening. This he solved, perhaps a little implausibly, by supposing that the author of the Succession Narrative had grafted the latter on to the Ark Narrative.

Fundamentally, Rost offered the same picture as Wellhausen. His Succession Narrative was still a political document, justifying the Davidic dynasty, and answering the insistent question, 'Who shall reign after David, and who shall sit upon his throne?' (1 Kgs 1.13, 17, [20], 24, [27], 30, [46, 48]). 1 Kings 2 completed the story of 1 Kings 1, and completed the history of many of the characters—David, Joab, Shimei, Adonijah, Abishag, Abiathar, Solomon. But the story which brought them all to these varying ends was a closely woven tissue extending back to David's kindness to Meribbaal in 2 Samuel 9, and before to Michal and Nathan. The Michal incident showed how none of her children came to the throne, and the 'house' prophecy set out the theme of the whole from the start, till it was referred to at 1 Kgs 2.45. Otherwise the plot was the plot which Wellhausen had descried half a century earlier.

Rost's originality was principally in extending the stylistic argument. There was a clear contrast between the simple, terse prose of the ark narrative and the longer sentences, fuller expression, sonorous language and richer imagery of the Succession Narrative. Its author was fond of parables—Nathan and the woman of Tekoa—of raising tension through the repetition of a story by a messenger—after the battle, or at Adonijah's feast—or of stock expressions for an ambitious man's retinue—Absalom and Adonijah. His speeches are finely wrought, with an ABA structure marking the end with an inclusio. He is a master of simile—'like a dead dog', 'like a fool', 'like water poured out on the earth', 'like an angel of God', 'like a bear robbed of its cubs'. Above all he is able, with his speeches, to portray character with high artistry: 'the unrestrained, sensual Amnon, the ruthless, ambitious and cunning Absalom, Adonijah eager for success, the calculating, merciless Solomon' (103). The multi-faceted David and the over-talkative, double-dealing Hushai especially drew Rost's admiration.

Like most contemporaries, Rost dated the Succession Narrative to the early years of Solomon. This was when Solomon's succession needed justifying, this was when many historical details, though now artistically overlaid, were still remembered, this was the time of peace, with no hint of the divided kingdom. The author was a courtier, perhaps Ahimaaz. Rost did not attempt a setting in life for the Narrative's use, but he gives this account of the Ark narrative: 'The story served the purpose of explaining the significance of the ark to the visitors to the shrine, most particularly the pilgrims . . . It could also have been told in answer to questions from members of the cultic community concerning the shrine' (26). So perhaps he thought the Succession Narrative was read by courtiers, who could then answer their own and other people's doubts about Solomon.

There were hesitations about Rost's thesis from the beginning, notably in a review by Otto Eissfeldt,[4] but it established itself over the years as a standard solution to the problem the chapters present. In recent times it has been criticized in two main directions. In continental scholarship the unity of the Narrative has been questioned, and attempts have been made to discriminate two contrasted tendencies within it as an earlier and a later hand. In Anglo-Saxon scholarship there has been a greater willingness to treat the Narrative as it stands, partly from distrust of the criteria offered for dividing it, and weariness with the source-critical method. But along with this have gone strong doubts over the central Wellhausen-Rost hypothesis of the political motivation for the Narrative, and new proposals for its setting, its date, its opening and other matters.

The movement towards seeing two redactions (and more) in the narrative has been exemplified in the monograph of the Finnish scholar Timo Veijola,[5] the writings of Ernst Würthwein,[6] and a succession of articles by François Langlamet.[7] The three authors have in common an underlying document of political tendency whose basic cast is however *anti*-Solomonic and even anti-Davidic: Solomon was merciless and sacrilegious, David was lustful, treacherous, murderous, weak, sentimental, self-pitying and senile. This is then revised in the direction of both a more religious and a more pro-dynasty view, whether by a seventh-century theological-sapiential author (Langlamet) or a series of Deuteronomic editors (Veijola). The criterion of distinction is basically, for each scholar, the tensions or contradictions within the story, and it is largely this which has made the approach distrusted. David Gunn[8] made a critique of it, emphasizing the complexity and ambiguity of events and characters in both life and art, and the circularity of argument in eliminating them. It has been felt besides that for all David's sins and Solomon's hardness, there is no clear underlying anti-dynastic tendency visible. The value of the approach has been rather, to my mind, twofold. First it has stressed properly that the final form of the Narrative is not a secular, historical, political document, but a religious production, like everything else in the Old Testament. Second, it has correctly sensed that Rost oversimplified the history of the tradition. There is something more to it than a contemporary work of genius imposed on an already existing Ammonite War narrative, and later taken over by the Deuteronomists who interpolated seven or eight verses.

A different line has been taken elsewhere, with questioning of the nature and purpose of the Narrative. Already in 1951 Morton Smith suggested briefly that it was not primarily a political, but a moral tract, a warning of the evil consequences of sin.[9] In 1968 Norman Whybray[10] argued for giving the work a setting in the Wisdom area, itself a focus of interest in Solomon's time. Whybray argued convincingly that the Narrative could not be seen as history in any modern sense but was rather (in Eissfeldt's phrase) 'a good historical novel'. It had all the features of such a work: unity of theme (the Davidic succession), structure, the drawing of character, dialogue and style. In all this Whybray was only developing Rost, and he retained Rost's idea that the main drive of the work was 'political propaganda'. His originality was in the suggestion that it was a production of the Solomonic enlightenment, in line with the teaching of Proverbs: it was a didactic narrative, like the Joseph story, and its aim was to inculcate the importance of wisdom and counsel, the inevitability of retribution, the action of Yahweh within the decisions and actions of men, the perils of illicit sex and treachery, and sundry other topics. In this way the Narrative was a production of the court scribes for the education of their pupils. Whybray has in fact two central motivations for the Narrative, which he has not quite resolved: it is both political propaganda for the Solomonic dynasty, and also a didactic tract to teach the young how to succeed in life.

Whybray's 'wisdom' proposal has been criticised, first by J.L. Crenshaw[11] and later by Gunn:[12] the wisdom themes are so general, and almost any story—especially any story of life at court—is bound to overlap them. But Whybray's analysis of the artistry of the Narrative is approved warmly by Gunn, as is his dismissal of its claim to be 'history-writing'. Gunn extends this analysis in a most attractive way. He points to the presence of certain stereotyped traditional motifs, and certain evidence of oral tradition behind the story. The traditional motifs are the recurrence of tales where Abishai and Joab are 'too hard for' David, wanting death where he would spare, outside as well as within the Narrative; or judgment-eliciting parables (the woman of Tekoa and Nathan); or women whose activities bring death in their train (Bathsheba, Tamar, Abishag, Rizpah); or the woman who hides the spies; or the two messengers; or the letter that brings command to kill the bearer. All these are traditional patterns of folk-story, and the suggestion is that rather than thinking that the letter Uriah carried happened to be rather like the letter Bellerophon carried, or that Jonathan and Ahimaaz happened to be helped by a woman rather like Rahab, we should think that the Narrative has been developed, like the Iliad or the Chanson de Roland, by the inclusion of such standard tales. Similarly there are stereotyped accounts of provisions being supplied to David's 'young men' (Abigail, Ziba), or of battles, or reports of defeat; and it is easy to see these as having been told orally over time rather than written down by the standard eyewitness. They show just those features of similarity and difference which are characteristic of oral narration.

> Gunn's analysis of these literary features leads him to three novel conclusions. (1) The Narrative does not come from Solomon's reign, but from a later period unspecified. The concrete details are no more evidence of near dating than such details would be in a modern historical novel; and the later idealization of David in orthodox circles need not exclude other 'warts-and-all' portraits. Besides, there are other features as well as those just outlined which distance the Narrative from its subject: Absalom's monument 'to this day' (2 Sam. 18.18), the robes that virgin princesses used to wear (13.18, perhaps reading *mē'ôlām*, in days of old), the vagueness over Judah's participation in the rebellion. (2) There is a block of similar literary material in 2 Samuel 2–4, and the inclusion of this would alter the whole thrust of the story: it would no longer be a *Succession* Narrative, but 'The Story of King David' from the days at Hebron when he was first made king till his death and Solomon's succession. In this way the lost beginning of Wellhausen and Whybray, and the unconvincing link with the Ark story made by Rost, can alike be dispensed with. (3) This would then free us from the 'political propaganda' view, whose uncertainty is evident from the presence of anti-David and anti-Solomon elements noted by Würthwein, Veijola and Langlamet, The Story was written to provide serious entertainment: it is a gripping, moving tale of giving and grasping, and it was told and written to grip and to move. Perhaps its setting was originally the court, perhaps the harem, perhaps a wider public.[13]

I do not think that Gunn's arguments for a later date[14] are very convincing. Fashions for unmarried princesses may change, and there are other amendments suggested for *m*^{ec}*îlîm* if the MT is found unsatisfying. Absalom's monument need only have been standing for twenty years 'to this day'. There is a more obvious answer to the problem of the vagueness over who participated in the Rebellion: the author of the Narrative was a Judahite (cf. 19.40, 'and all the people of Judah brought the king over, and also half the people of Israel'), and he wishes to suppress the fact that most of the Judahites were in it too. I will return to the mention of 'the *house* of Yahweh' (12.20) below (p. 81). On the other hand I think he has made a good case for thinking that many of the 'good story' elements are standard folk-tale material, and that the atmosphere of the Narrative is in many ways rather similar to Herodotus' account of the Persian Wars. There is a sound historical base, but enough time has elapsed for them to be glossed with fiction, and the great story-teller has a crowd of willing Athenian listeners fifty years after the crises of Marathon and Salamis. There is a historical base here too, but the wise woman of Tekoa, and the woman who hid Jonathan and Ahimaaz, are as much the products of the haze of time as Rhampsinitus and Gyges.

A better argument for a later date, hinted by Edward Ball, is the similarity between Sheba's rebellion and the Secession of 1 Kings 12. '(Sheba) said, We have no portion in David, neither have we inheritance in the son of Jesse: every man to his tents, O Israel' (2 Sam. 20.1): 1 Kgs 12.16 is nearly identical. The 1 Kings story gives an account of why the (northern) Israelites thought that they had no portion in David: Solomon had 'chastised them with whips', and Rehoboam was proposing to do so with 'scorpions'—they had suffered from taxes and levied labour, and gained nothing from it. But no such rationale is provided for Sheba's proclamation, which indeed is flatly contradicted by the loyal men of Israel in 19.43; and the whole episode of Sheba's rebellion is recounted in a vague and unsatisfying way. It is easy to think, therefore, that it is a misty memory told long after the event, and that its opening phase has simply been modelled on the familiar story of Jeroboam's secession. This would give a date not earlier than 920, if the Division is dated c. 926; and that would give time for the accretion of Gunn's folk-motifs to the Narrative in general.

But although I think that Gunn is right about the texture of the Narrative, and its dating, there persists a suspicion that justice has not been fully done to Wellhausen's appeal—and that of so many later scholars—to the concreteness of parts of the story. Three features in particular seem to strike the reader.

(1) For much of the story in 2 Samuel 15ff. very specific topographical details are provided. David reviews his evacuating troops at Beth-Merhak, at the crossing of the Kidron (15.17, 23), ascends the Mount of Olives (15.30), to the top, where God was worshipped (15.32), on to 'a little past the top' (16.1), and to Bahurim (16.5). He is bound for 'the fords of the wilderness' (15.28; 17.16), and thence to Mahanaim (17.24), while Absalom's forces camp 'in the land of Gilead' (17.26). All this detail stands in marked contrast to a more general neglect of topography in the Narrative. We are told that Joab's 'field' was near Absalom's (14.30), but we do not know

where. David's forces march out of Mahanaim to battle in 18.1-5, and we expect the battle to be on the East Bank (where, indeed, many commentators site it); but the Narrative tells us that it took place in 'the forest of Ephraim', which is on the West Bank, as all Ephraim is (cf. Josh. 17.15, 18). We are given no indication why this should be so. In ch. 20 we have no idea where Sheba's rebellion began, or why it ended up in Abel-Beth-Maacah.

(2) There is a similar specificity over the principal supporters on both sides. This applies not only to Ahitophel and Hushai who have a part in the story, but to other characters who have no further part to play. In 17.25 we hear not only of Amasa, Absalom's general, but of the four members of his family by whom he was first cousin to Joab. The following verses give names, patronymics and home-towns of three East Bank nobles who provided for David's army: Shobi ben-Nahash of Rabbah, Machir ben-Ammiel of Lo-debar, and Barzillai the Gileadite of Rogelim. These details are more specific than is necessary, and more specific than what the Narrative tells us of many other characters—Joab, Abishai, Meribbaal, Ziba, Hushai, Ahitophel: they are likely to stem from an account soon after the event. We have a similar contrast between the characters of the Gospels, hardly any of whom have come through with personal details, and those of, say, Corinth in Acts, where Luke, from more recently, knows what work people did and where they lived.

(3) On the whole the author of the Narrative is a skilled story-teller who builds up his account of events with forethought. We hear about Jonadab because he advised Amnon to rape Tamar, and it was this that led to Absalom's murder of Amnon, and so his exile, and so his rebellion, and so the fulfilment of Nathan's prophecy that the sword should never depart from David's house. Hanun's arrogance leads to the Ammonite War, and so to Uriah's absence, and so to David's adultery, and Bathsheba's conception, and Uriah's murder, and so to Nathan's prophecy. We have confidence in such a narrator, who can lead us on from scene to scene, and only after a while do we realize the connections which have been laid for us so imperceptibly by the hand of a master. It is therefore a surprise to us to find an occasional loose end to the story. How did Absalom come to make a vow to sacrifice in *Hebron*? What was the reaction of the two hundred men who went to Hebron 'in their simplicity', and found themselves implicated in the conspiracy? Why, if David thought he should 'make

speed to depart' from Jerusalem, does he stop at Beth-Merhak and hold a parade and march-past? Who was lying, Ziba or Meribbaal?

All these three features combine to suggest that the Succession Narrative is a fuller version, with a higher artistry, of an earlier account, whether written or oral, of the same essential story. The earlier form will have included topographical and personal details which were significant at the time, but which were not relevant to the later Narrator; and occasional details which did not at the time require explanation, and which have survived into our text. It will have been comparatively brief and factual. The Narrator of the fuller form will then have added the colourful material—the conversations, the character of the participants, the folk-motif scenes, the imagery—all that makes it a great work of art. This suggestion is in fact virtually entailed by Gunn's proposal, for it is hardly conceivable that a historically based 'story' should have been composed more than fifty years after the event without drawing on *some* prior formulation. In addition, it is in part in line with the proposals of Würthwein, Veijola and Langlamet: it provides for a (non-Deuteronomic) revision of a prior text, and the 'revision' is 'pro-Davidic'. But it differs from them in seeing the original version as merely factual, not anti-dynastic; and in seeing the central creative work as in the 'revision'.

This hypothetical earlier version is confirmed by the following further features:

(4) Both the detailed topographical information and the loose story-ends begin from the conspiracy story in 15.7 (Hebron, the sacrifice, the two hundred men in their simplicity). Now 15.7 is a notorious textual crux, for the MT, supported by LXX^{BAMN}, opens: 'And it came to pass at the end of forty years' (*miqqēṣ 'arbā'îm šānâ*). This is 'impossible' (McCarter), and almost all commentators prefer the easier reading of LXX^{L} Syr. Vg., 'four years', which is already known to Josephus (*Ant*. 7.196). But not only is it rather implausible that Absalom should have got up early for four years to grease his way into popular favour (15.1-6); it is also a scandalous denial of the principle, difficilior lectio potior. It is easy to see why the Josephus-Lucian tradition should have felt that 'forty years' was wrong, and might have substituted 'four years': suggestions of how 'forty' came to be substituted for 'four' are less obvious. Other recourses have been to suppose 'forty days', for which there is the evidence of two manuscripts, and which is a still easier reading, or that the -m was

enclitic (in which case there was likely to be a muddle over all numbers between 20 and 90). Surely a more satisfactory solution is obtained by taking the MT and main LXX tradition to be original. There was an account of what we may provisionally call the Passion of David, beginning with Absalom's conspiracy; and it was tacked on to an account of how David became king, with the opening clause, 'And it came to pass at the end of forty years'. The author of the Succession Narrative has been building up towards the conspiracy with chs. 13–14, and has provided his own (general, popular-tale) version of the basis of the revolt in 15.1-6; with 15.7 he introduces the detailed, specific, topographically accurate, loose-end account from the Passion story (PD). This must have been either written, or else in fixed oral form, and he has carried over the 'forty years' which makes no sense in his context.

(5) It has for long been noticed that the Succession Narrative veers between calling David by name, and calling him 'the king'. It is clear that no simple correlation of the names by attribution to sources can be correct, because of at least two factors. First, no speaker can address David with courtesy without using some such phrase as 'my lord the king', even if he normally preferred 'David'. Second, where some personal action is involved (as throughout ch. 12), it might be more natural to speak of 'David', even if one normally preferred 'the king': thus, 'And David comforted Bathsheba his wife'. We have also to consider that when two names are in use (as with 'Jesus' and 'Christ'), people may use both, but have a clear preference for one or the other; and that a later reviser may import his preferred use into the pattern of his predecessor.

This being said, it is open to us to examine the pattern of usage of 'David' and 'the king' in the PD and the remainder of the Succession Narrative along the lines marked out above. Since the PD began at 15.7, we have a good length of the Narrative before the PD's opening; and if we exclude the 'personal' matter in ch. 12, there is still at least 13.1–15.6 on which to try the distinction. Over these seventy-eight verses David is called 'the king' thirty-four times (plus twenty-seven times in dialogue), and 'David' six times, of which four (13.1, 1, 3, 32) are to express relationships, as in 'Absalom the son of David'. The remaining two are at 13.7 when David sends to Tamar, and 13.30 when word comes to David that all his sons are murdered. We have a similarily prolonged passage in chs. 18–19, where the Narrative tells the 'good stories' of Absalom's death in the battle, of the two messengers, of David's grief and his return: in all this there is little sign of the specific and detailed reminiscences of the PD. Over these seventy-six verses David is called 'the king' forty-five times (plus thirty-four times in dialogue) and 'David' six times (plus once in dialogue), as well as 'King David' twice (19.11, 16). Of the uses of 'David', four come in the battle and its preparations (18.1, 2, 7, 9) before the story of Absalom's death is reached: the other two are at 18.24, 'Now David sat between the two gates', and 19.22, David's word to Abishai. There seems therefore to be prima facie evidence that the Narrative has a strong preference for 'the king'.

The PD is to be found in 15.7–17.29, as well as in the later passages, but it has been overwritten by the author of the Narrative. For example, 17.15-29 tells how Hushai sent word to David to cross the Jordan, and how he came to Mahanaim: the passage is full of specific details, but 17.17-21a gives the Narrative's folk-tale of Jonathan and Ahimaaz in the well. David is called 'King David' in the folk-tale, at 17.17, 21, but 'David' at 17.16, 21b, 22, 24, 27, 29: he is never called 'the king' in the narrative of 17.15-29, and he is always 'David' in the non-folktale narrative. A second passage in which exact details are given of David's movements is 15.30-37, ascending the Mount of Olives, and at the shrine at the top; and this should therefore be ascribed to the PD. Here also there is no reference to David as 'the king': he is 'David' at 15.30, 31 (x2), 32, 33, 37, and 'the king' refers to Absalom in 15.34, 35. Thus we seem to have the elements of a second criterion. The PD is marked by details of topography and names, and by loose ends in the story; and tends to refer to David by his name. The remainder of the Succession Narrative has a penchant for good stories of a traditional standard form, for dialogue and character and the rest; and tends to refer to David as 'the king'.

We can, on so small a sample, speak only of tendencies; and I have noted some uses of 'David' in the non-PD parts of the Narrative. Nonetheless we may suspect that the presence of both 'the king' and 'David' in other parts of 15.7–17.29 is a sign of the overwriting of the PD by the author of the Narrative. For example 16.1, 'And when David was a little past the top, behold Ziba . . . ', looks as if it belongs to the PD, since it has both the accurate topography and the name 'David'. But in the remainder of 16.1-4 David is 'the king' four times in narrative and twice in dialogue, and never 'David' again. However, there are two good reasons for thinking that the author of the Narrative has over-written the story. First Ziba has brought two asses in 16.1, but in 16.2 they are 'for the king's household to ride on'; and the bottle of wine in 16.1 is for 'such as be faint' in an army of some two thousand in 16.2. So it seems as if the PD saw Ziba as providing primarily for the king himself, but the story has been expanded by someone who saw the provision as for the whole army. Second, the continuation of the story in 19.24-30 uses 'the king' throughout, and the preparation for it in ch. 9 has 'the king' eight times and 'King David' once, against five uses of 'David'. It is easy to think therefore that the PD gave a brief and unexplained account of the coming of Ziba to support 'David' in 16.1: and that the author of the Narrative has prepared for the incident in ch. 9 and followed it up in 19.24-39, and in addition expanded it in 16.2-4. This would in turn explain the tension of sympathies. The PD thought that Ziba was telling the truth, and this impression still comes through in 16.1-4. But the Succession Narrator thought that Ziba was slandering Meribbaal, and this is what comes through in 19.24-30.

The same overwriting may be seen in the other sections of the Passion of David. In 15.7-12, the Conspiracy, David is twice 'the king': after so many uses of 'the king' in 13.1–15.6 the author of the Narrative continues his own preferred usage at first (15.7, 9), slipping into the PD's 'David' at 15.12, 13, 14 from fatigue.[15] In 15.13-29 we have a heavily expanded story, David's evacuation of Jerusalem. The essential story in the PD, as will be argued below (pp. 78, 82f.), is the evacuation (15.13f.), including Ittai's troops (15.17f., 22), the coming of Zadok and Abiathar with the ark (15.24), and David's sending them back (15.27-29). This has been expanded by the Narrator with (a) the story of the concubines (15.15f.), (b) edifying material in the interchange between David and Ittai (15.19-21), (c) David's edifying speech to Zadok (15.25f.), and (d) the mention of Ahimaaz and Jonathan, to prepare for the well story. The name 'David' comes only in the PD verses (15.13, 14, 22): 'the king' comes eleven times, eight of them in the expanded verses (15.15 (x2), 16 (x2), 19, 21, 23, 25), and the remaining three where there is evidence of editorial work (15.17f., 27).

We may similarly discriminate a basic story of Shimei's abuse at Bahurim (16.5-7, 13f.), which will have been in the PD, from the edifying expansion in which David refuses Abishai's offer to take Shimei's head off (16.8-12). We have 'David' or 'King David' in the basic story at 16.5, 6 (x2), 13, and also once in the expansion ('And

David said to Abishai . . . Behold my son, which came forth of my bowels', 16.11). He is 'the king' in the expansion (16.9, 10) and in the PD at 16.14. 'David' at 16.11 may be due to the personal context of the words, or to the echo of a similar interchange between 'David' and Abishai at 1 Sam. 26.8ff. There is hardly any reference to David in the Absalom-Hushai-Ahitophel scenes in 16.15–17.14, and there he has to be referred to by name (16.16; 17.1). But Sheba's rebellion in ch. 20 shows the same pattern of a basic story from the PD, which has been expanded (a) with the end of the concubines (20.3), and (b) with the tale of Joab and the wise woman of Abel-Beth-Maacah (20.16-22). David is called by name in the basic story (20.1, 2, 3a, 6), and 'the king' in the expansion (20.3b, 21, 22); he is also 'the king' in 20.4, as the Narrator rejoins his source.

In this way we seem to have a regular pattern of usage. Throughout ch. 9, 13–20 we seem to have the work of the Succession Narrator developing an earlier story with edifying speeches, folk-tales, apologetic matter and such; and he regularly shows a strong preference for calling David 'the king'—as might be expected from an author writing when the dynasty was established. In the underlying narrative, which runs from 15.7 to the early verses of ch. 18, with its accurate topographical and personal detail and its loose ends, the teller tends to use 'David', and the same is true of ch. 20. The situation is less easy in 1 Kings 1–2 because (King) David's name is sometimes required to distinguish him when Solomon has been crowned; but 'the king' is frequently used, and often in passages which provide the dialogue and character associated with the Succession Narrative. There is a regular correlation, 'the king' with the Succession Narrative, 'David' with the PD. Only in 2 Samuel 10–12 is this not the case, for there 'David' is invariable. In chs. 11–12, as I have already suggested, the reason is mainly the personal nature of the story. It was the thing that *David* had done which displeased Yahweh, not the thing that 'the king' had done. But there is something more to say on this, to which I will return shortly. For ch. 10 we have long-standing hesitations over ascription to the Succession Narrative. There is a fresh beginning at 11.1; the crude and implausible tale of the messengers' clothes being half cut off 'even to their buttocks' consorts ill with the high level of the rest of the Narrative; the military detail of 10.15-19 is similarly alien. It is easier to think that the chapter was prefixed to the Narrative's account of the Ammonite War to provide the latter with a pretext; and that the

Narrator makes no reference to it because he knew it not.

(6) Now that we have an outline of both the Passion of David and the Succession Narrative, based on a number of criteria, we may enquire into a further difference, the familiar distinction between the use of Yhwh and *ᵓᵉlōhîm*. The Succession Narrative without its PD elements has the following uses:

> ... that I may show the kindness of God unto him (9.3)
> But the thing that David had done displeased the LORD (11.27)
> And the LORD sent Nathan unto David (12.1)
> As the LORD liveth, the man that hath done this is a son of death (12.5)
> Thus saith the LORD, the God of Israel (12.7)
> Wherefore hast thou despised the word of the LORD (12.9)
> Thus saith the LORD, behold I will raise up evil (12.11)
> I have sinned against the LORD (12.13)
> The LORD also hath put away thy sin (12.13)
> ... great occasion to the enemies of the LORD to blaspheme (12.14)
> And the LORD struck the child (12.15)
> ... and he came into the house of the LORD (12.20)
> Who knoweth whether the LORD will not be gracious to me (12.22)
> And the LORD loved him (12.24)
> And he called his name Jedidiah, for the LORD's sake (12.25)
> ... let the king remember the LORD thy God (14.11)
> As the LORD liveth, there shall not one hair of thy son fall (14.11)
> ... devised such a thing against the people of God (14.13)
> ... neither doth God take away life (14.14)
> ... for as the angel of God, so is my lord the king (14.17)
> ... and the LORD thy God be with thee (14.17)
> ... according to the wisdom of the angel of God (14.20)
> As the LORD liveth, and as my lord the king liveth (15.21)
> if I shall find favour in the eyes of the LORD (15.25)
> the LORD hath returned upon thee all the blood of the house of Saul (16.8)
> the LORD hath delivered the kingdom into the hand of Absalom (16.8)
> the LORD hath said unto him, Curse David (16.10)
> for the LORD hath bidden him (16.11)
> It may be that the LORD will look on the wrong (16.12)
> the LORD will requite me good (16.12)
> For the LORD had ordained to defeat... Ahitophel (17.14)

... that the LORD might bring evil upon Absalom (17.14)
... how that the LORD hath avenged him of his enemies (18.19)
Blessed be the LORD thy God, which hath delivered up ... (18.28)
for the LORD hath avenged thee this day (18.31)
for I swear by the LORD, if thou go not forth (19.7)
my lord the king is as the angel of God (19.27)
why wilt thou swallow up the inheritance of the LORD (20.19).

From this table it may be seen that the Succession Narrative has a strong preference for Yahweh, by 32 uses to 6; three of the six are in the phrase 'the angel of God' (14.7, 20; 19.27), and we also have 'the kindness of God' (9.3) and 'the people of God' (14.13). Yahweh is also used extensively, and 'God' not all, in the final sections of the Narrative in 1 Kings 1–2.

The PD sections are much shorter, and also more factual than the main Narrative, and include the following uses:

... which I vowed unto the LORD in Hebron (15.7)
If the LORD shall indeed bring me again Jerusalem (15.8)
then will I worship the LORD (15.8)
... bearing the ark of the covenant of God (15.24)
and they set down the ark of God (15.24)
Carry back the ark of God into the city (15.25)
Zadok therefore and Abiathar carried the ark of God again (15.29)
David was come to the top, where God was worshipped (15.32)
the counsel of Ahitophel ... was as if a man inquired at the word of God (16.23)

This gives us six uses of 'God' to three of 'Yahweh'. The latter are all in oratio recta in the opening two verses, and might be due (like 'the king' in 15.7, 9) to the Narrator's redaction. Four of the uses of 'God' come in 15.24-9 in the phrase 'the ark (of the covenant) of God'. 'The ark of God' is common, and the standard expression for it, in 1 Samuel 3–6; 2 Samuel 6; but we may contrast the Succession Narrator's 'the ark' at 2 Sam. 11.11, and we have 'the ark of the covenant of Yahweh (of hosts)' at 1 Sam. 4.3, 4, 5, and 'the ark of Yahweh' at 1 Sam. 4.6; 5.4; 6.1, 2, 8, 11, 15, 18, 21,; 7.1. It would appear therefore that it was open to the PD author to use a phrase for the ark with Yahweh rather than *ᵉlōhîm*, so far as general usage is concerned, but that the latter was natural to him. 'The ark of the covenant of God' (15.24) is rare (Judg. 20.27; 1 Sam. 4.4; 1 Chron. 16.6). The number of uses, and the concentration of them in descriptions of the ark, make too small a base for any firm conclusion; but the occurrence of *ᵉlōhîm* at 15.32 and 16.23, and the absence of Yahweh after 15.8, enforce the suspicion that the PD author spoke most naturally of 'God'. If this is so, we have a further distinction from the main Succession Narrative, with its clear preference for Yahweh.

(7) Now that we have sufficient (if provisional) criteria to identify the PD, we may ask the more difficult, but crucial question, what was *its purpose and function, and its setting in Israelite life*? I have attempted a reconstruction of the text in sections later in this book, but it may suffice here to give an outline. The PD is a series of episodes forming a semi-continuous sequence:

1.	Absalom's Conspiracy	15.7-12
2.	David evacuates Jerusalem	15.13-29 (heavily edited)
3.	David and Hushai	15.30-37
4.	David and Ziba	16.1-4 (edited)
5.	David and Shimei	16.5-7, 13f.
6.	Absalom's Court	16.15–17.14 (heavily edited)
7.	David withdraws to Mahanaim	17.15f; 21–29
8.	The Battle of the Forest of Ephraim	18.1-7 (edited)
9.	Sheba's Revolt	20.1f., 4-15 (edited)
10.	Adonijah and Solomon	1 Kings 1 (heavily edited)

We may note first the almost *liturgical* nature of the first part of the sequence. Aspects of this are noted in many commentaries: I cite Kyle McCarter, who himself takes up points from others.

> The king is marching into exile, but his flight seems sometimes to have the character of a religious pilgrimage rather than a strategic military retreat (Gressmann) . . . Indeed, as many commentators stress (Caspari, etc.), details of the narrative suggest that his journey over the Mount of Olives was made as an act of penance: 'All the land was weeping aloud' (16.23), and as for the king himself, 'His head was bare and he went along barefooted' (15.30). Ackroyd sees in these details evidence that 'the story of an actual rebellion is being told under the influence of forms which belong to worship, in which the humiliation and triumph of the king are celebrated not as historical events but as indications of the king's relationship to God'.

In particular, a problem is posed by the repeated mention in chs.

15–16 of very *specific locations* near Jerusalem, where David encounters a sequence of a significant people:

15.17	Beth-Merhak, by Kidron	Ittai, Zadok and Abiathar
15.30	The Ascent of Olives	Ahitophel's Treachery
15.32	The top, by the shrine	Hushai
16.1	A little past the top	Ziba
16.5	Bahurim	Shimei

It is not very likely that such a succession of detailed locations was preserved casually, as memories of the event which hung on because the places were familiar; such a succession is unparalleled in the OT, although many events take place around Jerusalem. We are reminded rather of the Stations of the Cross. Religious processions were a feature of Israelite festivals. We have a description of Nehemiah's celebration of the autumn festival with a double procession ringing the city to west and east after the completion of the walls (Neh. 12.27-43). Psalm 48 is associated with a procession round Jerusalem ('Walk about Zion, and go round about her . . . '), as is Psalm 87 (with dancing, v. 7). A number of psalms imply a procession to the Temple (24, 47, 68, 95). Hence arises the suggestion: the procession-like account of David's withdrawal is due to its being celebrated in subsequent years with liturgical processions,[16] Ackroyd's 'forms which belong to worship'.

But why should anyone wish to rehearse in later years the unhappy tale of David's tribulations? We do not lack evidence that an important theme at the Israelite autumn festival was a session of penitence in atonement for the sins of the year past, with an aspiration to happier times to come; and this has often been linked with suggestions that the king took a significant part in the atonement rituals. But it has equally seemed implausible to think that great kings like Solomon and Ahab submitted to very gross indignities: would it not then be far more credible to suppose that each year a day was given to the memory of royal sins long ago, and long ago atoned for, and of the golden age which issued from their atonement? A religious community needs a liturgy of penitence; and it needs a myth to go with its ritual. The story of the Passion of David supplies just such a myth. The day's ceremonies can recapitulate the sufferings of the noble and pious Israelite hero whom God chose to be the founder of a perpetual dynasty. Later kings can lead the procession from the palace barefoot, and with their heads covered, and weeping as they go. As they leave, the story of Absalom's conspiracy is recited; at Beth-Merhak there is a pause by the Wadi Kidron for the tale of Ittai's loyalty, and of Zadok and Abiathar with the ark; halfway up Olivet is told the coming of word that Ahitophel is with the enemy; at the shrine on the peak the faithfulness of Hushai; a little further, on the track, the support of Ziba; at Bahurim, the insults of Shimei. Each stage of the procession would be about a kilometre. On some eminence, perhaps Mt Scopus, the story is recited of the withdrawal to Mahanaim, the siege, and the final victory in battle. The procession returns to the city and concludes in the Temple, with the tale of the enthronement of Solomon, and the inauguration of a time of just government, national peace, wealth and plenty.

In this way we should have an explanation for the extent and form of the PD. It begins with the beginning of David's humiliation, as he is forced to leave his capital and flee. It ends with David's abdication, and the prospect of an era of happiness for all, under their vine and under their fig tree. It covers in accurate topographical detail the course of David's retreat over the first two miles, with an incident every half mile. It covers with considerable, but less specific detail, the events of Mahanaim and the Forest of Ephraim. It includes the later tribulations of Sheba's rebellion and Adonijah's usurpation.[17] It does not include an account of David's adultery and murder: *de regibus nil nisi bonum*. But this story, known to all, provides the key and resolution of the whole complex. As the Narrator was to express it, putting the words in the mouth of Nathan: 'Thou hast smitten Uriah the Hittite with the sword, and hast taken his wife to be thy wife, and hast slain him with the sword of the children of Ammon. Now therefore, the sword shall never depart from thine house; because thou hast despised me' (12.9f.). David sinned, and in his trials atoned for his sin, and so brought in an age of peace and prosperity: we re-enact his trials, in hope to atone for our sins, and to bring in a happier time. 'Thou hast set our iniquities before thee, Our secret sins in the light of thy countenance. For all our days are passed away in thy wrath: We bring our years to an end as a sigh ... O satisfy us in the morning with thy mercy; That we may rejoice and be glad all our days' (Ps. 90.8f., 14).

The need for such rituals of penitence, and of a myth to recite alongside them, is too obvious to need pressing. Good Friday, and the story of the Passion of Christ, supply it in the Christian tradition. There has been a pre-Paschal fast in the Church, with an associated reading/telling of the Passion story from the beginning (Eusebius, H.E., 5.23.1). Here is Egeria's description of Maundy Thursday night in Jerusalem in 381:

> Then everyone hurries home for a meal, so that, as soon as they have finished it, they can go to the church on Eleona which contains the cave which on this very day the Lord visited with the apostles. There they continue to sing hymns and antiphons suitable to the place and the day, with readings and prayers between, until about eleven o'clock at night. They read the passages from the Gospel about what the Lord said to his disciples when he sat in the very cave which is in the church. At about midnight they leave and go up with hymns to the Imbomon, the place from which the Lord ascended into heaven. And there they again have readings and hymns and antiphons suitable to the day, and the prayers which the bishop says are all appropriate to the day and to the place.
>
> When the cocks begin to crow, everyone leaves the Imbomon, and comes down with singing to the place where the Lord prayed, as the Gospels describe in the passage which begins, 'And he was parted from them about a stone's cast, and prayed'. The bishop and all the people go into a graceful church which has been built there, and have a prayer appropriate to the place and the day, and one suitable hymn. Then the Gospel passage is read where he said to his disciples, 'Watch, lest ye enter into temptation', and, when the whole passage has been read, there is another prayer. From there all of them, including the smallest children, now go down with singing and conduct the bishop to Gethsemane. There are a great many people and they have been crowded together, tired by their vigil, and weakened by their daily fasting—and they have had a very big hill to come down—so they go very slowly on their way to Gethsemane. So that they can all see, they are provided with hundreds of church candles. When everyone arrives at Gethsemane, they have an appropriate prayer, a hymn, and then a reading from the Gospel about the Lord's arrest. By the time it has been read, everyone is groaning and lamenting and weeping so loud that people even across in the city can probably hear it all. Next they go with singing to the city.[18]

Egeria's procession had much of the same character as that which seems to underlie the Prayers of David in the Psalter and the Passion of David in Samuel-Kings. Its liturgy was substantially psalms—'hymns', *t^e^hillîm*—interspersed with readings from the Paschal story: some of them the same psalms, 55, 69, which seemed so clearly prophetic of the Lord's sufferings. The antiphons were probably often psalm-verses also. The route of the procession was in part the same as that implied in 2 Samuel 15. The Eleona church lay towards the top of the 'ascent of Olives'; the Imbomon was on the peak, perhaps the same site 'where God was worshipped' a millennium before, and Hushai displayed the same courage and loyalty that were later to characterize the Twelve. Probably, as I shall argue, both processions began in the evening, and returned to the Temple in the daylight. Beneath both lay the same profound religious drive: to unite the worshipping community, through procession, ritual, recitation and singing, with the passion and ultimate triumph of the cult-hero; to expiate the sins of time foregone; and to partake for the future in a life of divinely blessed happiness.

Chapter 3

SIN AND ATONEMENT (51)

I have now hewn out the seven pillars of my wisdom: the Prayers' Davidic ascription; the unsatisfactory reasons which led to its abandonment; the enduring stalemate in interpretation between the schools of Gunkel and Mowinckel; the unity of the Prayers as a group; the discrimination of an earlier Passion of David narrative behind the Succession Narrative; the linking of Prayers and Passion narrative in a processional liturgy; and the suggestions of a comprehensive sequential correspondence between the Prayers and the Passion story. It remains to welcome my reader to my exegetical banquet; for my wine is mingled, and my table furnished.

51 For the Chief Musician. A Psalm of David: when Nathan the prophet came unto him, after he had gone in to Bath-sheba.
1 Have mercy upon me, O God, according to thy loving kindness:
According to the multitude of thy tender mercies blot out my transgressions.
2 Wash me throughly from mine iniquity,
And cleanse me from my sin.
3 For I know my transgressions:
And my sin is ever before me.
4 Against thee, thee only, have I sinned,
And done that which is evil in thy sight:
That thou mayest be justified in thy speaking (*b^{e}ḏoḇ^{e}reḵā*)
And be clear in thy judging (*b^{e}šop̱^{e}ṭeḵā*).
5 Behold, I was shapen in iniquity;
And in sin did my mother conceive me.
6 Behold, thou desirest truth in the inward parts:
And in the hidden part thou shalt make me to know wisdom.

7 Purge me with hyssop, and I shall be clean:
Wash me, and I shall be whiter than snow.
8 Make me to hear joy and gladness;
That the bones which thou hast bruised (*dikkīṯā*) may rejoice.
9 Hide thy face from my sins,
And blot out all mine iniquities.
10 Create for me a clean heart, O God;
And renew a steadfast spirit within me.

The speaker of 51 has done something terrible. It is a personal psalm ('my mother', v. 5), and there is no other personal confession of guilt in the Psalter to compare with it, either in length or in strength of language. Indeed, it stands in vivid contrast with such psalms as 6, 32 or 38, in which confession is freely interlarded with pathetic accounts of the singer's plight: 51 is not a confession of sins unknown but presumed, to placate God's anger and achieve a return to health. It is entirely taken up with a deep and real sense of sin. The speaker cannot get away from what he has done: it 'is ever before' him (v. 3), it obsesses him. He prays for it to be 'blotted out' (*m*ᵉ*ḥēh*, vv. 1, 9), like the curses which the priest wrote down against the woman suspected of adultery, and washed them away (*māḥāh*) into the waters of bitterness (Num. 5.23). He prays to be 'washed throughly from' it (*herebh kabb*ᵉ*sēnî*, v. 2): not rinsed, as Uriah was to rinse his feet in a bowl (2 Sam. 11.8, *rāḥaṣ*), but *kibbēs*, trodden, as clothes are trodden in fuller's earth (Isa. 7.3, the fuller's 'field')—and trodden repeatedly (*herebh*, Q *hereḇ*, imper. hiph., K *harbēh*, inf. abs.) because they are impregnated with dirt. He prays to be cleansed (*ṭah*ᵃ*rēnî*), because he is unclean from it, as the incense-altar is cleansed in Lev. 16.19. He feels himself to be so deeply wicked that sin is in his very nature from his birth and conception (v. 5). The Hebrews hardly ever felt as badly as this. At the time of the flood Yahweh felt that 'the imagination of man's heart is evil from his youth' (Gen. 8.21), and Job occasionally speaks of himself as unclean (14.4; 15.14; 25.4); but the closest parallel is in the Prayers themselves, where 'The wicked are estranged from the womb; They go astray as soon as they be born' (58.3). The speaker of 51 feels that he is radically wicked, from his conception. His only hope is a totally new beginning: 'Create in me a clean heart, O God' (v. 10). There are few more radical words in Hebrew than *bārā'*, which is always used of divine action: he is asking for a new creation within him, like the new heavens and the new earth created in Isa. 65.17, or the transformed nature created in Isa. 41.20. He has done something really dreadful.

Gunkel took the bruised bones of v. 8 as an indication that the speaker was ill, but modern commentators stress the centrality of his guilt. Kraus[1] warns against 'das Dogma von der kausalen Zusammengehörigkeit von Krankheit und Schuld in alle Psalmen hineinzutragen', and cites J.J. Stamm, 'dem Psalmisten die Befreiung von seinen Sünden wichtiger als die wörtlich nicht erwähnte Genesung (war)'.

However, critics are almost unanimous in taking v. 5 to refer to the universality of human sin, transmitted from generation to generation; only Rogerson and McKay make an honourable exception in seeing the reference as personal—and they tremble. But the passages cited do not bear on our psalm, which speaks so personally of 'I was born . . . my mother', not of all men. God's despair over mankind after the Flood in Gen. 8.21 is quite exceptional. Job is being represented as in the extremes of suffering, so of course he sometimes says that he is unclean (14.4), or that man born of woman cannot be clean or righteous before God (15.14; 25.4). There are similar statements of man's unrighteousness before God in Ps. 143.2 or Prov. 20.9; and the prophets on occasion speak of Israel as corrupt (Isa. 43.27; Jer. 17.9; Ezek. 16; Hos. 2). But the general, and healthy instinct of Israelite thinking was that there was an inclination for good as well as an inclination for ill in man. It was seen that no one was perfect, and that humility before God was in order; but the prophetic comments are rhetorical, and should be seen as invective and not theology. Gunkel and Anderson cite Leviticus 12, 15 on the association of sex and childbirth with uncleanness; but children did not require purification after birth (except in Lk. 2.22, and Luke did not understand), so there was no sense of contamination from conception and birth as such. We have rather to see the speaker as using the strongest language available to him to express his personal guilt. He is wicked, like the wicked of 58, estranged from the womb. He is rotten to the roots, and even implicates his mother.

51.14. What then has he done? We seem to have the answer in v. 14: 'Deliver me from bloodguiltiness, O God, thou God of my salvation'—he has done a murder. The Hebrew plural *damîm*, 'bloods', carries this meaning elsewhere. Shimei cursed David, 'Begone, begone, thou *'îš haddāmîm* . . . the LORD hath returned on thee all the blood of (*d*e*mê*) the house of Saul' (2 Sam. 16.7f.). Shimel is calling David a murderer for the death of Ishbaal and others, and sees in his retreat Yahweh's 'returning' all the *damîm* of the house of Saul on his head. In the same way it seems that our speaker has committed a murder, and prays to be delivered from the 'bloods' that may be expected to 'return on' him. Similarly Exod. 22.2f. (Heb. 22.1) provides: 'If the thief be found breaking in, and be smitten that he die, there shall be no *dāmîm lô*. If the sun be risen upon him, there shall be *dāmîm lô*, bloodguiltiness for him'. The householder is not held to be guilty of murder if he kills the thief in the dark; but if he kills him in the light, there is 'blood' (-guilt) for him. Or again, both Abigail and David are grateful that 'the LORD hath withholden thee/me from bloodguiltiness' (*bô' b^e^ḏāmîm*, 1 Sam. 25.26, 33). God has returned the evil-doing of Nabal on his own head (25.39), and it has not been necessary for David to do evil (*ibid.*) and to 'come into blood', with the perils of such guilt, human and divine. We often hear similarly of a man's *dāmîm* being on his own head (Lev. 20.9, 11, 12, 13, etc.): that is, the guilt for his death is his own. So there is no lack of evidence for *dāmîm* meaning 'bloodguiltiness'; and such a meaning would consort well with the desperate feelings of guilt with which the psalm is laden. We may also note the overladen metre of v. 14a, 'Deliver me from bloodguiltiness, O God, thou God of my salvation', five stresses against the psalm's regular three. We ought not to strike out the last two *metri causa*, as is done by Gunkel and many: they are a further testimony to the speaker's anguish, which is most deeply felt as he comes to put into words the dreadful act that he has done.

Such an interpretation seemed obvious to the older commentators, and we still find it in Delitzsch and Kirkpatrick, with references to David's murder of Uriah. But once the Davidic tradition has been set aside, some other view may seem to be required; and many have been tried. I will mention five. (1) E.R. Dalglish[2] suggests an extention of the older view. The speaker is King Josiah, and he is anxious lest the guilt of the executions under his predecessors may fall on the nation in his time. (2) Eaton, followed by Rogerson and McKay, proposes a further extension. *dāmîm* means guilt in general, not just for murder, as may be seen in Isa. 1.18; 4.4; Hos. 12.14; Ezek. 16. (3) NEB translates *dāmîm* as 'bloodshed', i.e. being murdered: the action is taken to be passive, and in the future. (4) The most popular solution is that proposed by Duhm: '*dâmîm* kann hier nur dasselbe bedeuten wie in Ps. 30.10: den Tod durch die von Jahwe geschickte Krankheit, nicht etwa einen gewaltsamen Tod von der Hand der Feinde, die ja nirgends erwähnt werden'. This is followed by Kraus, Weiser, Anderson and others, and is adapted by Mowinckel, who does see a violent death at the hand of enemies, i.e. sorcerers, whether mentioned or not (*Ps. st.* I, 142). (5) Various proposals have been made to amend the text. Gunkel thought *dumâm*, silence, should be read, like *dûmâ* in Ps. 94.17, 'My soul had soon dwelt in (the land of) silence'. Dahood reads *dammîm*, tears, i.e. the tears of death. Jacquet thinks *dāmîm* is a later gloss.

I do not think that any of these proposals is viable. Dalglish's national view shares the weakness of all corporate views of the speaker: the language is so personal, especially v. 5. NEB's 'bloodshed' introduces an alien element into the psalm, which is elsewhere about the speaker's sins, not his fear of the sin of others, as Duhm correctly says. It has been said that he fears being killed because he has killed himself; which would bring us round the full circle. Neither Gunkel's change of vocalization nor Dahood's quite give the sense they want—'Deliver me from silence' does not necessarily imply 'from death', still less 'Deliver me from tears'; and with a corpus like the psalms, which have probably been preserved because of their continuous use in the liturgy, emendations can be persuasive only when the MT yields nonsense.

For (2), is Eaton correct that 'blood' can be used for guilt in general? Isa. 1.18, 'though your sins be as scarlet . . . ', and 4.4, 'when the Lord . . . shall have purged the blood of Jerusalem from the midst thereof' have to be read alongside 1.15, 'your hands are full of blood'. As so often, it is difficult to know if Isaiah is pointing to real murders (which happen in every community) or if this is more prophetic invective: he refers to Jerusalem as Sodom, but we should not think it likely that homosexual practices were widespread. But in any case it is quite unclear that *dāmîm* means guilt in general; and in 4.4 it is parallel to 'when the Lord shall have washed away the filth of the daughters of Zion', and may refer to menstrual blood. Similarly the blood of Ezekiel 16 arises from the image of the foundling child which was unwashed at birth. In Hos. 12.14, 'therefore shall his blood be left upon him', the issue is clearer: at 6.7f. it is said that Gilead 'is stained with blood' and that 'the company of priests murder in the way toward Shechem', so there is naturally *blood*-guilt on Ephraim. So there is really no adequate evidence that *dāmîm* can mean guilt apart from blood-guilt.

Duhm's solution, (4), is even less convincing. Ps. 30.9 (10) runs,

> What profit is there in my blood (*dāmî*), when I go down to the
> pit?
> Shall the dust praise thee? shall it declare thy truth?

'Blood' does not mean 'death through sickness sent by Yahweh' here at all: it is parallel to 'dust', and these together form the two elements of the live man—'for the life of all flesh is the blood thereof' (Lev. 17.14). The blood and dust are only of profit when united in the living man, to praise Yahweh in this world. Even though the context here associates 'blood' with dying, that meaning would never be suggested without such a context; nor is the singular *dāmî* quite the same as the plural *dāmîm* of Psalm 51, which almost always implies *violent* death.

But if the speaker is involved in the guilt of having killed, we are faced with a problem of a different kind. The killing can hardly be manslaughter or bloodfeud, or he would not feel so dreadful about it—'Behold, I was shapen in iniquity . . . ' It sounds ineluctably like murder, and Israelite law provided a clear penalty for murder: 'He that smiteth a man so that he die, shall surely be put to death' (Exod. 21.12; cf. Lev. 24.17; Num. 35.16-21). Murderers might not escape with making financial compensation (Num. 35.31), nor by fleeing to cities of refuge (Deut. 19.11f.), but must be put to death so as to 'put away the innocent blood from Israel' (Deut. 19.13). How then, we must ask, can the speaker *hope* to escape blood-guilt? Will he not automatically be stoned to death for his sin?

51.7. The text makes clear, however, that he is not going to be executed; indeed he is hoping for total restoration (vv. 10ff.), for an opportunity to teach sinners (v. 13) and publicly to praise God (vv. 14f.), and even in due time to offer sacrifice (v. 19). The atonement which he is required to make is limited to the rites mentioned in vv. 6-8. The first of these referred to is 'Unsin me (*t*^{e}*ḥaṭṭ*^{e}*'ēnî*) with hyssop'. This is usually understood to involve sprinklng with the twigs of a hyssop bush, whether with blood or water (Kraus, Eaton); for hyssop is mentioned as a means of sprinkling in other OT rites, whether at Passover (Exod. 12.22), or with leprosy (Lev. 14.4f.) or with the red heifer (Num. 19.18). Such a purgative ritual seems very mild, and can hardly be right. According to Michael Zohary,[3] hyssop is not (as is widely asserted) European hyssop (*hyssopus officinalis L.*), which does not grow in Palestine, but the Syrian hyssop (*origanum syriacum L.*); J.C. Trever comes to a similar conclusion (*origanum maru* L.).[4] Origanum is a powerfully tasting herb, and is sold as such in Arab markets today and used as a spice. It is much more likely that the speaker of 51 *drank* a strong potion of hyssop. (i) The preceding verse says, 'Behold, thou desirest truth in the inward parts: And in the hidden part thou shalt make me to know wisdom'. The singer is born in iniquity, conceived in sin (v. 5), he is rotten to the core (*sāṯum*, the shut up place; *ṭuḥôṯ*, the reins): but it is there that God wants truth, and from there alone that the knowledge of wisdom can flow. It is internal cleansing that the speaker needs (v. 6), and it is this which a strong draught of hyssop may be thought to provide (v. 7). In sufficient concentration it would have a violent effect on the digestive system. (ii) He prays to be 'sinned', as we speak of 'fleaing' a dog, that is to be rid of his sin (privative piel, G-K 52h), and we should expect that to be followed by the *means* of riddance, the water, blood, etc., rather than with the instrument of application, the hyssop-twigs, in the normal view; as in Exod. 12.22f., where it is the blood on the doorposts, not the hyssop it is sprinkled with, which is the Israelites' protection. If the hyssop is drunk, it is itself the means of 'sinning', and the meaning runs naturally. In any case the man cannot have been sprinkled with *blood* (the most common suggestion), for the blood would have to come from a sacrifice, and we are expressly told, 'thou delightest not in sacrifice that I should give it'. (iii) A parallel rite of purgation by drinking is given by Falkenstein and von Soden in a Babylonian prayer to Marduk, 'May the tamarisk purify me, may the . . .-plant redeem me, may the palm-pith do away my sins'.[5] Such practices are very widespread: the bishop offers Alexander a bottle of castor oil as an alternative punishment to the cane in Ingmar Bergman's 'Fanny and Alexander', and the Swedish director was himself able to redeem his sins each Friday in youth by his father's administration of both sacraments.

51.8. Bergman had both the bottle and the cane; and the same is suggested for our speaker by v. 8,'Make me to hear joy and gladness, That the bones which thou hast bruised may rejoice'. The root *dkh* is used of physical pounding: Israel has been crushed (*dikkîṯānû*) by defeat into an abode of jackals (Ps. 44.19), and the floods lift up their pounding waves (*dāḵîm*) in Ps. 93.3. So here: 'the bones which thou hast pounded (*dikkîṯā*)' implies that the speaker has been flogged. Flogging was a second-line penalty in Israel, limited in application in our biblical legal traditions, but its free use seems to be implied in Solomonic times by 1 Kgs 12.11, 14, 'My father chastised you with whips . . . ' Perhaps the merciful forty-stroke law was already in place (Deut. 25.1-3); and perhaps not. A believable picture thus emerges. The man is a murderer, and is obsessed with his guilt. He atones for his sin with a threefold expiation rite. First he is whipped; then he drinks the hyssop potion; finally he is washed—the blood runs off him, and he knows that his back will heal: he will be whiter than snow. He can look forward once more to being part of the national festival with its 'joy and gladness', the cheering and laughter that attended Israel's new queen as she was carried in her palanquin to the king's palace in Ps. 44.15, or David with the ark in 2 Sam. 6.12.

Gunkel took the 'pounded bones' to represent sickness (see above, p. 53), and this is still widely supported, whether as an accompaniment of spiritual distress (Jacquet), or as an alternative (Anderson). Eaton[6] is alone in suggesting 'blows', but he has in mind something rather gentle and symbolic, as at Babylon.

51.4. As the means of expiation become clear, so does v. 4. Someone has to say for the confessing sinner what his penance is to be, and this duty has probably fallen to the priest (Lev. 10.11; Hag. 2.11), or some prophet like Samuel (1 Sam. 15.33) or Nathan (2 Sam. 12.10f.) who spoke in the name of God. Hence 'That thou mayest be justified in thy speaking And be clear in thy judging': God has 'spoken' and given his judgment through the priest or prophet, so many lashes and a draught of hyssop—and after that no one is to complain that justice has not been done, and that the punishment has been too soft. This would be entirely natural in the case of a murder, since murderers were normally handed over to the relatives of the dead man for execution. It seems indeed to be hinted when the speaker says, 'Against thee, thee only, have I sinned, And done that which is evil in thy sight, That (*l^{e}ma'an*) thou mayest be justified...' Murder is, of course, like all moral fault, a sin against Yahweh, and David can say after the death of Uriah, 'I have sinned against Yahweh' (2 Sam. 12.13); but it is also, self-evidently, a sin against the dead man (and his family). It is true that the religious mind gives centrality to the relationship with God, and that elsewhere in the Prayers we find a similar stress: 'My soul is silent unto God only . . . He only is my rock . . . ' (62.1, 6); 'I will make mention of thy righteousness, even of thine only' (71.16); 'Give us help against the adversary: for vain is the help of man' (60.11). But it does seem rather convenient here that the concerns of the dead man should be totally overlooked; and the suspicion that this is the force of 'thee only', *l^{e}ḇadd^{e}ḵā*, is confirmed by the otherwise puzzling final particle *l^{e}ma'an*. The speaker is confessing his guilt against God *only, in order that* there should be no complaints about the sentence of expiation. Gunkel comments correctly, 'niemand anders geht meine Sünde an als dich; niemand kann Einspruch erheben wenn du vergeben willst'. But Gunkel did not suggest any reason for raising objections.

Both *l^{e}ḇadd^{e}ḵā* and *l^{e}ma'an* present critics with uncomfortable choices. If the sin is only against God, earlier critics took it to be idolatry. Gunkel dismissed this: rather the speaker was aware that 'sein Herz nicht ganz bei

Gott gewesen ist, nicht völlig rein, nicht in allem dankbar, folgsam und vertrauend', but he was not guilty of the immoral conduct which his relations (like Job's friends) took to be the cause of his illness. He confesses in order that God may be honoured, and so mercifully heal him. The picture is at least consistent, if implausibly pietist. Less admirable is the standard view of almost all commentators which appeals to Josh. 7.19, 'My son, give glory to Yahweh', and to 2 Sam. 12.13, David's, 'I have sinned against Yahweh', to justify the claim that somehow all sin is against God *only*. So Delitzsch: 'in the last analysis all sin is against Him alone', and H.H. Rowley, 'sin against man is not the infringement of rights which are man's by nature, but the infringement of rights which are his because God willed that they should be his'.[7] Delitzsch's (common) view is a pious evasion: if Uriah has been murdered, Uriah has been wronged as well as God. Rowley's exalted theological talk is an irrelevance: if God has given man rights, then those rights are his, and a sin against those rights is not a sin against God only.

There is similar trouble with *l^ema'an*. The particle is almost always final, but the meaning would run smoothly for the standard view if it were consecutive. Dahood makes it consecutive, as does Jacquet ('Oh certes . . . '). Kirkpatrick has a crypto-consecutive sense, 'The consequence of his sin is therefore in a sense its purpose (for nothing is independent of the sovereign will of God). . . ' Delitzsch, Anderson and many make the clause dependent on 'I acknowledge' in v. 3: the speaker 'says Amen to the penal sentence so that God may be in the right', says the former, citing Rom. 3.4. But is the psalmist's concern that God should be 'justified' and 'clear' in his sentence really as pure as the apostle's?

11 Cast me not away from thy presence;
And take not thy holy spirit from me.
12 Restore unto me the joy of thy salvation:
And uphold me with a royal (*n^edîḇâ*) spirit.
13 Then will I teach transgressors thy ways;
And sinners shall return unto thee.
14 Deliver me from bloodguiltiness, O God, thou God of my salvation;
My tongue shall sing aloud of thy righteousness.
15 O Lord, open thou my lips;
And my mouth shall shew forth thy praise.

51.11-15. All of this, however, only serves to reinforce our problem. The psalmist is guilty of murder, and he has been sentenced, not to death, but to a beating and a purgative; and he is pleading disingenuously that his fault is against God alone, and that God should not be blamed (!, *tiṣdaq*, *tizkeh*, v. 4) for the lenient punishment. How then can he get away with it? The answer must surely be: because he is the king. Only the king would have the position and influence to be above the law in this way; and we have an instance of the king's so being in that David was not executed for the murder of Uriah. Furthermore there are a number of indications elsewhere in the psalm that the king is the speaker. 'Cast me not away from thy presence; And take not thy holy spirit from me' (v. 11): ordinary Israelites did not have daily access to the divine presence, nor reckon to possess the holy spirit of God. It was the king and his priests who were day by day in the temple, and so in God's presence; it was the king and the prophets who might lay claim especially to His holy spirit—the king sacramentally, by virtue of his anointing (1 Sam. 10.1, 6, 10f.; 16.13; 2 Sam. 3.2ff.). 'Restore unto me the joy of thy salvation: And uphold me with a princely spirit' (v. 12). The joy which the speaker hoped to hear in v. 8, the joy and gladness of the Israelite festival, when sin has been atoned for, and God's blessing can be looked for in 'salvation', military, agricultural and in all kinds. The 'spirit' stands in the same position in each of vv. 10-12 (*w^e^rûaḥ* first word in the second hemistich). Here the spirit is *n^e^d̲îb̲â*, and *nād̲îb̲* normally (x20) carries the meaning of prince, or princely; only in the later texts Exod. 35.5, 22; 1 Chron. 28.21 does the meaning extend to generous, devoted. He wants the restoration of his former royal spirit—feminine as a human spirit, masculine in v. 10 as a newly-created divine spirit, which would be *nāk̲ôn*, steadfast in temptation.

With such a spirit ('Then') he will teach transgressors God's ways, and sinners will turn to Him (v. 13). It is difficult to see how this can refer to anything but royal action, either in the liturgy, or in the daily administration of justice. The Israelites did not have reformatories with Bible classes. Transgressors were taught God's ways in public recitals of the Law, or else when they were condemned by the king, and his just punishments might hope to turn them to better living. But he can only judge others if he has expiated his own guilt ('Deliver me from bloodguiltiness, O God', v. 14). Till then he must keep shamed silence: when that is done, his tongue can sing aloud of God's righteousness and show forth his praise, for the Lord will have opened his lips (v. 15). The context ties all these ideas together. Expiation of his guilt will enable the king alike to be present in the temple, to judge the guilty and to take the lead in national worship. Tradition represents all the kings from David (1 Chron. 29.11-19) and Solomon (1 Kgs 8) to Hezekiah (2 Kgs 19.15-19) as leading the liturgy.

Dalglish argued from Akkadian psalms that the speaker was the king in Psalm 51; and Eaton takes the same view. He appeals to the LXX translation of *n^e^ḏîḇâ*, ἡγεμονικῷ; to the use of 'holy Spirit' in connection with Moses as Israel's leader in Isa. 63.11; to the royal covenant implied in such expressions as *ḥasdeḵā* (v. 1), *ṣiḏ^e^kāṯeḵā* (v. 14) and *t^e^šû'āṯî* (v. 14); and to other arguments as well as those above (*KP*, 71f.). But this conclusion is uncommon. Gunkel sees 'thy holy spirit' as the 'seligen Erfahrung von der sanften und doch allgewaltigen Macht Gottes im Herzen der Frommen', which he acknowledges to be 'fast einzig' in the Old Testament. Healed of his 'Krankenheit', the speaker will 'ein fröhliches Danklied singen, das seinen Ruhm verkündet, und er kann, wenn er darin Gottes Walten in seinem Leben erzählt, "die Frevler Gottes Wege lehren"'. Such a picture reappears in many commentaries: but are the sinners imagined as hanging around the Temple waiting to hear testimonies, as at Hyde Park Corner? Or was a time allotted for such testimonies at the national festivals? Jacquet appeals to Hymn 2.7-9 from Qumran (Hod. col. 17.26), but the context shows that 'those who rebel . . . traitors . . . the wicked' are those outside the sect, while 'those who repent . . . the simple' are the members, and G. Vermes thinks it probable that the hymn was recited by the Guardian and newly initiated members at Pentecost.[8] Kraus compares 'thy holy spirit' with Ezek. 36.25ff. and passages in Jeremiah; but these concern a new gift of the spirit to Israel—the speaker here has the holy spirit, and does not want it taken away. Appeals to other David psalms such as 22 and 143 are not helpful, because they are also claimed to be royal psalms: it is entirely believable that the king (or the temple staff) testified of God's righteousness and 'taught the wicked' in the festal liturgy, but a plausible public setting is still to be given for private Danklieder.

51.4. We have now reached what might normally be considered a rather absurd situation. We have a psalm which tradition describes as 'For David', and for which it further prescribes the occasion: 'when Nathan the prophet came unto him, after he had gone in to Bath-sheba'. There appear to be powerful arguments from several features of the psalm for thinking that it is spoken in the name of the king; that the speaker has been responsible for a murder; and that he feels such extreme guilt for this that he is prepared to accept a public thrashing and other humiliations. The Succession Narrative, an account of events probably written within some fifty years, apparently takes up phrases from the psalm in its description of Nathan's interview with David:

Ps. 51.4	And done that which is evil in thy sight (*w^e^hāra' b^ec^êneîḵā 'āśîṯî*

2 Sam. 12.9	Wherefore hast thou despised the word of the LORD, to do that which is evil in his sight (*la'^{a}śôṯ hāra' b^{e}'ênaw*)
Ps. 51.4	Against thee, thee only have I sinned (*l^{e}ḵā... ḥāṭā'ṯî*)
2 Sam. 12.13	I have sinned against the LORD (*ḥāṭā'ṯî laYHWH*).

On almost any other question it would be asked, Why then should we so single-mindedly refuse to believe the tradition? Why should we not simply accept that the psalm was written, as it says, in the aftermath of David's administrative murder of Uriah, and composed either by him himself, or by his *m^{e}naṣṣēaḥ*, his Master of the King's Musick? Indeed, it might be thought obvious that this was the case.

Obvious, however, it has not been, and some reply must be made to a variety of objections.

(1) It may be felt that it is unlikely that a king should have submitted to a whipping, and that the text of 2 Samuel 12 gives no hint of such a penalty. However, we have to bear in mind Israelite belief in the corporate effect of sin, and especially of sin in the king, the channel through whom so much of the divine blessing must flow. Even adultery by a commoner was 'folly in Israel', and murder by a commoner must be expiated by death—'Thine eye shall not pity (the killer), but thou shalt put away the innocent blood from Israel, that it may go well with thee' (Deut. 19.13). How much more when it is the king! It is not surprising that we lack parallels for such penalties in Israelite history. When kings like Ahab or Jehoiakim had their private enemies stoned, or filled Jerusalem with blood, they did so 'with a high hand' and were not filled with remorse like our psalmist; and the D-historian felt that the disasters which later befell Israel and Judah were in part God's punishment of these unrepented sins. We have a distant but apt parallel, however, in Henry Plantagenet, King of England, who authorized the murder of Thomas Becket, Archbishop of Canterbury, in 1170, and who expiated his guilt with four hundred lashes. In Henry's case the penance was imposed by the Pope. But the common, driving force in both David's and Henry's cases was the appalling national feeling of offence against the primary law of God, which could not be defied with impunity—a feeling deeply shared by the king himself. Peoples do not expect their monarchs to condemn themselves to death (and nor do the monarchs); but they expect that some serious atonement be offered,

and the humiliation and pain of a flogging may be acceptable. It is not surprising either that the Succession Narrative does not mention the matter. It is royalist document, concerned with exalting the line of David and to please his descendants. Its central thrust is to tell how the sword would never depart from David's house in punishment for his taking Uriah's wife, and killing him with the sword of the children of Ammon (2 Sam. 12.9f.). It gives a second expiation in the rape of David's concubines by Absalom, and a third in the death of his child. To describe the king's humiliation under the whip might give the unfortunate impression that his successors could be liable to the same discipline.

(2) Gunkel thought a derivation of the psalm from David impossible.

> Die Anschauung jener alten Zeit über Opfer und Gottesdienst ist eine bei weitem derbere als die vergeistigte des Psalms vgl. II Sam. 21. Und welche Kluft liegt zwischen den urwüchsigen Geisteswirkungen von I Sam. 19.18ff. und denjenigen, an die der Psalmist denkt!

The crudeness, and perhaps the political motivation, of David in acceding to the Gibeonites' demand for blood vengeance, and the primitive ecstasies of the early prophetic guilds, are alike a long step from the civilised post-exilic times where Gunkel sets Psalm 51. But it is a simple error (to which Gunkel's generation was prone) to draw a graph from the barbarous and spiritually impoverished times of David through the moral insights of the great prophets to Christianity, and to plot all documents on this spirituality curve. A quite simple community may recognize the guilt of premeditated murder (2 Sam. 12.13), distinguish it from other killings (Exod. 21.12ff.), and recognize that deliberate and serious sins cannot be bought off with the sacrifice of an animal (Exod. 32.30-35). God would accept no atonement from Moses for the golden Calf; slaughter (in the oldest story), and plague (in E) were the only means to restoration. The inadequacy of sacrificing compared with obedience is attributed to Samuel in 1 Sam. 15.22, and tradition repeatedly credits David with novel spiritual insights (1 Sam. 24.6; 26.9, 19; 2 Sam. 12.22; 15.25f.; 16.10ff.; 19.22f.; 1 Chron. 11.19).

(3) Gunkel objects, secondly, that the prayer for the building of the walls does not fit David's time as (a) the king was responsible for the fortification of his capital, and (b) Jerusalem's walls are presupposed to be lying 'ganz oder teilweise in Trümmern'. This point seems

misconceived. Religious men have always called on God to forward projects understood to be his will, while at the same time accepting responsibility for carrying them out; and the text in no way implies that the walls were wholly or partially in ruins—see below on vv. 16-19.

(4) Finally Gunkel points to a tension between 2 Samuel 11f. and Ps. 51.4: 'David, der ein Weib verführt und ihren Mann schändlich zum Tode preisgegeben hat, darf doch wahrlich nicht sagen, er habe gegen Gott allein gesündigt'. There is indeed a tension here; and the resolution of it (see above, p. 58) is that David wishes to escape the penalty that might be exacted by Uriah's family, and limit his sin to that against (a lenient) God. Being Hittites, Uriah's relatives might be in a weak position to press their case for the king's blood, and we can think of reasons for his wife keeping silence; so David could expect to get away with confessing his sin against God alone.

(5) Further difficulties are urged by Jacquet: '*Le style et la pensée* apparentent le Ps. aux écrits *des grands Prophètes*, notamment d'Isaie (cf. 1.18, etc...), surtout de Jérémie (cf. 24.7; 31.33; 32.39) ... jusqu'à 5 des formules charactéristiques de l'un de ses Oracles (33.6-11)'. The verb *ḥiṭṭē'* in v. 7 is proper to Ezekiel (x4) and the Priestly Code, and the renewal of the heart is a repeated theme in Ezekiel (esp. 36.24-38). These features led Mowinckel and Kraus (and many, including Jacquet himself) to place the psalm in exilic times. What is surprising in these authors is the assumption, without any argument, that where there is style and content in common, the psalm must be later. We have to beware of unargued approaches which would make T.S. Eliot's phrase 'now and at the hour of our death' a source for the Book of Common Prayer, or Noel Coward's 'Perchance to Dream' an inspiration for Shakespeare. Behind the lack of argument stands the assumption—openly stated a century ago—that creative religious insight was the achievement of the prophets in Israel, and that priests and psalmists represented popular religion, limping along behind them. But there is no reason at all for thinking that this was so. King David's humble words, the natural and proper reaction of one responsible for a man's death so that he might cloak and perpetuate his adultery, might well be repeated for generations in the liturgy; and phrases from them could well seem applicable to Israel in later centuries—sins washed whiter than snow in Isaiah, a new heart in Jeremiah and Ezekiel, the forgiveness of sins and iniquities in all three. In fact the theory of prophetic creativity *ex*

nihilo is not as popular as it was; but its ghost lives on today from the great Psalms commentataries of the 20s.

(6) '*Les sentiments de "contrition parfaite"* du psalmiste s'ajustent bien difficilement sur les actes de repentir de David après sa faute, lesquels, selon II Sam. 12.13-25, manquent de spontanéité, demeurent foncièrement *intéressés* et *ne survivent pas à la mort de son enfant*'. Jacquet is hard on David. 2 Samuel 12 keeps a total silence on whatever David's spontaneous response may have been to Nathan's revelation, other than his confession. When his child is about to die, his fasting, prayer and sleeping on the ground seem quite spontaneous, and it is harsh to say of any father praying for his dying son that his religion is 'intéressé'. The fact that David ends his fast when the child dies is represented as his bowing to the will of God, and is admired by the author of the Succession Narrative. The incident may well have happened months or years after the interview with Nathan, and can allow no conclusions on the genuineness of David's repentance.

In view of all this, it is hard not to conclude that the case for associating the psalm with David, Uriah and Nathan is strong, and that the objections to it are weak. They rest in fact on the unspoken assumption that association with David is 'conservative' (i.e. dogmatic), and unworthy of serious discussion since the arrival of form-criticism; and on the conviction of earlier critics that tenth-century Israelite religion was too 'primitive' to have produced such high spirituality, which could be credibly derived only from the great Prophets. But conservatism and dogma are not the monopoly of evangelicals. Tradition always deserves to be treated seriously. Even the historical note in the heading, 'when Nathan the prophet. . . ' is not valueless. It is no doubt the *guess* of later generations, who have guessed incorrectly at the situation of seven of the other Prayers. But it is a testimony to the lingering on of a tradition that the David psalms were not merely associated with King David, but were the reaction of him or his court-poet to particular historical crises in his life, some of which are known to us from the accounts in Samuel-Kings. It is my conviction that this tradition was profoundly right, and that its rejection has meant the loss of the key to understanding the whole sequence.

Davidic authorship was still accepted by more traditional leading critics at the end of the last century, including Delitzsch and Kirkpatrick: more recently, it has been defended by Aubrey Johnson.[9] The association with David has usually been seen since Gunkel as a later misunderstanding, and without significance. A number of rather unsatisfactory middle ways have been suggested. Dalglish, working on the basis of numerous parallels from Akkadian psalms, thought the 'David' tradition signified that 51 was a royal psalm of penitence for the sins of the nation, spoken by King Josiah, or in his name; but the personal details make this implausible. Rowley[10] suggested that 'the Psalmist may have composed it with David in mind, to be used by others who were conscious of heinous sins' (cited by Anderson): but if the heinous sin is 'bloodguiltiness' it would not be much use to them, for they would be executed. Jacquet falls back on a proposal of the Biblical Commission of 1910 to have it both ways, with an original Davidic song of repentance which has been '*refondu, repensé*, par un pénitent de l'Ère des Prophètes, à la lumière d'une Théologie morale *plus évoluée du Péché*, de la Contrition et du Pardon'; but he offers no evidence for this comforting speculation.

16 For thou delightest not in sacrifice, that I should give it:
Thou hast no pleasure in a burnt offering (*'ôlâ*).
17 The sacrifices of God are a broken spirit:
A broken and a contrite heart, O God, thou wilt not despise.
18 Do good in thy good pleasure unto Zion;
Build thou the walls of Jerusalem.
19 Then shalt thou delight in the sacrifices of righteousness, in burnt offering and whole burnt offering:
Then shall they offer bullocks upon thine altar.

51.16f. do not express a general rejection of sacrificial worship, but rather the speaker's own unworthiness to offer sacrifice, and God's refusal of such cheap grace. I have already cited God's refusal of Moses' prayer of atonement, and his insistence on punishment with death in Exod. 32.30-35; and we have a similar early legend about David's numbering of the people in 2 Samuel 24—God refuses to 'put away' the king's iniquity, even when confessed in humility, and is satisfied only with the deaths of seventy thousand Israelites in pestilence. The J and E traditions of God's inexorable discipline through plague or defeat in the desert (Numbers 11, 14) show how ancient is the conviction that divine justice is not to be bought off with animal sacrifice. With time, religion becomes less uncomfortable and the entire nation's sins can be understood to be forgiven through the observances of a Yom Kippur; but those days are not yet. God will not accept a burnt offering, but he will accept a shattered (*nišbārâ*) and pounded (*nidkeh*) heart and spirit. It is an easy mistake to see these familiar words as the expression of a purely spiritual condition, of humility and contrition. But to the Hebrew, the spirit and the heart were but the inner aspects of the united, psychosomatic man; and the verb behind 'contrite' (*dkh*) is the same as in 'the bones which thou hast bruised' (*dikkîṯā*) in v. 8. David has been beaten, and as his bones have been pounded and shattered, so have his spirit and his heart. He is experiencing what David Lodge has called 'that laundered feeling'.

Gunkel had 'kein Zweifel' that the refusal of sacrifice 'auf die schroffe Abweisung alles äusseren Dienstes durch die Propheten zurückgeht'. He also thought the psalmist was 'arm und kostbare Dankopfer von Tieren nicht bringen könnte'. Nothing in the text supports the latter idea, and the former is now widely rejected.[11] Anderson has the main point: 'the Law simply does not prescribe any atoning sacrifices for such things as murder and adultery, and since these or similar grave offences may have been the cause of the Psalmist's downfall, it is clear that the only alternative was penitence'. But even Anderson misses the outward and visible aspect of the latter.

51.18f. As is usual in Hebrew poetry, the psalm ends on a happier note. In the present situation God will not accept animal sacrifice: the only thing he will accept ('the sacrifices of God') is the penitence which David feels after the flogging. But (the penitent must hope) if God has accepted such a sacrifice as this, then he will not withhold his blessing from the great work which David has undertaken in his name. David had taken Jerusalem, and had moved the ark of God into the shrine-area there; and the unmarred public rejoicing at the (final) introduction of the ark, and the subsequent unbroken series of military successes (2 Sam. 8) alike testified to Yahweh's approval. David had at once begun to extend the walls of the little town of Jebus: 'he built the city round about from the Millo inward' (2 Sam. 5.10). The 'Millo'—the Infill—'must refer to a major earthwork of some kind, a rampart perhaps or a platform produced by filling in a ravine'.[12] The extension was a large work not finished in David's lifetime, for Solomon had to use forced labour to build 'the house of the LORD and his own house and the Millo and the wall of Jerusalem...' (1 Kgs 9.15); 'he built the Millo, and closed up the breach of the city of David his father' (11.27; cf. 3.1). While the wall is unbuilt, much of God's city is unprotected, and he may be suitably distracted from the present unhappy interlude to his interest in 'doing good to Zion' and 'building the walls of Jerusalem'. The psalmist inserts tactfully *bir^{e}ṣôn^{e}ḵā*, 'when it shall please you'.

This then leads into a final contrast between the present sadness and future happiness. Verse 16, 'For thou hast no delight in a sacrifice that I should give it. . . ': verse 19, 'Then shalt thou delight in the sacrifices of righteousness. . . '. No animal sacrifice is acceptable now, but when God has shown his forgiveness of David's sin by permitting the completion of the city walls, *then* there will be sacrifices in plenty, and a good time will be had by all. Those will be 'sacrifices of righteousness', as in Ps. 4.5, for the king's guilt will have been 'blotted out', and he will be 'righteoused' in the full Pauline sense. The singer's enthusiasm at the vision of joy to come outruns his metre, as he piles *'ôlâ* and *kālîl* on his *z^{e}bāḥîm*.

An admiration for the 'profound spirituality' of vv. 1-17, allied to a belief in the prophetic rejection of sacrifice, has induced almost all commentators to excise vv. 18f. as an 'appendix' added later. Thus Kirkpatrick: 'This anticipation of the restoration of material sacrifices in Jerusalem seems a poor ending to a Psalm of such profound spirituality'. Kraus thinks of an editor in Nehemiah's time looking to a reformed cult which would no longer incur prophetic protest: 'er übersieht das gewaltige Bekenntnis in [v. 17], das zu R[om.]. 12.1 schon hindeutet'. Kraus's extensive citations from Luther on the psalm suggest that his influence has something to do with it. Weiser's condescension is especially revealing: 'It is understandable that this lofty religious conception [of vv. 1-17]. . . could not be fully grasped and borne by the piety of a later period deeply rooted in cultic ritualism'. The integrity of the psalm is defended among moderns only by P. Bonnard[13] and Eaton. But the references to hyssop and washing (not to speak of bruised bones) in the body of the psalms show that the author of that is deeply rooted in cultic ritualism: and the sacrifices of v. 19 are but an aspect of the joy and gladness of v. 8. Once critics have rejected a Davidic context (or dismissed it as unworthy of consideration), they have a psalm whose first seventeen verses make a profound religious appeal as a statement of personal contrition for sin. They have some difficulty with *dāmîm* and they find it a minor problem to explain how the speaker will be in a position to teach sinners; but the words speak to the heart, and seem a clear foreshadowing of Christian, Pauline and Lutheran religion. The only part that does not fit is vv. 18f., fortunately the last two verses, which can then be treated as a later addition by a man of inferior spiritual insight. But the 'bloodguiltiness' and the teaching of transgressors (and the *n^{e}ḏîḇâ* spirit, and 'thy holy spirit') and the unbroken ancient tradition, all point to a Davidic association for the psalm; and this enables us to treat the text as a whole, and not break off the part which does not fit our exegesis. The whole psalm is a noble statement of King David's desolation at the evil which he has done, first in the seduction of Bath-sheba, and then, much more, in the constructive murder of her husband in battle. He has submitted to a painful and humiliating expiation, which he hopes will secure God's forgiveness; and he ends, most suitably, with a glance to better times to come, when the walls of God's city are complete, and sacrifice can be offered once more with a joyful heart.

Chapter 4

THE EVACUATION: FROM ZION TO OLIVET (52-55)

David hoped that he had expiated his sin with the whip and the hyssop potion; but far worse troubles lay ahead of him, which he and his contemporaries came to see as the real atonement exacted by Yahweh. For in his later years the sword was never to depart from his house: his eldest son Amnon was to be murdered by his brother, he would be driven from his throne by his favourite son Absalom, the latter would be killed in battle to his great grief, and there would be further violence with the rebellion of Sheba and the usurpation of Adonijah. The Succession Narrator would in time credit Nathan the prophet with the foresight of these disasters ('thou hast smitten Uriah... Now therefore the sword... ', 2 Sam. 12.9f.); and would supply him with an apocryphal 'parable', the ewe-lamb, like the apocryphal 'parable' of the widow's sons which he places on the lips of the wise woman of Tekoa. It is more likely that in history Nathan did indeed face the king with his wickedness, urged to it by an outraged public opinion; but that his further comments were limited to a decision on the (minimum) number of strokes ('thy speaking... thy judging', 51.4).

52 For the Chief Musician. Maschil for David (*l^eḎāviḏ*): when Doeg the Edomite came and told Saul, and said to him, David is come to the house of Ahimelech
1 Why boastest thou thyself in mischief, O mighty man?
The mercy of God *endureth* continually.
2 Thy tongue deviseth very ruin (*hawwôṯ*),
Like a sharpened knife (*ta'ar m^eluṭṭāš*), O worker of treachery (*'ọśeh r^emiyyâ*).
3 Thou lovest evil more than good;
And lying rather than to speak righteousness. (Selah

4 Thou lovest all devouring words,
O thou (RV) deceitful tongue.
5 God shall likewise break thee down for ever,
He shall take thee up and pluck thee out of the tent (*mē'ōhel*),
And root thee out of the land of the living. (Selah

Psalm 52 belongs securely within the family of the Prayers. Its uncommon form, a reproach to a menacing sinner, is shared with 58. The main gravamen of this reproach is the sinner's deceit, lying, devouring words and evil tongue, and these are a recurring feature of the Prayers; cf. 55.9, 12ff., 23; 57.4; 58.3; 59.6, 12, 14; 63.11; 64.3, 8. Here they are compared to a whetted razor, as to swords in 55.21, sword, spears and arrows in 57.4, arrows in 58.7, sword and arrows in 64.3. The rare word *hawwōṯ*, engulfing destruction, is used in 52.4 (cf. v. 9) as in 55.12; 57.2. The sinner is apparently a military figure, *gibbôr*, in a tent; and if so would recall 'him that encampeth against thee' in 53.5, those who go round about the city in 59.6, 14, and other military passages as in 60 or 68. He trusts in his wealth, as do the opposition of 62.10; we may contrast the professed need and poverty of 69.29, 33; 70.5, of which 69 has a national context (vv. 35f.). The speaker, on the other hand, is like a green olive tree in the house of God, which may imply an association with the Temple; we hear similarly of the speaker of 57.1 taking refuge under the shadow of God's wings; cf. 61.4; 63.2; 65.4, or the frequent vows of continual sacrifice. In particular 'I will give thee thanks for ever. . . I will wait on thy name, for it is good, in the presence of thy saints' recalls 54.6, 'I will give thanks unto thy name, O LORD, for it is good', and 61.8, 'So will I sing praise unto thy name for ever' along with 'those that fear thy name' in 61.5.

The speaker's invective is addressed to a *gibbôr*, a 'mighty man'; the word is used much the most commonly of physical and military prowess (Gen. 6.4; 10.8; 1 Sam. 14.52 and often; 2 Sam. 23.8, David's 'mighty men'), and it is natural to read it in that sense here. A military context may also underlie 'out of the tent' (v. 5): we should have expected a wealthy man (*'ośrô*, v. 7), if he were a civilian, to be living in a house; and although the tent may sometimes be used poetically for the home (Isa. 16.5, etc.), and perhaps archaically ('To thy tents, O Israel'),[1] the normal meaning is the movable dwelling of a nomad (Ps. 120.5, 'the tents of Kedar', and throughout Genesis) or a soldier (1 Sam. 17.54; Jer. 37.10). The lack of a suffix, *mē'ōhel*, 'from (the) tent', strengthens this impression: God will pluck the man from the tent where he is encamped, and destroy him. This would be in line with two texts later in the sequence. In 53.5 God has scattered the bones of 'him that encampeth against thee' (*ḥōnāḵ*), and camping is done in tents. In 55.11 day and night the enemy surround (*yᵉsôḇᵉḇuhā*) the city to its wall (p. 102), and this implies tents also.

The principal thing which the speaker has against the *gibbôr* is his deceit, and he holds it very bitterly. He boasts of the evil (*rāʿ*) he is doing (v. 1). His tongue devises *hawwôṯ*, ruin, engulfing destruction such as overwhelmed Job (Job 6.2); it is like a whetted knife in the hand of Joab (2 Sam. 20.10) that kills unseen and does not strike a second time. As *lāšôn* is feminine, it is the *gibbôr* himself who is the worker of *rᵉmiyyâ*, treachery (RSV). He has abused a position of trust, and has double-crossed the speaker. He loves evil more than good, and lying rather than speaking the truth (v. 3). The same verb in v. 4, 'Thou hast loved' shows that the meaning there is the same: this time he loves 'all words of destruction'—*bālaʿ*, swallowing, as Hushai warned David to move lest the people be swallowed up (2 Sam. 17.16), and the wise woman of Abel persuaded Joab not to swallow up her city (2 Sam. 20.19f.). The final phrase in v. 4 is best taken as a vocative, as with v. 2, 'you deceitful tongue'. There can be little doubt that the deceit and treachery, which are thus so repeatedly attacked, are deeply feared as a threat to the speaker's existence. Otherwise he would hardly expect God to take the man's life and extirpate him. This is the force of the *gam* in v. 5. The man has spoken words of destruction: God will *also*, 'likewise', demolish him (*yittāṣᵉḵā*).

The only other hint which we have of the *gibbôr*'s position is in v. 7: he trusted in the abundance of his riches and strengthened himself in his lust (*hawwātô*). The expression is vague, but we have a good parallel in Psalm 49 where the enemy 'is made rich, When the wealth of his house is increased' (v. 16); but 'they are appointed as a flock for Sheol', and the upright, that is the Israelites, 'shall have dominion over them in the morning', when the battle takes place (v. 14). I have argued elsewhere[2] that Psalm 49 is not a wisdom psalm, as is often thought, but a warning to Israel's enemies; and that the money in 49.16 is the tribute of subject peoples, and is being used to hire and finance the enemy army. In this way we have an explanation for 49.6, 'They that trust in their wealth, and boast themselves in the multitude of their riches', alongside the refusal to ransom prisoners in 49.7ff.; and this verse is very close to 52.7, 'Lo, this is the man that made not God his strong hold, But trusted in the abundance of his riches'. The *gibbôr* of 52 need not, of course, be a foreign enemy; his treachery and deceit rather suggest that he is an Israelite.

What situation then emerges from all these details? It would seem that *a rebellion is in progress*. The *gibbôr* is a trusted figure of the Israelite elite, a fighter, and a man of considerable resources which he is using to finance a coup. He has betrayed his trust, and is a traitor to the government; he has plotted ('devised') the overthrow ('very ruin') of the latter behind a front of smooth talk ('lying', 'deceit'). If he is successful, he will no doubt execute ('swallow up') the present rulers, of whom the speaker is one. But the rebellion, though formidable, is not yet successful: the *gibbôr* is still in 'the tent'—his army is advancing but has not yet taken power. If we give any credit to the Davidic reference in the heading, we can think of a suitable situation from David's life, though it will not be connected with Doeg the Edomite. In 2 Samuel 15 Absalom 'prepared him a chariot and horses, and fifty men to run before him': he trusted in the abundance of his riches—and no doubt even more so when he had to supply food and pay for a small army. He was guilty of deceit in that he rose up early and 'stole the hearts of the men of Israel' with the tale that he would give better justice than the king; and he told more lies about his vow in Hebron, where he raised his revolt. So the *gibbôr* could very suitably be Absalom; but the use of the word will be strongly ironic, as is *'ēlîm* in 58.1. Absalom has taken in hand to turn the king off his throne, but has never fought in his life.

Our psalm is twice punctuated by a Selah, after verses 3 and 5; and in an earlier work I have argued that Selah (*sollâ*, a lifting up of the voice) stands for an interlude in the psalm (LXX διάψαλμα), in which a relevant story was cantillated. Thus 87.2, 'Glorious things are spoken of thee, O city of God. (Selah', made good sense if the psalm was interrupted at this point to allow the recital of the foundation legend of the city (of Dan, originally), with the promise of its glorious future. Or if 44.1-8 is closed with a Selah and opens, 'We have heard with our ears, O God. . . ': the Selah could well be the recital of the taking of the land, perhaps in line with our Joshua 24, which has a number of phrases in common with Ps. 44.1-8.[3] I was able to conjecture suitable stories for nineteen Selah's in the Korah psalms, and I propose to follow the same line of explanation consistently through the Prayers. The Prayers are a more taxing test because we have in part a given text in the Passion of David, with a given opening point and a fixed order. If the hypothesis is wrong, the special pleading should soon be apparent.

The opening section of the Passion of David ran as follows, and it is this which will form the first Selah of the Prayers, at 52.3:

> And it came to pass at the end of forty years that Absalom said unto (David), I pray thee, let me go and pay my vow, which I have vowed unto Yahweh, in Hebron. For thy servant vowed a vow while I abode at Geshur [in Aram], saying, If Yahweh shall indeed bring me again to Jerusalem, then I will worship Yahweh. And (David) said unto him, Go in peace. So he arose, and went to Hebron. But Absalom sent spies throughout all the tribes of Israel, saying, As soon as ye hear the sound of the trumpet, then ye shall say, Absalom is king in Hebron. And with Absalom went two hundred men out of Jerusalem, that were invited, and went in their simplicity; and they knew not anything. And Absalom sent Ahi[ezer] the Gilonite, David's counsellor, from his city, even from Giloh, while he offered the sacrifices. And the conspiracy was strong; for the people increased continually with Absalom. (2 Sam. 15.7-12, 'David' for 'the king' in vv. 7, 9, see pp. 42f.; Ahiezer, see p. 78).

It would not be difficult to imagine the indignation and fear of a priest in David's court expressing themselves in the face of these events in the words of Psalm 52. Here is the 'mighty man' who trusts in his wealth and has deceitfully plotted his treason, who means to overthrow the king and his advisers, and to put them to death, who has been the king's trusted darling too long, and who is now under canvas, outside Jerusalem. The Selah has been inserted at the ideal place: after three verses of vituperation for his treachery, and leading into v. 4, 'Thou lovest all words of devouring, O thou deceitful tongue'. The speaker knows that the words of devouring intend his own death, among others.

A Davidic reference also gives force to v. 1 which is otherwise weak: 'Why boastest thou thyself in evil, O *gibbôr*? The mercy of God *endureth* continually'. The *ḥeseḏ* of *'El* is his *steadfast* mercy which he promised to David eternally in 2 Sam. 7.15, and which is as old a concept as Ps. 18.50 = 2 Sam. 22.51. This covenanted mercy is *kol-hayyôm*, for ever (100.5, Delitzsch): so how vain are the boasts of the rebel in his brief initial successes! There is a strong parallel of contrast between the two cola: the vacuous confidence of the pampered Absalom with his pretensions to soldierliness, set against the eternal promise to David by God.

Such an interpretation is not totally novel: Jacquet, II 191, 'on lui préfère (sc. à Doëg) celui de la trahison d'Achitophel'. But it is not represented in modern commentaries. The association with Doeg was a fourth-century guess: Doeg was the 'mightiest' (*'abbîr*) of Saul's herdsmen, and brought about much destruction with his malicious tongue. Delitzsch still believed in him, but the psalm lacks any reference to the massacre of the priests at Nob. In his place have come a variety of shadowy theories. The villain is often, following Gunkel, a wealthy man oppressing the godly poor with false accusations. Mowinckel at first took him to be a sorcerer bewitching a sick man with spells (*Ps.st.* I 21f., 118-124). Often the evil he does seems trivialized: NEB speaks of 'cruel gossip' and 'wild lies', and Jacquet of 'un cas concret d'effronterie obstinée et méchante'. Eaton at least provides a plausible setting for the psalm in the festal liturgy: it is a commination pronounced by a prophet to ward off an enemy who has begun a war of words, as in Numbers 22f.

But aside from the difficulty of a setting for Individual Laments, the theories do not fit the text very well. Gunkel amended *haggibbôr* to *haggeḇer*, 'O man', comparing v. 7, 'Lo, this is the man (*haggeḇer*) . . . ' and Isa. 22.17, where Shebna the royal steward is addressed with the same word. But Dahood notes effectively that Psalm 120 seems to be an imitation of 52, and speaks of the 'sharp arrows of a *gibbôr*'. Others (Moffatt, Anderson) take the word to mean a tyrant, for which there is no warrant. Or it is understood sarcastically: but without the military context the sarcasm seems pointless and flaccid. *mē'ōhel* similarly creates difficulties. Anderson says it means 'your dwelling place', comparing Job 18.14 and Ps. 132.2; but Job is a book set among nomads who live in tents, and in Ps. 132 'the tent of my house' is in parallel with 'a place for Yahweh', and may mean a tent. Weiser and Jacquet speak of the Tent, i.e. the Temple: the rich sinner is to be expelled from the cultic community before being executed. The *gam* in v. 5 is an embarrassment because it implies that the *gibbôr*, like God, was intending death: *bāla'* can be watered down (NEB 'slanderous talk'), but not *gam*. Kirkpatrick says, 'We might have expected *therefore*', and Dahood translates 'with a crash'. Most ignore the problem. The apparent weakness of v. 1 has led to the reversal of *ḥesed̠ 'ēl* to *'el-ḥāsîd̠*, boasting 'against the pious': this is recommended by BHS, and the difficulty was already countered so by the Syriac.

A different line is taken by Walter Beyerlin.[4] The psalm has a number of standard features—the contrast of the proud man who trusts in his wealth and the speaker who trusts in God, the correlation of action and its reward, the blessing of the righteous as like a flourishing tree, etc. These standard themes recur, often with the same vocabulary, in Psalms 49, 73, 34, 107 etc.; and in certain texts in Proverbs. All of these are Wisdom documents, and Psalm 52 should be taken as coming from the Wisdom tradition: it hails like them from the world of the post-exilic Temple. Beyerlin is surely right in the similarity of 52 to Psalm 49 (which soon drops out of view) and 73; but he does not note that the 'well-known' classification of these as Wisdom poems depends upon massive emendation. Kraus makes nine conjectures with the text of 49, mostly with the consonants, accepts four easier readings from the versions, and despairs completely of v. 14;[5] and Beyerlin, like many, sacrifices the text of 73.1, 'Surely God is good to Israel' on the altar of his Wisdom theory. The method is vitiated by its concentration on similarities and its neglect of differences. There is a sharp difference of tone, for example, between the warnings, the fear and the threats of divine punishment addressed to the enemy by 52 and 49, and the counsel of patience addressed more relaxedly to the faithful in 34 and 37; or between the hostile attitude to the *gibbôr* in 52 and statements in Ecclesiastes that the wise man can do more for an imperilled city than the *gibbôrîm*.

The Selah passage contains few problems. The formal opening with its 'forty years' cannot be due to the Succession narrator, who has brought the story to within a few weeks of the Revolt in 15.1-6; it will have been the opening of the PD, and may reflect the use of earlier parts of the Davidic history, say 2 Samuel 6–7, in the liturgy. Stanley Cook[6] says, 'vs. 7 ("And Absalom said") reads like another account of the commencement of the revolt, and may be older than vs. 1'. As the PD regularly writes 'David', I have taken it that the Succession narrator changed this in vv. 7, 9 to his favoured 'the king'. McCarter[7] hyphenates Yahweh-in-Hebron; as the ark is in Jerusalem this may be necessary—but perhaps Absalom is understood to have vowed in Hebron to sacrifice to Yahweh there. Also the preference for *ᵉlōhîm*, and even *'ēl*, in the Prayers may imply that these names were more commonly used than Yahweh in Jerusalem.

The whole unit presupposes factors which are not explained but are taken to be familiar to the original audience: hence there is no reason to excise v. 8 with its reference to Absalom's exile in Geshur.[8] Cook suggests plausibly[9] that 'in Aram' is a gloss. There was a less well-known Geshur in the Negeb where David had campaigned in his freebooting days (1 Sam. 27.8). His first two wives were from southern Judah, and the sons of all his first six wives were born in Hebron (2 Sam. 3.5): it would certainly be easier to think that Maacah, Absalom's mother, came from neighbouring Geshur than from Geshur in (western) Syria, where David had at the time no contact that we know. The name Maacah recurs as a concubine of Caleb in 1 Chron. 2.48, and a namesake of Talmai, her father, was a Hebronite driven out by Caleb in Josh. 15.14. We should then have an explanation for Absalom's raising the Revolt in Hebron: he could expect his mother's family—who had every reason to abominate David, 1 Sam. 27.8-11—to provide troops.

The nationwide disaffection, including both Judah and (much of) Israel, is undoubtedly accurate, as the Prayers will testify. The two hundred 'simpletons' are no doubt Judaean or Jerusalem notables whom it was politic for David to reinstate after the conflict, and whose excuses were accepted.

'Ahitophel' is a joke-form. 'The element *tōpel* is otherwise unknown in the Hebrew onomasticon. It seems to mean "foolishness, insipidity", suggesting that *'ahîtōpel* might be a deliberate distortion satirizing the man's ill-used wisdom'.[10] Other such distortions suggest that the Ahi- prefix is original; cf. Ishbosheth/Ishbaal, Jerubbesheth/Jerubbaal. The true form of some names is preserved in Chronicles, e.g. Eshbaal in 1 Chron. 8.33; 9.39, Meribbaal in 1 Chron. 8.34; 9.40; which encourages us to think that the reviser who distorted the names limited his work to Samuel. 1 Chronicles 12 gives a list of David's *gibbôrîm* who came to help him at Ziklag. Only one of these bears the prefix Ahi-, and he is the first mentioned: 'The chief was Ahiezer' (12.3). It would seem likely therefore that the real name of 'Ahitophel' was Ahiezer.

52.5 (Selah
6 The righteous also shall see *it*, and fear,
And shall laugh at him, *saying*,
7 Lo, this is the man that made not God his strong hold;
But trusted in the abundance of his riches,
And grew strong (*yā'ōz*) in his ambition (*b^ehawwāṯô*).
8 But as for me, I am like a green olive tree in the house of God:
I trust in the mercy of God for ever and ever.
9 And I will hope in (*wa^a qawweh*) thy name, for it is good, in the presence of thy loyal ones (*ḥ^asîdeîḵā*).

There is a second Selah after v. 5, and this then will be the following pericope from the Passion narrative:

And there came a messenger to David, saying, The hearts of the

> men of Israel are after Absalom. And David said unto all his servants that were with him at Jerusalem, Arise, and let us flee; for else none of us shall escape from Absalom: make speed to depart, lest he overtake us quickly, and bring down evil upon us, and smite the city with the edge of the sword. [ ] And [David] went forth, and all the people after him; and they took their stand (*wayya'am^{e}dû*) in Beth-merhak. And all his servants passed on beside him; and all the Cherethites, and all the Pelethites, and all the Gittites, six hundred men which came after [Ittai] from Gath. [ ] And David said to Ittai, Go and pass over. And Ittai the Gittite passed over, and all his men, and all the little ones that were with him. [ ] And lo, Zadok also [ ] and Abiathar went up; [ ] And [David] said also unto Zadok, [ ] Seest thou? return into the city in peace; [ ] I will tarry at the margins (*'aḇ^{e}rôṯ*) of the wilderness, until there come word from you to certify me. Zadok therefore and Abiathar [returned] to Jerusalem: and they abode there (2 Sam. 15.13f., 17f., 22, 24a, 27ff.).

The Revolt forces the issues of loyalty. The covenant that *'ēl* (v. 1), *^{e}lōhîm* (v. 8), made with David was permanent, and the speaker will be loyal to it ('trust in' it) for life; and he will do this, and praise God for it, in company of other loyalists (*ḥ^{a}sîdeîḵā*, the men of thy covenanted mercy). These men are being faithful to the promise of allegiance which they have made to the king, so they are 'righteous'. Their 'laughter' should not be spiritualized: they are in fear of their lives, and a good laugh at the expense of the rebels, when God has seen to their defeat, will not be out of place. The psalmist's comment follows most suitably on an account of those who were loyal to David at his lowest hour—his 'servants', Joab, Abishai and his personal retinue; his private army of Philistines, including the newly come Ittai and his battalion from Gath; Zadok nd Abiathar.

There is however a further point in common between v. 6 and the Selah. Psalm 52 is a *maśkîl*, and in *PSK* I proposed a solution to the problem of this technical term (pp. 88-91): that it meant a 'clever psalm' as in 2 Chron. 30.22 *maśkîlîm*, skilled, and that the skill consisted in including a pun on the name of the principal person referred to. Two psalms in the Korah series seemed easy to date, 44 and 89. 44 seemed to reflect the disasters of the last days of the Northern kingdom, when Hosea was king, and we find four uses of the related verb *yš'* in the opening section:

> Neither did their own arm save them (*hôšî'â*), v. 3
> Command salvations (*y^{e}šû'ôṯ*) for Jacob, v. 4

Neither shall my sword save me (*hôšî'ēnî*), v. 6
But thou hast saved us (*hôša'tānû*), v. 7.

The king is called 'Saviour', and the poet prays that God will make his name effective. Similarly 89 seems to come from the last days of the Southern kingdom when Jehoiachin was the deported king, and we find four uses of the verb *kûn* with Yahweh as subject understood:

Thy faithfulness shalt thou establish (*tāḵîn*), v. 2
Thy seed will I establish (*'āḵîn*), v. 4
With whom my hand shall be established (*tikkôn*), v. 21
It shall be established (*yikkôn*) for ever, v. 37.

Despite all appearances Yahweh will establish the king whom he has so named. We seem now to have a similar appropriateness in the language of 52.6. Having heard the tale of those who stood by David in the crisis, culminating in Zadok, *ṣāḏôq*, and Abiathar, the psalmist responds, *w^{e}yir^e'û ṣaddîqîm*, in the words following. Zadok was being true to his name; he was indeed among the righteous. The psalmist's liking for such assonances may be seen from the following word also, *w^{e}yîrā'û*, 'and will fear'—almost the same as *w^{e}yir^e'û*, 'and will see'. The *gibbôr* preferred lies to 'speaking *ṣeḏeq*' in v. 3.

52.7ff. The remainder of the psalm now falls into place. The derided Absalom did not make God his strong hold—so far from being loyal to God's covenant with David, he did not even honour his father but rose in arms to kill him. He put his trust in his wealth: he used the income from estates David had given him, first for pararoyal display (2 Sam. 15.1) and then to hire Geshurite auxiliaries. He grew strong (*yā'ōz*) as the conspiracy gained force (*'ammis*) and the hearts of the men of Israel turned after him (2 Sam. 15.12f.); strong in his *hawwâ*, his devouring ambition—cf. Mic. 7.3, 'The great man utters the *hawwaṯ* of his soul'; Prov. 10.3, 'He thrusteth away the *hawwaṯ* of the wicked'. The same word was used in the plural in 52.2 of devouring destruction.

The speaker reveals his own background in v. 8. He is a priest on the Temple staff, and he sees himself as blessed by God for his loyalty, and flourishing like the evergreen olive trees in the Temple courts, themselves the symbol of the eternal divine blessing. Here we may see a further reason for his admiration for Zadok; and perhaps there is also a wistful look back as the royal army sets out on its bleak retreat up the ascent of Olives (2 Sam. 15.30). But more significantly, we have here an explanation for the steady preference for *ᵉlōhîm* through the Prayers, and the two uses of *'ēl* in this psalm (vv. 1, 5). Zadok and his colleagues had been priests in Jebus before David took the town, and these were the names by which they had been accustomed to address the deity. Yahweh was a new and strange name to them, more familiar in Hebron (2 Sam. 15.7f.), to be used more freely in company of the victorious loyalist troops in Psalm 68. In the meantime 'thy name', v. 9, Yahweh, is the hope of David's forces: he has 'done it' in his covenantal promise, and therefore the victory is assured—all they have to do is to 'wait on' (*qwh*) that name together, for it is good, and will bring them home in safety. The frail confidence is repeated at 54.6, 'I will give thanks unto thy name, Yahweh, for it is good'. Hope springs eternal.

The speaker's association with the Temple is claimed by Weiser ('a priest') and Jacquet ('familier du Sanctuaire'); though this consorts ill with the theories that the man is ill, or oppressed by the wealthy. Without the Absalom context the parallelism of v. 7bc, 'his riches/*hawwaṯô*', is obscure, and the Syriac and Targum follow a tradition which has amended it to *hônô*, his substance; and this is then followed by Gunkel and many. For rejoicing over the downfall of the enemy, cf. 58.10; 69.30; or Allied feelings on VE Day. From Hitzig on, commentators have not been able to understand *ᵃqawweh*, which supposes Yahweh's action to be in the future, and have amended to *ᵃḥawweh*, I wil proclaim; once the Davidic key is thrown away, the Hebrew has constantly to be improved.

Gunkel and Kraus reject the David link because the (Solomonic) Temple was not yet built; but this comment seems hasty. Jebus had been an independent city-state with a priesthood; and it is really unthinkable that it should not have had a full sacral panoply, with *bāmâ*, altars and some image as a cultic focus, housed in a suitable building. It is quite likely that the image was the bronze serpent discovered by Hezekiah in 2 Kgs 18.4, and legitimated by the legend in Numbers 21. David must have brought the ark into some established sacred area in 2 Samuel 6, and the altars on which he sacrificed in 2 Sam. 6.17f. will have been the ancient city altars. If he accepted the old priesthood, why should he reject the old altars? In 2 Sam. 12.20 David 'came into the house of Yahweh, and worshipped'. In fact he simply took over the established arrangements as they stood, and no doubt installed the ark in the 'house of Yahweh' too. He planned, and his son built, a much grander temple on an extended site; and later writers, shy at the thought of the ark in a heathen temple (cf. 1 Sam. 4f.), had the ark of God within curtains.

The reconstruction of the PD is not simple, as it has been elaborated by the Succession Narrator with a number of themes. (1) The *loyalty* theme has been amplified, so as to edify the hearer and make him more loyal: so v. 15 is introduced, the loyalty of the king's servants; and the whole conversation between the king and Ittai in vv. 19-21; the weeping of 'all the country' in v. 23; and the inclusion of the ark with the party from the temple in vv. 24-29. (2) The *concubines* element in chs. 15, 16 and 19 is also due to the Succession Narrator, who has a strong sexual interest. His narrative includes seduction (Bathsheba), menstruation (2 Sam. 11.4), marital coition (11.11; 12.24), rape (Tamar), multiple enforced semi-public sexual union (the concubines), sexual stimulation (Abishag) and infatuation (Adonijah for Abishag). There is no other biblical author who can compete with this record outside the Song of Songs. (3) We have the impression of a *review of troops* as the king 'stands' (v. 19) at Beth-Merhak; but there is much repetition and overlap as various people 'go forth' and 'pass on' (vv. 16, 17, 18 (x2), 22, 23 (x2)). It is not possible to penetrate clearly behind this improbable and edifying sequence, which probably masks a certain amount of panic, disloyalty, mutiny and chaos. It is not very likely that David's army 'tarried' (RV), 'halted' (RSV, NEB) at Beth-Merhak in face of the urgency of v. 14. *'md* means to 'take one's stand' for battle in 2 Sam. 2.25; Judg. 6.31; Exod. 32.26, and *'br* means to cross over to attack an enemy in 1 Sam. 14.1, 4, 6, 8; Judg. 11.32; 12.3. Ps. 53.4f. make it clear that David's forces had to fight their way out of Jerusalem which was encircled (55.10) by an enemy 'encamped against' them (53.5). The hostile force of these verbs has been lost in the welter of loyal speeches, little ones, mourning, etc., superimposed by the Succession Narrator. All we can say is that it is likely that Ittai emerged with credit, as he is given a surprisingly large command in 2 Sam. 18.2. (4) David shows *humble spiritual insight*, both with Ittai and in declining Zadok's offer to bring the ark. This is in line with the character of David presented throughout the Succession Narrative: we may compare the scene after Yahweh struck his child in 12.16-23; or when Shimei curses him in 16.10ff.; or at Shimei's petition in 19.22f. (5) The mention of *Jonathan and Ahimaaz* is to prepare for the 'good story' of their escape in the well at Bahurim. All these amplifications are signalled by the use of 'the king' rather than 'David', and of 'Yahweh'. 'God' is used in the expansions only in the phrase 'the ark (of the covenant) of God', as often in 1 Samuel 4–6.

Some of these units are noted as expansions (of the Succession Narrative) by earlier scholars. Würthwein[11] and Langlamet[12] take the concubines to be secondary; Würthwein,[13] Langlamet,[14] and Veijola[15] all see a duplication in 15.25-27, and excise David's 'spiritual' words as 'pro-David' (Würthwein), 'sapiential' (Langlamet), or Deuteronomistic (Veijola). The Levites carrying the ark are also widely suspect; but then Zadok cannot have carried the ark himself, and we can hardly have an interruption between Zadok and Abiathar in v. 24. The ark itself belongs with the expansion: the critics are too cautious.

'aḇᵉrôṯ hammiḏbār is often mistranslated 'the fords of the wilderness' (RV, RSV, NEB). *'aḇārâ* never means a ford: in its only other occurrence, at 2 Sam. 19.19, it means a ferry-boat or convoy. The priests' sons are understood as going repeatedly, from En-Rogel to David (17.17), and a rendezvous closer to hand than fifteen miles away, by the Jordan, is presupposed. A halt by the Jordan would in any case be pointless. David camped at 'the crossing places of the wilderness', i.e. the point where the cultivated land stopped. In this way he would be able to organize his forces by camping near to hand, to restore morale, and to ambush any hasty thrust by the enemy, while defending the household party's rear. The place chosen was called the Far Oaks Dovecot (Ps. 56, Heading).

Psalm 52 raises one last question. Was the psalm then a contemporary response to Absalom's advance and the loyal support which David received as he left Jerusalem, with the two Selah's inserted later so that people could understand the original context? Or was it a later composition written to provide a suitable liturgical accompaniment to the recital of the story, like a Bach Oratorio? The issue is not a clear one, but perhaps we may prefer the former view. The story elements have been inserted into the psalm, and not vice versa; and with a liturgical theory one would have expected one psalm per Selah, not two Selahs within two verses of a single psalm. One may also cite, through with much hesitation, the existential impact of the text.

53 For the Chief Musician; at (*'al-*) Mahalath. Maschil
for (*lᵉ*) David.

1 The fool hath said in his heart, There is no God.
Corrupt are they, and have done abominable iniquity;
There is none that doeth good.

2 God looked down from heaven upon the children of men,
To see if there were any that did deal wisely,
That did seek after God.
3 Every one of them has defected (*sag*); they have rotted (*ne'ᵉlāḥû*) together;
There is none that doeth good, no, not one.
4 Did they not know (*hᵃlō' yāḏᵉ'û*), the workers of iniquity?
Who ate their bread by eating up my people (*'ōḵᵉlê 'ammî 'āḵᵉlû leḥem*),
On God they called not (*'ᵉlōhîm lō' qārā'û*).
5 There were they in great fear, where no fear was:
For God hath scattered the bones of him that encampeth against thee;
Thou hast put them to shame because God hath rejected them.
6 Oh that the salvation of Israel were come out of Zion!
When God reverses (*bᵉšûḇ*) the captivity of his people,
Then shall Jacob rejoice, *and* Israel shall be glad.

There is a closely similar version of 53 at Psalm 14: there are a number of small differences, and major ones in vv. 5b-c, where the military aspect of 53 is absent in 14. The original form is 53. (1) The obscure and allusive military passage of 53 can easily be understood as being improved and replaced by the standard piety of 14.5f, 'For God is in the generation of the righteous. Ye put to shame the counsel of the poor, But the LORD is his refuge'. A change in the reverse direction is difficult to account for, and is generally not attempted by critics, Kirkpatrick being an exception. (2) *'ᵉlōhîm* is invariable in 53: in 14 it occurs three times (including v. 1, 'There is no God', where it is unavoidable), with Yahweh four times. As *'ᵉlōhîm* comes a total of only fifteen times in the whole of Book I, we have the impression that it has been carried over inadvertently from an alien Elohist psalm at 14.2, 5. For the weakness of the alternative view of an Elohistic redaction of Books II and III, cf. p. 22. (3) It appears that the editor of Book I is making a sequence of Davidic psalms to cover the whole of David's life, and that he thinks Psalm 14 is about Nabal the Carmelite (see below). (4) There are four duplicates in the Psalter, with one of each pair coming from the Prayers of David: 53 = 14; 57.7-11 = 108.1-5; 60.5-12 = 108.6-13; 70 = 40.13-17. It will be argued below that the other duplicates have their earlier version in the Prayers, most evidently with 108.

Most commentators take 14 to be the earlier form, (i) on the Elohistic redaction theory, and (ii) because the exclusion of the military matter allows the psalm to be more easily given a *Gattung* as an (aberrant) Individual Lament. Gunkel is an honourable exception, in that he sees the text of 53 as normally prior; however the crucial 53.5 is 'stark verderbte'. Kirkpatrick explained 53 as an adaptation of a Davidic 14 to the invasion of Sennacherib, when the Assyrians encamped against Jerusalem and their bones were scattered. Dahood swings between Sennacherib and difference of dialects for any explanation. Anderson says the duplicate points to the independent existence of two Davidic collections, but I do not think this is so: I hope to explain 14 as a revision of 53, taking the *nāḇāl* as Nabal.

[It would take us too far afield to expound the whole of Book I in this sense, and a brief table must suffice. I take the editor of Book I to have selected a series of psalms to correspond (artificially) with David's whole career, on the model of the Prayers' correspondence with the story of his Passion. Thus:

Ps. 2	'against his anointed'	1 Sam. 16	David anointed by Samuel
3	'I will not be afraid of ten thousands of people'	1 Sam. 17f.	'David his ten thousands'
14	*nāḇāl* said, No God	25	Nabal's folly
18	David delivered from all enemies, and from Saul	31	Saul killed, persecution ended
20	'his anointed', 21 'The king'	2 Sam. 1ff.	David king in Hebron
22	'bulls of Bashan beset me'	2ff.	Civil war: Ishbaal in Mahanaim
23	'valley of shadow of death'	5	Valley of Rephaim
24	'King of glory shall come in'	6	Ark brought into Jerusalem
32	'sin acknowledged, forgiven'	12	Nathan and David
37	'I have been young and now am old': bows of wicked broken	18	David old, Absalom's rebellion broken
39	'before I go hence, be no more seen	24	Plague

41	'When will he die'	1 Kgs 1	Adonijah's conspiracy
	'Blessed be Yahweh...'	1.48	Solomon to be king

These would be a selection of a comprehensive correspondence between David's career and Psalms 2–41.]

Psalm 53 is a wartime psalm, and the war has been going badly. The 'workers of iniquity' have been 'eating up my people', that is, the enemy has slaughtered the king's army. 'There they feared a fear'—presumably this means that there was a panic in the king's army 'there', i.e. on the battlefield where the people were 'eaten up', since there is rarely a panic among the victorious troops. This is followed however by 'God hath scattered the bones of him that encampeth against thee', and 'Thou hast put them to shame'. The enemy has encamped against the king in his city, and there has been an engagement in which at first the royal forces suffered heavy casualties, and panicked. Such panic was not necessary though, because in the end the king's army defeated ('put to shame') the enemy, and left many of them dead ('scattered their bones'). The name of the city is given in v. 6 as Zion. It is not any ordinary enemy which has been involved. They are godless traitors to a man; they have defected (*sāg*), and have apparently carried the whole people with them. The situation is extraordinarily like that which we have been considering for 52: the hearts of the men of Israel were after Absalom, and David has had to 'take his stand' at Beth-Merhak and force his way across the Kidron, 'crossing over'.

When expounding the Korah psalms, I suggested that the series of *'al*-phrases in the Headings denoted different locations around Dan where the psalms were originally chanted. Thus 'At (*'al*) the Lilies' in the Heading of 45 meant that that psalm was sung in the royal courtyard beside the palace (45.8), where the ashlars were decorated with lilies as the royal symbol;[16] or 'At *'alāmôṯ*' in the Heading of 46 meant 'at the Deeps', *viz*. at the source of the Jordan by Dan.[17] Now *'al-māḥ^alaṯ* occurs in the Heading of the Korah Psalm 88 as well as in 53 (and in them alone): the speaker of 88 has apparently been left overnight in some underground chamber, and this suggested a connection with *m^eḥillâ*, a cave. We should consider therefore the possibility of translating *'al-maḥ^alaṯ* in the Heading of 53 'At the cave' also; and this recalls the passage from Egeria cited on p. 49—'the church on Eleona which contains the cave which on this very day the Lord visited... when he sat in the very cave'. There is, of course, no reference in the Gospels to any cave, and the Eleona church was near the peak of the Mount of Olives, where there was a second church, the Imbomon, at the traditional site of the Ascension. It is likely that the 'cave' was a traditional holy site in Egeria's time,[18] which has come to be included in the Christian Passion procession. Perhaps then this is the place which David came to in 2 Sam. 15.32, 'at the top of the ascent where God was worshipped', and where he met Hushai the Archite. The meeting with Hushai shows that the place is not the peak itself, the Imbomon site: it is a wayside shrine where the path up from Jerusalem turns north along the crest to Bahurim and Archite territory.

The topographical understanding of *'al* (= 'At') will then supply a credible setting in Israelite life for both the Prayers and the PD narrative. David's evacuation of Jerusalem had been punctuated in history by a series of incidents at different points—Beth-Merhak, the ascent of Olivet, the cave-shrine at the top, a little past the top, Bahurim; and in the years following the Rebellion the king's humiliation and reinstatement were 'remembered' in a procession over the same territory with suitable psalms and recitals at the various stations. With time however, and with increasing numbers of participants, the frequent stations were found to be unmanageable, and the procession was simplified. It began from the Temple area, to the north of the City of David: here were sung Psalm 51, the king's cry of penitence for his sin, first expiated in the old Jebusite temple. This was followed by 52 on the same location, looking down on the crossing of the Kidron at Beth-Merhak, a hundred metres further north where the modern road crosses the stream from St Stephen's Gate. The psalm was broken off twice, to recall the treachery of Absalom (52.3), and the faithfulness of Zadok and Ittai (52.5). These psalms have no topographical (*'al-*) note in the Heading because they were chanted in the primary sacred area, the Temple court. The procession then set out over the same crossing at Beth-Merhak, and had its first station *'al-māḥ^{a}lat*, at the Cave, where 53 was chanted, and 54 and 55, which have no *'al* note. Psalm 53 had been the Prayer of David's priest after the bloody forcing of the crossing of the Kidron, and we shall find further references to the trials of the retreat up Olivet in 54 and 55. The Cave was a particularly significant point on the route. It was where David reached the ridge, 'at the top', and so was able to regroup his forces momentarily without being shot at from above; it was a holy place, 'where God was worshipped'; and it

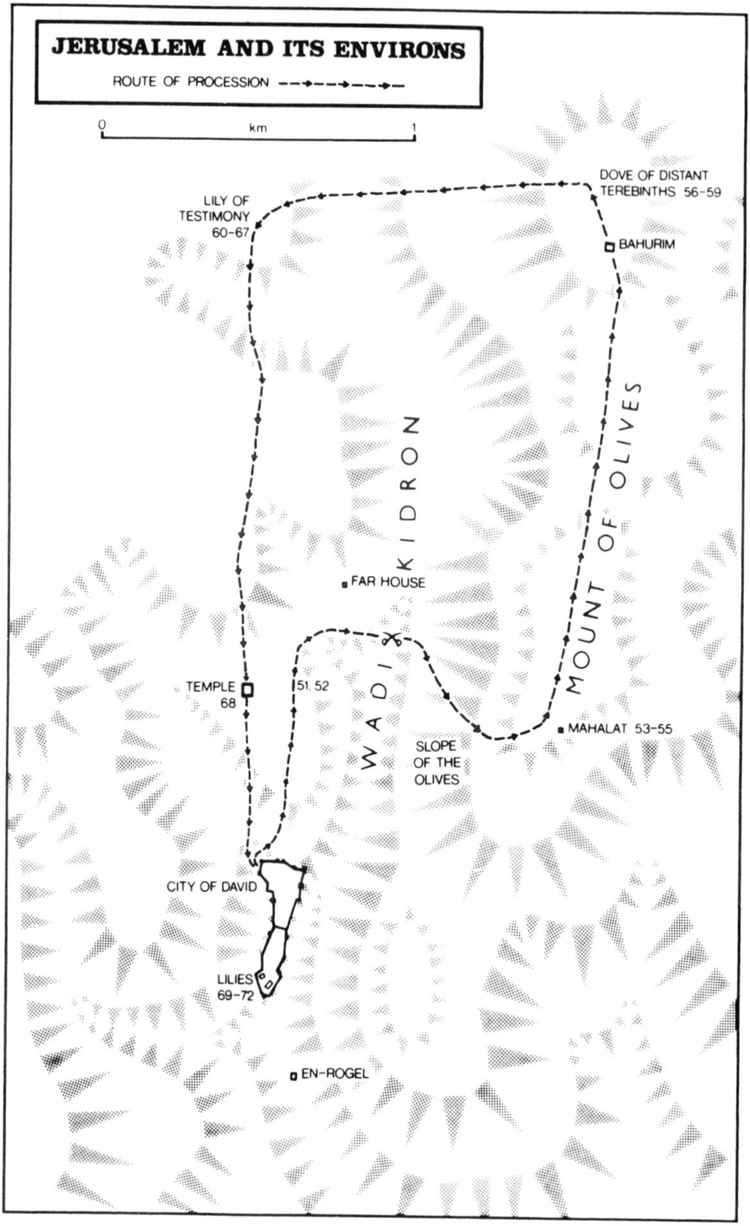
JERUSALEM AND ITS ENVIRONS
ROUTE OF PROCESSION
0
km
1
DOVE OF DISTANT TEREBINTHS 56-59
LILY OF TESTIMONY 60-67
BAHURIM
MOUNT OF OLIVES
WADI KIDRON
FAR HOUSE
TEMPLE 68
51, 52
MAHALAT 53-55
SLOPE OF THE OLIVES
CITY OF DAVID
LILIES 69-72
EN-ROGEL

was where Hushai met David, and set in train events pregnant with hope for the future. The distance from the Temple to the Eleona church, the site of the Cave, is about a kilometre.

53.1-3. The 'fool' is a follower of Absalom, who has thought (Dahood) in his heart that God would allow the prince to succeed in his treachery, and intended treachery himself. He is tantamount to an atheist, because he thinks that God will not act to support his chosen one; whereas the faithfulness of God in fact is for ever (52.1). Similar 'folly' had been with Nabal in earlier days. What he has done is *'awel*, iniquity; *hišḥîṯû*, they have acted corruptly, and *hiṯ'îḇû*, abominably—they have broken their oath of loyalty. What is so shocking is that virtually everyone has gone along with it: no one does good, i.e. stands by the king. God is pictured as looking down from heaven to see if there was a single man of understanding, i.e. a loyalist and no 'fool', like the 'wise' of later times in Dan. 12.3, one who sought God by obeying his king. Not a man: the hearts of the men of Israel were after Absalom. Each one of them has deserted (*sāg*); another psalmist was to vow, 'So shall we not desert (*nāsûg*) you' (Ps. 80.19), and the verb often means 'to be faithless' in the niph. The root *'lh* is used of milk going sour in Arabic, and with 'together' here suggests the rotting of good fruit by bad. The whole country has joined the rebellion.

53.4f. The bitter words are powered by the peril in which the speaker stands. Among the enemy he can see men he knows, of whom the story was that two hundred of them had been invited by Absalom to Hebron and had gone in their simplicity, 'and they knew not anything' (*wᵉlō' yāḏᵉ'û kol-dāḇār*, 2 Sam. 15.11). 'Did they not know (*hᵃlō' yāḏᵉ'û*)', he asks caustically, 'the workers of iniquity?' 'Devouring my people' means slaughtering them, as when later in the story 'the forest devoured more people (*leᵉ̆ḵōl hā'ām*) than the sword devoured' (2 Sam. 18.8). To 'eat bread' can mean to earn one's living, as in Gen. 3.19, 'in the sweat of thy face shalt thou eat bread', or Amos 7.12, 'flee thee away into the land of Judah, and there eat bread'. Those who have deserted the king had left a tale that they knew nothing about the rebellion, but in fact they are drawing their rations for slaughtering the speaker's soldiers. 'My' shows that he is in a position of high authority.[19]

The old city of David, which was built to the southeast of the modern Old City, drew its strength in part from following the contour of the hill above the Kidron to its east. David will have broken out of the north gate and advanced a little less than a kilometre to the Far House, which must have stood near the present St Stephen's Gate. Here there is the easiest crossing of the Kidron, where the modern road goes over and up the Mt of Olives to Bethphage. The rebel force were 'encamped round the town (53.5, 55.10), and defended the crossing. David 'took his stand' (2 Sam. 15.17), and ordered his Cherethites and Pelethites to attack (to 'pass over', *'br*). The situation was little short of desperate. David had a force of around twelve hundred men, half of them his longstanding Philistine bodyguard (1 Sam. 23.13; 27.2), half of them the newly-arrived Gittites, and not one single Israelite, if we may believe the psalmist. He also had an indeterminate number of women and children, both his own large family and the dependants of his soldiers, none of whom might fancy being massacred or raped by the incoming rebels. The city behind him was hostile (55.9ff., see below), which was largely why he was forced to leave. He will almost certainly have opened the gates before dawn, with his vanguard advancing at the double to achieve maximum surprise. The women and little ones must follow as fast as they might through the cold half-light of the misty October dawn (p. 107). With good fortune they might cut down the opposition encamped nearby and make their way quickly up Olivet. In the event the rebels were able to withdraw in good order over the Kidron and present a firm front. They will no doubt have sounded the *šôpār* to summon the assistance of the rest of their army, much larger than David's.

The initial assault was a failure. The front-line troops had either to pass over the narrow causeway or fight their way up the steep bank, and they were 'eaten up'. Small wonder then that panic broke out, 'they feared a fear', with defeat before and hundreds of women behind beginning to shriek, and the knowledge that in a matter of minutes detachments would be arriving from the neighbouring rebel encampments. But the royal forces were probably better armed (1 Sam. 13.19-22), and were disciplined professionals, and they had seasoned commanders in Joab and Abishai; and with time they forced their way through. 'There was no (need for) fear', for they won with time enough. 'God scattered the bones of him that encampeth against thee', says the psalmist to David, 'Thou hast put them to shame because God hath rejected them'. The God of battles has been on the side of the righteous this time at least. The scattering of the enemy's bones unburied (cf. 79.3; Ezek. 6.5) is an understandable hyperbole.

53.6. As he sets off up the Ascent, the *m^{e}naṣṣēaḥ* looks back to the shrine on Zion where *^{e}lōhîm* has for so long resided, and now is present in his ark; and he looks forward to the deliverance which he will bring in his faithfulness. Perhaps we should translate 'when God reverses the captivity of his people', with the thought of those who now must live under enemy oppression, and perhaps, like Zadok, in prison. If 'his people' means the royal army, as in v. 4, then we need a more general translation, 'when God turns the fortunes' as in Job 42.10, Ezek. 16.53. The psalmist knows that hitherto Israel has gone over to the rebels to a man; but he may still hope, and with justice, that there will be faithful hearts among the more distant tribes. He can still think that when victory comes, Israel and Jacob will rejoice, the people as a whole will exult. We cannot but admire his courage in a moment of great weakness. Like Claverhouse he can say, 'Ere the king's crown go down, there are heads to be broke'; he knows there are hills beyond Jordan, and before he owns a usurper he will couch with the fox. But he served a better king than James Stuart, and the battle at Zalmon would bring him a happier issue than Killiecrankie.

Psalm 14. The Prayers have frequent occasion to speak of the opposition they contend with: they are the enemy, the wicked, the doers of iniquity and the like. Here alone do we find the so-called Wisdom motif: the man is *nāḇāl*, a fool. The coincidence with a famous passage in David's earlier career has caught the editors.' attention: there is an echo of Nabal the Carmelite. Fool was his name and folly was with him; he refused David's rightful claims and the Lord struck him. This verbal play is shown by the fact that the psalm is a Maschil, and one of a series of four Maschils, 52–55.

This opening line has led to the psalm's re-use as a response to the Nabal story, now as Psalm 14: the editor has changed the unsuitable words skilfully, retaining as much of their sound as he can. Nabal did not really do any *'āwel* (v. 1), iniquity; he just did *'alîlâ*, a deed. Nor did he apostatise, *sag*; he just turned aside, *sār*. The redactor adds *kol* twice, in vv. 3, 4. He sees Nabal and all his followers as eating up David's men by refusing them food, and fearing a fear when Abigail tells of David's approach. But there was indeed cause for fear then, so he omits *lō'-hāyâ pāḥad*; and in place of 'for God has scattered, *pizzar*', he puts the stock 'for God is in the generation of the righteous', *b^{e}ḏôr ṣaddîq*, i.e. with David. The military *'aṣ^{e}môṯ ḥōnāḵ h^{e}ḇîšōṯâ* he transmutes to *^{a}ṣaṯ-'ānî tāḇîšû*, you have put to shame the counsel of the poor—Nabal and his men refused David's humble proposal of help. The now meaningless *m^e'āsām*, God has rejected them, becomes *maḥsēhû*, Yehweh is his refuge. The editor has done a very neat piece of assimilation.

The allusiveness of 53, and the presence of a civilian near-doublet at 14, leave the critics in some disarray: 14 is usually preferred as being more comprehensible, and comments on 53 may be sparse, or even absent (Weiser). Delitzsch thought 53 was Davidic, but without ascribing a context; Kirkpatrick that it was about Sennacherib; Gunkel that it was a prophetic attack on the priesthood ('eating the bread of Yahweh'); Mowinckel that the 'fool' and his fellow 'workers of iniquity' are sorcerers 'eating up my people' with spells; Kraus and Weiser that it is an individual lament with the wealthy 'fool' eating up the poor and righteous; Anderson is, perhaps wisely, uncertain. Those who follow St Paul in taking vv. 1-3 as about the universality of sin, with references to the Flood and the Tower of Babel, may end by finding v. 5 'somewhat obscure' (Rogerson and McKay).

These results are not obtained without some violence either to the Hebrew or to the text. In v. 5 NEB's 'shall they not rue it?' is popular, following D. Winton Thomas's conjectured vowels *yēḏ^{ec}û*, and conjectured link with the Arabic *wadu'a*, to be submissive.[20] RV's translation, followed by most, 'Who eat up my people *as* they eat bread' is hard to justify; and parallels for eat = oppress are difficult to find - Jacquet offers Jer. 10.25 which is about the devastation of enemies, and Mic. 3.3, which is about flogging. Gunkel ingeniously takes the (for him) difficult *šām* in v. 5 as *š^{e}mô* with v. 4; and with two such different texts for v. 5bc many commentators are happy to use the hatchet. NEB says the Hebrew is obscure, and describes its translation, 'the crimes of the godless are frustrated' as from a probable reading.

54 For the Chief Musician; on stringed instruments.
Maschil for (*l^e*) David: When the Ziphites came and
said to Saul, Doth not David hid himself
with us?
1 Save me, O God, by they name,
And vindicate me (*t^{e}ḏînēnî*) in thy might.
2 Hear my prayer, O God;
Give ear to the words of my mouth.
3 For strangers are risen up against me,
And violent men have sought after my soul:
They have not set God before them.
(Selah

4 Behold, God is mine helper:
The Lord is with them that uphold my soul.
5 He shall requite the evil unto them that lie in wait for me:
Destroy thou them in thy truth.
6 With a freewill offering will I sacrifice unto thee:
I will give thanks unto thy name, O LORD, for it is good.
7 For he hath delivered me out of all my trouble:
And mine eye hath looked (*rā'ᵃṯā*) upon mine enemies.

Psalm 54 has much in common with its two predecessors. 52.9, 'I will give thee thanks... And I will wait on thy name, for it is good'; 54.6, 'I will give thanks unto thy name, Yahweh, for it is good'. 53.1-4, 'There is no God... (none) that did seek after God... call not upon God; 54.3, 'They have not set God before them'. Like 52–53 it is a wartime psalm, in which disaster is not far away. 'Strangers', probably foreigners, who are men of violence, are the speaker's enemies: they lie in wait for him, and seek his life. But as with the preceding psalms, it is not felt that the war is a fair contest. It is perhaps a rising, in that the strangers have 'risen up against me'; cf. 2 Sam. 18.31f., 'the LORD hath avenged thee this day of all them that *rose up against* thee'. What they have done is 'the evil', and they will be destroyed in return for it, under the righteous judgment of God. It is best therefore to try to read the psalm as a continuation from 52–53.

54.1-3. The Ziphites are a guess, arising from the context of 1 Sam. 23.15, 'And David saw that Saul was come out to seek his life'; cf. v. 3b. But good sense can be made from the later context, as David's little army goes up Olivet. God is called upon to save and to vindicate by his name—'thy name, Yahweh' in v. 6. The priesthood hails from pre-David times at Jebus, and calls God *'ᵉlōhîm* or *'ēl*; he has yet to use the name Yahweh, and even here in v. 6 it may be in apposition to 'thy name', and not in the vocative. The name is something of a novelty, and its knowledge gives the speaker a quasi-magical hope of salvation from the enemy; or perhaps we should think that the ark has been left behind in Zion, but God can still act through his name—rather as the D-Historian would come to rely on Yahweh's name (e.g. in 1 Kgs 8) when temple and ark had been lost. The enemy are *zārîm/'ārîṣîm*. The former word is commonly, though not always, used of foreigners; in association with the latter it always is—Isa. 25.2f., 5; 29.5; Ezek. 28.7; 31.12. The speaker sees them as an alliance of mercenaries from the southern deserts and Israelite traitors who will stop at nothing: the former are spoken of in 68.30 as 'the peoples that delight in war', and are associated with Egypt. The phrase *qûm ʿal* is used of Absalom's rising at 2 Sam. 18.31, 32, and the phrase *biqqeš napšî* of Absalom's attempt to kill David at 2 Sam. 16.11.

54.4-7. The three cola of v. 3 are not an indication of a lost line (Duhm, Gunkel), but of a coming Selah, as not uncommonly (cf. 52.5; 59.5, 13; 62.4). The Selah marks a change in the tone of the psalm, from prayer and complaint to confidence and vow. The next section of the Passion of David Narrative is the brief incident as the king goes up Olivet:

> And David went up by the ascent of the *mount of* Olives, and wept as he went up; and he had his head covered, and went barefoot: and all the people that were with him covered every man his head, and they went up, weeping as they went up. And one told David, saying, Ahi(ezer) is among the conspirators with Absalom. And David said, O LORD, turn the counsel of Ahi(ezer) into foolishness (2 Sam. 15.31f.).

I suggested above that the distorted name Ahitophel ('Brother is folly') was likely to have been originally Ahiʿezer ('Brother is help'), the first of David's supporters in 1 Chronicles 12, and the only one to bear the prefix Ahi-. This proposal seems now to be borne out. Psalm 54 is a Maschil, and the previous two psalms have contained a play on a name; as 'Ahitophel' is the person at the centre of the Selah, we are expecting a play on his name. Further, the play in 52, *ṣaddîqîm*, came directly after the Selah about Zadok, in 52.6; and the play in 53, *nāḇāl*, came in the opening line, there being no Selah. We should therefore expect to find some play on the name Ahiʿezer, if that is 'Ahitophel''s real name, after the Selah in 54.4: and the text runs, 'Behold, God is mine helper (*ʿōzēr*)'. The word has come that David's wisest counsellor 'Brother is help', is to be his help no more: never mind, says the psalmist, God is helper to me; and with him as my ally I shall not lose the fight.

Delitzsch, and most, take the b^e in v. 4b as *beth essentiae*: God is of my upholders (and he is the only one). But this loses some of the force of the context, and arises from jealousy for God's uniqueness—as Anderson says,

'RV renders... as if God were one among many helpers'. The psalmist means, God is on the side of the loyalists.

The speaker's immediate response to the news of Ahiezer's treachery is to comfort himself with the thought of his divine ally; but his mind then turns naturally to 'the evil' which will surely rebound (*yāšûḇ*, K, Gunkel, Kraus), or which God will make rebound (*yāšîḇ*, Q, Delitzsch, Kirkpatrick) on its perpetrators. The latter are spoken of as *šōrᵉrāi*.The participle is usually derived from *šûr*, to watch—'those who watch me', and so lie in wait for me (so BDB, Anderson). But W.F. Albright[21] defends a translation 'to trick, betray'; and 'those who betray me' would give the best sense to all the passages where the form occurs (Pss: 5.9; 27.11; 56.3; 59.11).

54.6f. The psalm ends with the rosier thought of the celebration of victory. King and followers will offer sacrifice with a free will—a free will offering in fact—to thank God for his promise. They will give thanks to his name 'for it is good': the emphasis on the 'goodness' of Yahweh's name, repeated from 52.9, testifies to the novelty of its use. He means 'for it is effective', a matter not doubted in later times. Its effectiveness may be seen in two deliverances already achieved. First, it has rescued the royal party 'from all *ṣārâ*, constriction'; they had been in Jerusalem with a disloyal population inside the town and a triumphant enemy without, and they have now escaped into open country, and may hope to raise further support and fight again. Second, 'mine eye has looked on my enemies': the word has come to me of the treachery of Ahiezer, and I know what I am up against.

The lack of context has driven translators to take the last phrase as 'has seen *my desire* upon my enemies', a forceful extension of the Hebrew, justified by the parallels in Pss. 59.11; 92.11; 112.8; 118.7. But what ancient leaders often needed—like Her Majesty's forces in N. Ireland—was information; cf. 92.11, 'Mine eyes also have looked on them that lie in wait for me, Mine ears have heard of the evil-doers that rise up against me'.

Delitzsch supported the Ziphites, and Kirkpatrick hesitated; but most critics have followed Gunkel in taking the psalm as an Individual Lament. Gunkel, Kraus, Anderson and Jacquet see the traditional poor and pious Israelite persecuted by the wealthy; Weiser specifices a lawsuit (v. 1) with a favourable judgment (v. 4). But this view seems to go against the grain of the psalm. Not only does it involve reading *zēḏîm*, proud men, for *zārîm*, strangers in v. 3, they are also 'enemies' who are either watching for the speaker or have betrayed him; they want to kill him ('sought my life') and are to be killed ('destroyed') by God in consequence. There are manuscripts which read *zēḏîm*, and the reading is testified from the Targum; and there is a close parallel with *zēdîm* at 86.14. But 86 is a late psalm combining units from other psalms, and is likely to have amended *zārîm* to its domestic situation, just as 14 was an amendment of 53. The parallels with Isaiah and Ezekiel, where five times *zārîm* stands in parallel with *'ārîṣîm*, strongly suggest that they are a stock pair; and as Dahood says, the form *zarîm* is now confirmed by the Isaiah A scroll from Qumran.[22]

Mowinckel, Eaton and Dahood see 54 as a national psalm spoken by the king against his enemies abroad. If the psalm is taken in isolation, that is quite plausible.

Weiser does not admire the psalmist. He is 'neither able nor ready to give himself up wholly to God... Human self-will and man's low instincts of vindictiveness and gloating retain their power over his thoughts... (He) thinks of God in a rather human fashion and wants to make use of God's might in the service of his human sentiments'. I hope that a clearer historical context will do something to restore the writer's reputation. His loyalty to the king, and his trust in the divine covenant with David, seem to me admirable and for the time religious; and his expectation that those who plotted parricide and rebellion would be paid out for their treachery appears quite apposite.

55 For the Chief Musician; on stringed instruments.
Maschil for (*l*^e^) David.
1 Give ear to my prayer, O God;
And hide not thyself from my supplication,
2 Attend unto me, and answer me:
I break loose (*'ārîḏ*) in my complaint, and will moan (*'ąhîmâ*),
3 Because of the voice of the enemy,
Because of the harrying (*'ąqaṯ*) of the wicked;
For they cast trouble (*'āwen*) upon me,
And in anger they pursue me (*yiśṭ^e^mûnî*).
4 My heart reels (*yāḥîl*) within me:
And the terrors of death are fallen upon me.
5 Fearfulness and trembling are come upon me,
And horror hath overwhelmed me.
6 And I said, Oh that I had wings like a dove!
Then would I fly away and be at rest.
7 Lo, then would I wander far off,
I would lodge in the wilderness.
(Selah

8 I would hasten my escape
From the stormy wind and tempest.

The enemy's shouting (v. 3), the hostile pursuit (v. 3), the imminent peril of death (v. 4), the need to escape (vv. 6ff.), already suggest forcefully a military, and a desperate, situation. In later verses we find violence and strife in the city (v. 9), with hostile troops day and night at its walls (v. 10), and all manner of wickedness going on in it (vv. 10f.), and a near-battle (v. 18). It is easy to see the situation as of an army which has been driven out of its city; and the address to a human being in v. 22, 'Cast thy burden upon Yahweh', as well as of other verses to God, makes it likely that the king is with the retreating forces. The speaker has been betrayed by a close friend in vv. 12-14, and by someone—perhaps a different person—who had a covenant with him in vv. 19-21. The underlying situation becomes more and more like David's retreat and the treachery of Ahiezer, which indeed is already asserted in m.Aboth 6.3, and by the inclusion of Ahitophel's name in the Targum at v. 16: the detail confirms this.

55.1f. The opening hemistich echoes 54.2, but is now more insistent, requiring attention, and an answer; and we shall have the psalmist reassuring himself in v. 17, 'he shall hear my voice'. Nor is he merely offering a finely wrought poetic psalm as his prayer: he feels himself to be breaking loose (*rûḏ*, hiph.) as Esau was to break loose in Gen. 27.40, or Israel in Jer. 2.31, and determines (cohort.) to give rein and to utter loud moaning cries without restraint. The strength and bitterness of the psalm's feeling is, as usual, an index of the military predicament. The rebel forces have had to give way at the crossing of the Kidron, but they and their comrades from encampments further south have scattered on to the high ground above the road. The royal forces are moving up the road, and are too strong to be challenged to battle; but their morale can be lowered by abusive shouting ('the voice of the enemy'), by well-directed arrows and stones ('the pressing of the wicked'), and by dropping (*mûṭ*, Delitzsch 'roll') trouble upon them, no doubt in the form of sizable boulders. The rebels hold the upper ground, and the retreat can be effectively harried both with angry words and with missiles. We are reminded of a slightly later episode with Shimei. *śṭm* means to pursue relentlessly in Job 16.9; 30.21.

55.4-8. Under such circumstances the sensation of rising panic, all too familiar to those who have been under damaging fire, is easily understood. As one comrade and then another goes down, the speaker's heart reels, and he is looking his own death in the face. Shudders (*pallāṣôṯ*) take hold of him: it is a thing infinitely terrible. The image of the dove, the symbol of escape, perhaps arises from the presence of dovecots on the hillside farms opposite Jerusalem: we have apparent reference to such in the heading of 56, 'At the dove of the Far Terebinths', and the keeping of doves has been part of the Palestinian economy for many centuries.[24] The light-winged creature can flutter away and sleep peacefully in the untilled scrub beyond the crest, where, God willing, there will be camp and rest for the psalmist at the margins of the wilderness (2 Sam. 15.28). His imagination lingers over the pleasant thought of the bird flitting hither and thither in the distance to take its rest in safety from the howling gale. Perhaps we should think of a physical strong wind adding to the singer's distress as the column winds up the track towards the top (v. 8). *miplāṭ* may be either an abstract (as in RV) or a concrete escape—'I would hasten to an escape (-place) for me'.

The Selah will be the next piece from the Passion narrative. In 2 Sam. 15.30f. David was going up the Ascent of Olives, and the people with him 'went up, weeping as they went up'. We may think of our psalmist breaking loose and moaning aloud, though the narrative does not mention the shouts of the enemy, or the stones and boulders, which would take away something of the dignity, and the penitential air of the occasion. But now we have reached the following passage, whose incident takes place at the top of the Ascent:

> And it came to pass, that when David was come to the top *of the ascent*, where God was worshipped, behold, Hushai the Archite came to meet him with his coat rent, and earth upon his head: and David said unto him, If thou passest on with me, then thou shalt be a burden unto me: but if thou return to the city, and say unto Absalom, I will be thy servant, O king; as I have been thy father's servant in time past, so will I now be thy servant: then shalt thou defeat for me the counsel of Ahi(ezer). And hast thou not there with thee Zadok and Abiathar the priests? therefore it shall be, that what thing soever thou shalt hear out of the king's house, thou shalt tell it to Zadok and Abiathar the priests. Behold, they have there with them their two sons, Ahimaaz Zadok's son, and Jonathan Abiathar's son; and by them ye shall send unto me every

> thing that ye shall hear. So Hushai David's friend came into the city; and Absalom came into Jerusalem (2 Sam. 15.32-37).

Psalm 55 is the fourth of a series of Maschils, and we have become accustomed to finding the name of the central character of the Selah played upon in the following line of the psalm. The central character here is Hushai (*ḥûšaî*); and the word following in 55.9 is *'āḥîšâ*, I will hasten, from *ḥûš*, hiph., to hasten. No doubt Hushai's name is quite unrelated etymologically to *ḥûš*,[25] but the sound is quite close enough for popular Hebrew derivations, and the unlikelihood of such a closely sounding word occurring in the right place by accident is striking. We have had plays on the names of Zadok, Nabal, Ahiezer and Hushai for the four Maschil-psalms, and each has come in the line after the Selah (or the first line of the psalm where there was no Selah). If Maschil involves a name-play, there had to be a play on Zadok and Hushai in the relevant line (Ahiezer is a reconstruction, Nabal was not necessary); and added to the Korah Maschils (Hosea, Ahab, Jehoiachin) the case seems strong.

The mention of the shrine 'where God was worshipped' as David's meeting-place with Hushai, is suggestive for the pattern of the later procession. The marshalling of a large procession, the need for silence and the practicalities of open-air acoustics all suggest that the number of stops will have been limited. There are three events on the Ascent—the notice of Ahiezer's treachery, and the meetings with Hushai and Ziba—and it is likely that these will have been simplified into a single stop at the shrine by the ridge. The liturgy will have begun (p. 87) with the chanting of 51 and 52 in the Temple court overlooking the Kidron; the two Selahs in 52 told of the raising of the rebellion and David's withdrawal from the city. The procession then formed and filed up the Ascent, with the people 'covering every man his head, and they went up, weeping as they went up' (2 Sam. 15.30). When they reached the shrine (*'al-māḥ^{a}laṯ*) they chanted 53, 54 and 55. 53 had no Selah. 54 included the report of Ahiezer's defection, and 55 had two Selah's; the first of these covers the meeting with Hushai, and the second the encounter with Ziba. We then have an explanation for the absence of an *'al* phrase in the heading of 54 and 55: the procession is already at the shrine for 53, 'at the Cave', and there is no need for further direction. We may notice also the musical direction *bin^{e}gînōṯ* at the heading of 54 and 55 (and also 61 and 67), 'on stringed instruments'. While the procession has been mourning up the slope, there has been no music, and that includes 53 which was sung at arrival at the shrine. Now that the ridge is gained, the mourning ceases, and the music can begin, at first only the thin accompaniment of the strings. We shall find a crescendo in the musical directions as the procession continues to its end, and this is no time for the joy of the percussion instruments and the trumpets. But although the strings may be piano, they are a welcome symbol of hope.

The site of 'the place where God was worshipped' is not certain. McCarter[26] notes that there are three summits to the Mount of Olives, and thinks that David would be making for the middle one, the Jebel-eṭ-Ṭur, as being the most direct route to Bahurim. J. Murphy-O'Connor[27] comments: 'The lie of the land permits only one route if the traveller wants to avoid climbing in and out of wadis: from Gethsemane straight up the hill to et-Tur'. Murphy-O'Connor is writing about Jesus' route to Bethphage and Bethany, which are reached by continuing eastwards: the way to Bahurim turns north along the ridge. The Eleona church is close to the fork: thus far David and Jesus will have been covering the same ground. Egeria's comment, 'There they continue to sing hymns and antiphons suitable to the place and the day, with readings and prayers between' (35.3) will then strike a familiar note. Little did she think how similar a procession had passed the same way to the same place thirteen centuries before, and with psalms and readings and prayers suitable to the place and the day likewise.

Langlamet[28] thinks that the whole theme of Hushai's counter-counsel is a later, sapiential addition, and omits much of vv. 31, 34 as well as 17.5-14. I concur with him (and Würthwein[29]), in thinking 17.5-14 to be later (part of the Succession Narrative, in my case); but the 'defeating of the counsel of Ahiezer' could be effected merely by reporting it to David.

But the thought of Hushai's mission stirs deeper thoughts than the play on his name in v. 8.

55.9 Destroy (RV), O Lord, *and* divide their tongue:
For I have seen violence and strife in the city.
10 Day and night they encircle it (*y*^{e}*sôḇ*^{e}*ḇuhā*) to (*'al*) the walls thereof:
Iniquity also and mischief are in the midst of it.
11 Wickedness is in the midst thereof:
Oppression and treachery (*mirmâ*) depart not from her streets.

12 For it was not an enemy that reproached me;
Then I could have borne it:
Neither was it he that hated me that did magnify himself against me
Then I would have hid myself from him.
13 But it was thou, a man mine equal,
My companion, and my familiar friend.
14 We took sweet counsel together,
We walked in the house of God with the throng.
15 Let death come suddenly upon them,
Let them go down alive into Sheol,
For wickedness is in their dwelling, in their inward part.
16 As for me, I will call upon God;
And the LORD shall save me.
17 Evening, and morning, and at noonday, will I complain and moan
And he shall hear my voice.
18 He hath redeemed my life (*napšî*) in safety (*b*ᵉ*šālôm*) so that none came nigh me:
For with archers (*b*ᵉ*rabbîm*) they *strove* with me.
19 God shall hear, and afflict them,
Even he that abideth of old.
(Selah

Hushai is to insinuate himself into Absalom's counsels; and the hope rises that in some way he may sow doubt and ultimately frustration in the rebel camp: God is prayed to swallow up (*balla'*), to cleave (*pallag*) their tongue, i.e. their counsels (BDB). The phrase carries the echo of the dramatic confrontation between Hushai and Ahitophel in 2 Sam. 17.5ff., which may owe something to its suggestion.

55.9b-11. The verses give us a more detailed insight into the circumstances of David's evacuation of Zion. The psalmist prays for the rebels' destruction because of what he has himself 'seen' in Zion, so we have a first-hand account. While David was still there rioting broke out. There was violence (*ḥāmās*) and public quarrelling (*rîḇ*), trouble (*'āwen*) and ado (*'āmāl*), injury (*tōḵ*) and treachery (*mirmâ*) in the town; while Absalom's forces were to be seen by day, and with their fires by night, encircling (*y^e^sôḇ^e^ḇû*) it. The poel of *sbb* means to surround or encircle, either protectively (Deut. 32.10; Ps. 32.10) or in adoration (Pss. 7.8; 26.6, the altar), or menacingly (Jon. 2.4, 6, the waters; Ps. 59.7, 15); Cant. 3.2 gives a late extension of meaning, to circle round. One does not encircle a city *upon* its walls, the normal translation of *'al*, but *by* them (BDB *'al* 6a; cf. Prov. 14.19 'by the entrance'), or even *against* them (*ibid.* 7d; cf. Gen. 34.25, 27 'upon the city'). The arrival of the rebel forces in strength, and encamped (53.5) on all sides of Zion, had been the signal for a rising of sympathizers within.

No doubt David would have preferred to sit out a siege if he could: the moving of women and children must be a hazardous business, the opportunities for sniping and ambush must be legion once he left the safety of his walls (55.3ff., 18; 56.1f., 6; 57.6), the force of inertia is always strong, and if he left Zion, he must only go and be besieged somewhere else. What drove him out was the rising within the town. David had deeply offended Israelite feelings in many ways—with his taxes, with his dynastic ideas of kingship, with his desertion of the old Israelite cities and shrines for his Canaanite capital and his Canaanite priesthood, with his trampling on traditional Israelite morals with Bathsheba and Uriah. Now in the moment of crisis David is isolated. Only his family (Joab and others), a few loyalists, his mercenaries and his Canaanite friends stood by him. The hearts of the men of Israel were with Absalom, and as those Israelites within the town took arms, and were likely to open the gates to the enemy, there was nothing for it but to go. David went from the north gate, but he had to force his way through the besiegers as he went; and they could withdraw up the hill and plague his column as it climbed. The people had better reason to cry out and to cover their heads than the dignified grief attributed to them by the Succession Narrative. But the PD narrative tells us accurately that within an hour or so of David's departure 'Absalom came into Jerusalem' (2 Sam. 15.37). There was time for David to go up the Ascent, and time for Hushai to come down. The rebel army had been encircling the city night and day, to its walls; and with the king's going, their friends within could open the gates to them.

Without the Davidic context the sense is difficult. It is common to see a reference to the Tower of Babel in the confusing of the 'oppressor's' tongue (so Eaton, Rogerson and McKay). If v. 10a is rendered 'they go about (the city) upon the walls thereof' (RV), following the unique meaning *sôḇēḇ* in

Cant. 3.2, it becomes impossible to imagine a motive for such a bizarre human activity; and recourse is had to capital letters, turning Violence, Mischief, etc. into personifications (so Kirkpatrick, Gunkel and many). This is thin; and Gunkel's appeal to 43.3, 'O send out thy light and thy truth; let them lead me', is inadequate, for light and truth are thought of as good angels—demons are not so easy to parallel.

55.12-15. The psalmist is moved more especially by the treachery of his friend. The Selah has told of the coming contest between Hushai and Ahiezer, and it is the thought of the latter's betrayal which is boiling over in his heart. Ahiezer did not just go over to Absalom secretly; he 'reproached' the speaker—that is, he appealed to him publicly in 'her streets' (v. 11) to support the rebellion. As in the English Civil War, there were men of high principle on both sides. Ahiezer, like Fairfax and Essex, could see the king as obstinate in misgovernment, and unfaithful to the nation's ethical, religious and social ideals; his loyalty lay with Israel, and he could publicly reprove the psalmist for denying those ideals in siding with the king. But to the latter, as to Sir Jacob Astley, the issue was the divine right of kings, and such talk was *tōḵ ûmirmâ*, violence and treachery. The *kî* in v. 12 is not a 'loose' but a direct connection: it was treachery that was abroad in Jerusalem, *for* it was no enemy advocating disloyalty to the king, but Ahiezer himself.

The 'reproaching' clearly took place in Jerusalem in the last hours before the king left; and this resolves the problems of 2 Sam. 15.12, 'And Absalom sent (*wayyišlaḥ*) Ahitophel the Gilonite, David's counsellor, from his city, even from Giloh, while he offered the sacrifices'. *šlḥ* does not mean 'sent for' (RV text), but 'sent' (RVmg); he sent Ahiezer to Jerusalem in just the same way that David sent Hushai, to be a double agent. 4Q Sam^c has eased the difficulty by supplying *wayyiqrā'*, 'sent and summoned' Ahitophel, sc. to Hebron. *šlḥ* means to send off, without a specified destination, at Gen. 28.5; Judg. 11.38; in both passages, as here, the destination is implied by the context. No doubt Ahiezer went out to greet Absalom when Zion fell, as in ch. 19 so many come to greet David on his return: 2 Sam. 16.15 tells us that he then entered the city with Absalom.

Ahiezer reproached the psalmist and 'magnified himself against him': he took an aggressive line. Had it been an enemy, the speaker would have put up with it and moved off ('hid myself from him'). 'But it was thou'—the traitor is addressed in indignation, as the *gibbôr* was in 51, and the 'mighty ones' will be in 58. He was a man on a par with the psalmist in rank (*k*^{ec}*erkî*), a comrade (*'allûp*) from the same community (*'elep̄*), and an intimate friend (*m*^{e}*yuddā'î*). They had shared happily together in the royal cabinet ('we sweetened counsel together'); they had processed (cf. 42.4) side by side through the Temple courts before the populace. No doubt hard words passed between them at the hour of parting: now the bitterness of betrayal is overwhelming. Death (following Q) is called down on the turncoat—worse than death, Sheol to devour him and his fellows alive, as befell Dathan and Abiram. Wickedness is in their dwelling, in their heart: he calls their home a *māgûr*, a sojourning place—it will not be their home for long.

55.16-19a. As elsewhere in the Prayers (52.8; 69.29), bitter thoughts of the wicked end with a contrasted aspiration by the speaker, 'As for me'. Again the use of Yahweh seems a little unfamiliar: 'I will call upon God, And Yahweh shall save me' (cf. 52.9; 54.1, 6). The prayer which began so insistently in 55.1f., with its complaining and moaning cries, will be continued three times a day, evening, morning and noon; and God *will* hear his voice. Already—since they reached the top with the Selah at v. 7—the terror of death is abated. God has redeemed his life in safety: a Selah may bring about a sharp change of tone in a psalm (cf. 57.7), and it is better to treat the perfect as realistic than as prophetic. RVmg points *miqq*^{e}*rob̲-lî*, infinitive, 'from (anyone) coming near me', cf. G ἀπὸ τῶν ἐγγιζόντων; and this yields an easier sense than *miqq*^{a}*rāb-lî*, 'from the battle (set) against me'. That would also fit well with the second hemistich, where the translation of *b*^{e}*rabbîm* as 'many' (beth essentiae) has long raised difficulties. *rabbîm*, from *rab̲* an archer (*rbb* II, to shoot), is found in Job 16.13, Jer. 50.29 in the plural, and this gives a clear force, 'for with archers were they against me' (cf. Gunkel's emendation *rōb̲îm*). The 'trouble' that was 'let fall' in v. 3 included arrows as well as stones (and far more dangerously); as long as the archers were in range, death was a present threat, and its horror was felt as overwhelming. Once God redeemed his life from their approach, the psalmist knew he was safe. It is also easier to understand *'immāḏî* as 'with me' in a hostile sense if the subject is hostile ('archers') instead of neutral ('many'); elsewhere the hostile sense is always implied by some other word in the sentence ('indignation', Job 10.17, 'contend', Job 13.19; 23.6; 31.13).

God will hear my voice (v. 17); he will hear and afflict the enemy (v. 19)—the similarity to v. 2 (*ya'anēm/'anēnî*) makes a conscious play on the words likely. The force of *wᵉyōšēḇ qeḏem* is not very clear. Perhaps 'even he who is enthroned eternally', in contrast to the changes and chances of this fleeting life.

In view of the closeness with which the text fits the long-running Jewish interpretation that the traitor is Ahitophel, it is extraordinary how easily interpreters have rejected it. Kirkpatrick and Jacquet note that Ahitophel was not of David's rank; a comment which shows little flexibility of imagination, for it is easily possible that the psalmist was the Chief Musician or such, writing 'for David'. In fact David has not been taken very seriously this century; even among Catholic exegetes only Herkenne has opted for him in 55. But without him, and the military peril that goes with him, there are many aporias: personified demons going round the battlements, or a procession of magical efficacy (Weiser); a dreadful curse of death on a false friend who has slandered the speaker ('flying into a helpless rage', Weiser); the intrusion of a poem about Ishmael and other desert tribes in vv. 19-22 (Gunkel; cf. Kraus, NEB). The old is best.

55.19b They who had no change of clothes (*'ên ḥᵃlîp̄ôṯ*),
And who fear not God,
20 He hath put forth his hands against such as were at peace with him:
He hath profaned his covenant.
21 His mouth was smooth as butter,
But his heart was war:
His words were softer than oil,
Yet were they drawn swords.
22 Cast thy burden upon the LORD, and he shall sustain thee:
He shall not for ever (*lᵉᶜôlām*) suffer the righteous to be moved.
23 But thou, O God, shalt bring them down to the pit of destruction:
Murders and traitors (*'anšê ḏāmîm ûmirmâ*) shall not live out half their days;
But I will trust in thee.

These final verses are preceded by the psalm's second Selah; and the next incident in the Passion of David is the encounter with Ziba near the pass at the top of Olivet:

> And when David was a little past the top *of the ascent*, behold, Ziba the servant of Me[ribbaal] met him, with a couple of asses saddled, and upon them two hundred loaves of bread, and an hundred clusters of raisins, and an hundred of summer fruits, and a skin of wine. And [David] said unto Ziba, What meanest thou by these? And Ziba said, The asses be for the king's household to ride on; and the bread and summer fruit for the young men to eat; and the wine, that such as be faint in the wilderness may drink. And [David] said, Where is thy master's son? And Ziba said unto [David], Behold he abideth in Jerusalem: for he said, Today shall the house of Israel restore me the kingdom of my father. Then said [David] to Ziba, Behold, thine is all that pertaineth to Me[ribbaal]. And Ziba said, I do obeisance; let me find favour in thy sight, my lord, O king (2 Sam. 16.1-4).

The tale of faithless ingratitude evokes the bitter words of 55.19b-23. After the death of Ishbaal, his nephew Meribbaal,[30] still a minor (2 Sam. 4.4) and a cripple, had been taken in by the kindly Machir ben-Ammiel in Lo-debar (9.5). He had no income from his estates during the civil war, and no ability to earn: he had, as our psalmist puts it a little harshly, 'no change of clothes'. The standard meaning of *ḥ^a^lîp̱â* is a change of clothes—usually with a word for clothes, as in the stories of Joseph (Gen. 45.22), Samson (Judg. 14) or Gehazi (2 Kgs 5), but also absolutely, as here, in Judg. 14.19. Indignation draws the psalmist into anacoluthon: '*Those* who had no change of clothes and who fear not God, *He* hath put forth his hand. . . ' Meribbaal had, without too much hyperbole, a covenant (v. 20) with David: that is, David had restored him his lands, made Ziba responsible to deliver the income to him, and provided him with daily meals at the royal table—with so much kindness, he might be understood to have undertaken loyalty in response. This covenant he has now profaned by going over to the rebels: David was at peace with him(to put it mildly)—note the generalizing plural as in v. 19b—and he has 'put forth his hand against him' by his failure to send support. Basically this is irreligion: he 'fears not God', like the fool of 53.1. V. 21 draws an effective contrast between his unctuous toadying and his inner hostility and secret treachery.

With *55.22f.* the speaker turns to the king. He should cast his *y^e^hāḇ* on Yahweh: the word is found in the Talmud meaning a burden laid on a camel (b R.H. 26b; cf. Delitzsch). Yahweh will support him in his hour of utter exhaustion, betrayal and peril; he may try the righteous for a while, but his load will not be upon him for ever. But as for the rebels, God will see them down to death before half their allotted span. RV's 'bloodthirsty and deceitful men' is much too weak: they are men of blood and treachery, murderers and traitors. The description is not exaggerated, and the prophecy was to err on the generous side. Absalom would be dead in three months, Amasa in a couple of years, Ahiezer in a week; only Meribbaal was to survive the current upheavals.

Cook,[31] denies 16.1-4 its present place in the original narrative, but this is in favour of his theory of dating the rebellion before David was king in Jerusalem. Langlamet[32] sets all the Ziba-Meribbaal matter together in an independent Benjaminite source; but this seems speculative and unnecessary. The topographical detail, and the use of 'David' in 16.1, suggest that the section belongs with the other PD passages. I have taken it that the Succession Narrator has substituted 'the king' and 'Mephibosheth' in 16.2-4. It is possible that the limited amounts of food were all originally for the king's household, and that v. 2 is also the Succession Narrator's redaction; but even limited supplies might be very welcome to an army in low water. The 'summer fruits' (*qaîṣ*) is interesting in that it tells us the time of the rebellion: it was at harvest-time. Jeremiah told the people to gather and store their *qaîṣ* after the fall of Jerusalem in 586, and the setting up of Gedaliah's regime at Mizpah (Jer. 40.10, 12); the word comes several times in parallel with 'vintage' (Jer. 48.32; Mic. 7.1; Isa. 16.9—cf. Amos 8.1f. with play on *qeṣ*, 'the end', cp. the end of the year). The rebellion took place in October, and 'the men of Israel' were available to support it because the year's work in the fields was done. Very likely Absalom's sacrificing at Hebron was a thanksgiving for harvest as well as other things.

The final passage in the psalm is a source of perplexity. 'The men who have no changes' are a particular puzzle: Delitzsch, following the Targum, took this to mean no repentance, Gunkel (and NEB) no respect for oaths, Kirkpatrick no vicissitudes of fortune, Kraus no exchange of prisoners, Dahood no variation in the Godhead. The clause is often construed with v. 19a in defiance of the Selah (which is 'quite inexplicable and must be misplaced', Kirkpatrick): a subject has then to be supplied for v. 20 ('My companion', RSV), or a transposition supposed. Gunkel thought v. 19a was about Ishmael and Ja'alam and he who dwells in the east, and that vv. 18-22 were a different psalm which had been intruded; Kraus has these nomads attacking the speaker in S.E. districts, and not surprisingly finds the situation hard to supply. NEB has made it a similitude.

Chapter 5

THE RETREAT: FROM OLIVET TO MAHANAIM (56-59)

56 For the Chief Musician. At (*'al*) the Dove of the Distant Terebinths. For (*l^e*) David: Michtam: when the Philistines took him in Gath.

1 Be merciful unto me, O God; for man panteth after me (*š^e'āpanî*):
All the day long he fighting harrieth me (*yilḥāṣēnî*).

2 They that lie in wait for me pant (*šā^{'a}pû*) all the day long:
For archers (*rabbîm*) fight against me from above (*mārôm*).

3 In the day (*yôm*) of my fear (*'îrā'*),
I will put my trust in thee.

4 In God will I praise his word:
In God have I put my trust, I will not be afraid;
What can flesh do unto me?

Psalm 56 belongs comfortably in the Prayers sequence. It shares its initial 'Be merciful unto me, O God' with 57.1, and its 'panting' enemies with 57.3; its 'liers in wait' (*šôr^erai*) with 54.5 and 59.10; its *rabbîm* with 55.18, and their 'going down' to Sheol (v. 7) with 55.23 and 59.11; its foreign enemies (v. 7) with 54.3, 59.5 and other texts; their 'gathering' with 59.3, their watching 'my steps' with 57.6, and their waiting for 'my soul' with 54.3. Even when the vocabulary is not the same, or is common, the enemies, the fear, the vows and many other matters are the leitmotifs of the psalm-sequence.

The first point for which David's column made was the ridge of Olivet, and it was here in later years that 53-55 were recited, at 'Mahalath' (53, Heading), the psalms covering the events of that fraught ascent. Once the ridge was gained, the column turned north towards Bahurim (2 Sam. 16.5), and on to 'the crossing of the wilderness' (15.28; 17.6), to which it is implied that David came, weary, soon after he had passed Bahurim (16.14). The weariness can hardly be exaggerated. There are few experiences more wearing on the nerves than leaving one's home before dawn for an unknown destination, forcing a passage over a river with heavy casualties, climbing a hillside under a constant hail of stones and arrows, with repeated halts, ambushes and skirmishes, marching a further distance under similar conditions, and with constant verbal abuse, while at the same time escorting and encouraging some hundreds of wailing women and terrified, exhausted children. David will have been as fresh as a British soldier on the Somme who had survived July 1st, 1916; and it is the obverse of this condition that he has not advanced far. The Passion Narrative account makes this clear. At 16.5 'king David came to Bahurim', and Shimei came out of the village to pelt and abuse him from 'the hillside over against him': David and his men were marching along the road as he did so (16.13), 'and the king, and all the people that were with him, came weary; and he refreshed himself there' (16.14). 'There' can only refer to a place already mentioned, that is Bahurim. Bahurim is near the hilltop, and David will have made his camp on the crest so as to escape the plague of being shot at from higher ground. The Bahurim hillcrest is visible from Jerusalem, and was no doubt wooded at the period. This will be the 'Distant Terebinths', distant that is from Jerusalem. The site was christened 'The Dove of the Distant Terebinths' in recognition of the dove imagery of Ps. 55.6ff., the symbol of the company's escape.

The 'there' of 2 Sam. 16.14 is a well-known puzzle. McCarter[1] has David's company 'winding down finally to the Jordan' in this verse; but this is in no way hinted, and it must surely have been stated. I do also feel that there has been some failure of imagination by those who suppose a twenty-mile march to be practicable in a day under such conditions. RVmg suggests that *ᵃyēpîm* is the name of a place: 'came to Ayephim; and he refreshed himself there'. But the name is not testified elsewhere, and it would be an ironic coincidence for a party as weary as David's to arrive at a place called Weary. I have accepted the standard (Olshausen's) changing of vowel points, *'ēlim* (terebinths) for *'ēlem* (silent), and suppose that a pious lector took *'ēlim* for a piece of polytheism.

We may picture the downcast royalists then as encamped for the night under the trees. A part of the food they have carried is eaten, a fire is lit, the children are laid to sleep, sentries are posted. The enemy is gone away, and our psalmist strikes up with 56 and 57, two psalms that he has been praying under the day's fire. Small wonder if in years to come the old comrades will relive their experiences under the magic of his music, and will teach their children's children to participate by joining in a procession to the same spot each year, and to join in the same Prayers. Psalm 56 is the first of a series of Michtam's, 'inscribed psalms' (*ktm* Jer. 2.22, to incise or stain; LXX στηλογραφία): Delitzsch[2] notes that the Michtams (16,56-60) have in common the reprise of the psalms' theme, and we may think that this was written down, so that all could join in, but without music. The theme of 56.3f. is taken up in vv. 10f. In this way we should have a musical crescendo from the chanted refrains of 56-60 via the string of 61 to the mizmors, 62-68, and the Songs, 65-68. It has nothing to do with the Philistines taking David in Gath—a late guess arising from David's fear in 1 Sam. 21.12.

56.1-4. The singer describes graphically the trials of the day. Kirkpatrick notes the stress on 'all the day' (vv. 1, 2, 5) and 'the day of my fear' (v. 3); and the stress has a reason—from dawn to dusk the column has been under virtually uninterrupted assault. As the slave panted (*š'p* I) after the shadow in Job 7.2, or the wild ass in heat in Jer. 2.24, so have company after company of the enemy come panting up the hill after them (Dahood, 'hounding them'). All day they have fought with the speaker and pressed him. If we take *šôrᵉraî* with RV to mean 'those who lie in wait', there have been numerous ambushes (but cf. p. 95)—and this is extremely likely. After their losses at the Kidron crossing, the rebels have not felt strong enough to try a battle, but they have been unpleasantly effective with their archers (*rabbîm*, as in 55.18, q.v.) firing down from higher ground (LXX ἐξ ὕψους), Heb. 'fighting *mārôm*', above. It has indeed been a day of fear for him—panic at the dawn crossing (53.5), fearfulness and trembling, terror of death and horror (55.4f.) during the ascent of Olivet. Now that the long strain is over, and he and the bulk of those who set out with him so many hours ago are encamped in safety, he lifts his voice in trembling trust in the God who has seen him through. He will trust in God, he will not be afraid; with such a Protector, mortal man (*'ᵉnôš, bāśār*) cannot touch him.

A second feature of 56 is its repeated stress on 'words': 'In God I will praise his word' (vv. 4a, 10ab), 'All the day long they wrest my words' (v. 5). A plausible explanation of this will be that 'the voice of the enemy' (55.3), whose 'tongue is a sharp sword' (57.4) has in fact been citing David's own words against him. The psalmist veers between speaking in his own name (55.13f.; 61.6ff.; etc.), and in the king's name (53.4, 51 throughout), and here he speaks for David. Perhaps they cited phrases from 51, like 'Against thee have I sinned, And done that which is evil in thy sight' (cf. 2 Sam. 12.13); this might very suitably be spoken of as 'They wrest my words'. Such attacks would be the more understandable if the year had borne a poor harvest. Yahweh's blessing on the crops was understood to be contingent upon national, and especially on royal, obedience: the God Yahweh would not dwell (in the land) unless his norms were observed (68.18). A failure of the harvest would be likely to bring other grievances to a head; and David's sins with Bathsheba and Uriah would make him an easy scapegoat for a superstitious generation. The psalmist's response to this onslaught is to take refuge in 'God's word', that is the oracle pronounced by Nathan, 'Yahweh also hath put away thy sin' (2 Sam. 12.13): in God he will praise his word. Since the whole structure of the Prayers sequence is set up on the premise that David's sin over Uriah was the cause of all his troubles, and since the Succession Narrative has adopted the same basis for its story, it can only be plausible that the same ideas were current, and expressed, during the actual events.

Psalm 56 raises many problems. With its military language, it was still honoured as a Davidic psalm by Delitzsch and Kirkpatrick, even with the Gath. context. Most modern commentators have followed Gunkel in seeing it as an individual Lament, but this has involved a formidable amount of emendation, down to NEB. Gunkel placed the sufferer in the Diaspora, in view of 'In anger cast down the peoples, O God'; Kraus and others, not very convincingly, take this as a general assertion of God's judgment of mankind. Furthermore, individual interpretations involve treating the insistent military phrasing as imagery (fighting, panting, pressing, hiding, 'waiting for my soul', wandering, enemies, the light of the living). Mowinckel followed by Eaton and Dahood, sees a national situation with the king as speaker;[3] but this involves treating the tears, etc. as rites of contrition. The 'word' which is praised is also difficult for these views, and is often taken to imply an oracle, whether private or public. Weiser sites the psalm between the oracle and the thank-offering; but it reads rather as if the speaker has had a terrifying day, and that he will be duly grateful when God's expected deliverance takes place in the future (Kraus). It is difficult to relate God's 'word' to 'my words' without the Nathan context.

There are numerous smaller problems. *mārôm* is an especial difficulty without the archers on the higher ground: Dahood and Anderson favour 'O Exalted One', Kirkpatrick and RV 'haughtily': Gunkel is right to be suspicious of these as Hebrew and he and Kraus treat it as 'unintelligible', and emend. There are two verbs *š'p*: Anderson and Rogerson and McKay follow the old versions with 'trample', but most commentators prefer 'pant after', as I have for a different reason. The dove of the distant *'ēle(i)m* is a conundrum for all; but perhaps my copse on the hill top by Bahurim is more plausible than the standard name of a tune, or Mowinckel's release of a dove in penitential rites (cf. Eaton).

56.5 All the day long they wrest my words:
All their thoughts are against me for evil.
6 They encamp (*yāgûrû*), they hide themselves,
They mark my steps,
Inasmuch as they have waited for my soul.
7 Shall they escape (RV) in view of (*'al*) iniquity?
In anger cast down the peoples, O God.
8 Thou tellest my wanderings:
Put my tears into thy bottle;
Are they not in thy record?
9 Then shall mine enemies turn back in the day that I meet them (*'eqrā'*):
This I know, for God is for me.
10 In God will I praise *his* word.
In the LORD will I praise *his* word.
11 In God have I put my trust, I will not be afraid;
What can man do unto me?
12 Thy vows are upon me, O God:
I will render thank offerings unto thee.
13 For thou hast delivered my soul from death:
Hast thou not *delivered* my feet from falling?
That I may walk before God
In the light of life.

56.5f. The dire plight of the retreating royalists comes through in brilliant colours. 'All the day long' there has been fighting, harassing, and the calling of abuse. RV's 'they wrest my words' is justified by Anderson on the basis of *'ṣb* II = shape, twist (Koehler-Baumgartner): this will then correspond to wounding, ironic cries of 'Behold, I was shapen in iniquity', 'Deliver me from bloodguiltiness, O God', or such, which have dismayed the speaker and his comrades. All their actions have been indeed thought out for David's ruin. *yāgûrû* can hardly mean 'they gather themselves together' (RV), though this is defended by Delitzsch: the mention of 'the peoples' in the following verse suggests that we take the normal meaning, 'they sojourn' or encamp. The most effective of the rebel troops have been the desert mercenaries, 'the peoples that delight in war' (68.30). Ishmael, who dwelt in the wilderness of Paran, their homeland beyond the Negeb, grew up to be an archer (*rôḇeh qaššeṯ*, Gen. 21.20), and it is the archers who have plagued the retreat (55.18; 56.2). They have settled, encamped on Israelite soil; they have hidden themselves behind rocks or mounds; they—*hēmmâ*, emphasized, the archers—they have marked my heels, that is, they have shot down the rearguard. It makes little difference whether we read *yiṣpînû* with K or *yiṣpûnû* with Q: the hiding is for ambushing in any case, and the most effective ambushing is shooting from behind. David's column felt like the British Afghan expedition retreating from Kabul in 1842.

56.7f. They have 'waited for my soul' in their rocky foxholes, firing volleys of arrows into the thinning rearguard, shooting down any counter-attack, and then panting over to the next outcrop. We can well understand David's refusal of Abishai's offer to go and take off Shimei's head, in the Succession Narrative (2 Sam. 16.10f.): the Narrator attributes it to David's noble and religious humility, but military prudence is a more likely motive. In such a predicament there is little option but to press on regardless; and the consequent anger comes out in appeals for divine vengeance. '(Will there be) escape for them in view of (their) iniquity?' seems the best rendering of difficult Hebrew; or perhaps 'in view of (the) trouble (they cause)'. God is called on to cast them down (to Sheol) as at 55.15, 23, and the specification of them as *'ammîm* shows that the whole psalm (and much of its predecessor) has been concerned with mercenary bowmen. God's memory is dependable: 'Thou (*'āttâ*) countest my wandering'—God adds up every night spent camping here and there away from the palace. Every tear shed at the loss of position, of comrades, of womenfolk, he will store in his divine lacrimary; though such luxuries were not yet perhaps invented on earth, they may be imagined in heaven, and *nō'ḏ*, a skin-bottle, makes a good play with *nōḏ*, wandering. Is not all this suffering recorded with God? He will surely repay.

56.9ff. Then, *'āz*, on the day that God casts the peoples down, David's enemies will turn back. RV translates *b^eyôm 'eqrā'* 'on the day that I call', and this is general: but the sense is then obscure—surely the psalmist is calling now? Also *'āz* has then a very weak meaning, 'Then... on the day that I call'. It is better to take *'eqrā'* as from *qr'* II, to encounter, so often to encounter in battle, though usually in prose with an object. There is no pitched battle today. The royal forces do not want it because they are heavily outnumbered; the rebel army cannot force it against an enemy on the move, and whom their vanguard can only harass from a distance. But the day will come when David does encounter his enemies, and then they will indeed turn back (68.12). The speaker knows this because God is on David's side. He chose David to be king, and promised the kingdom to his dynasty (2 Sam. 7);[4] and he assured him that his sins were forgiven (2 Sam. 12). So for the second time the psalmist praises God for his oracle (*dāḇār*). We had God... Yahweh in parallel hemistichs at 55.16, and they come again at 58.6. With trembling self-reassurance he vows to put his fear behind him for tomorrow: with God on his side, what can man do to him? But unwelcome reflection tells him that God was on their side today, and the casualties have been heavy.

56.12f. God can be encouraged by the thought of rich sacrifices to come. David and his priest have undertaken such in vows from 54.6 on, probably from 52.9 on, and the Prayers make constant reference to these vows. God has indeed, in this day of peril, delivered both king and psalmist from death: the arrow that flieth in the noonday has killed some dozens, but it has not come nigh them. Their legs have been knocked (*dḥh*) from under them, but the singer has come through, has he not? God meant him to walk before him in the light of life, in loyal service to his Anointed, and perhaps also in the administration of the sacrifices, if, as it seems, he is a priest.

The most serious problem of the psalm is to account for the rise in confidence of the last verses. Jacquet exaggerates when he speaks of the text taking 'un accent de plus en plus assuré et triomphant', but the feeling at the end is better. Jacquet's own explanation is that he 'atteint le sommet (de confiance en Dieu) dans un acte de remise de soi à son Dieu'; but this purely spiritual solution is hardly convincing. The hypothesis of a liturgical event is not much better. Weiser writes, 'the experience which has given rise to the worshipper's assurance that his petition has been granted is not explicitly mentioned, but only alluded to; presumably it was the promise of divine grace, pronounced in public worship'. Mowinckel and Eaton think on similar lines, though their ideas of liturgy are more colourful than Weiser's. It seems more plausible to account for the change of feeling by positing a genuine change of situation: the harassment of the day is over, and the spirits rise; God's promise that he would put away David's sin now seems believable once more, and fear can be laid aside.

The same problem of a psalm beginning on a low note and ending on a high tone of confidence is posed in a more acute form by 57.

57 For the Chief Musician. *'al-tašḥēṯ*. A Psalm for (*l*^{e})
David: Michtam: when he fled from Saul, in the cave.
1 Be merciful unto me, O God, be merciful unto me;
For my soul taketh refuge in thee:
Yea, in the shadow of thy wings will I take refuge,
Until calamities (RV) be overpast.
2 I will cry unto God Most High;
Unto God that performeth *all things* for me.
3 He shall send from heaven and save me;
He that panteth after me (*šō'*^{a}*pî*) reproacheth.
(Selah
God shall send forth his mercy and truth, my soul
(*napšî*).
4 I will lie down (*'ešk*^{e}*ḇâ*) among lions;
The sons of men burn fires (*loh*^{a}*ṭîm*):
Their teeth are spears and arrows,
And their tongue a sharp sword.
5 Be thou exalted, O God, above the heavens;
Thy glory above all the earth.

Psalm 57 belongs securely within the sequence 52–59; Duhm even thought 56–59 had the same author. The opening phrase, 'Be merciful unto me, O God', is the same as that of 56; the *hawwôṯ* of v. 1 are the same pit of destructiveness as in 52.2 and 55.11; the *šō'*^{a}*pî* is the same as in 56.1, 2; the comparison of words to swords is as in 59.7, and like 52.2 and 55.21; the enemy are spoken of as lions in v. 4 and as lion cubs in 58.6. 'The shadow of thy wings' in v. 1 is like 'the covert of thy wings' in 61.4. The names of God, *'ēl*, *'*^{e}*lōhîm*, *'elyôn*, are to be found in many of the Prayers (pp. 22f.).

A satisfying meaning can be given to the psalm on the basis that it is a continuation of the cycle. Psalm 56 was the psalmist's response to the first part of the march from the peak of Olivet to Bahurim: 57 is his prayer now that the fighting is over for the day, and camp has been set up. But although the stress of the day is over, the peril remains acute. The king has eleven hundred soldiers and a mass of dependants sleeping out, without stone wall, palisade or ditch between him and a much more numerous enemy; who may, even now be planning a mass attack at dawn. Eaton suggests that *'al-tašḥēṯ*, do not destroy, stands for some rites of lamentation which accompanied the psalm: we may think of Deut. 9.25f., 'So I *fell down before the LORD*... And I prayed unto the LORD, and said, O Lord GOD, *destroy not* thy people' (Dahood). Psalm 57 then will be chanted with ritual prostrations, as are suited to a moment of dire crisis; and as the company will continue to be exposed to such danger while they are at the Far Terebinths, so do 58 and 59 find utterance amid the same physical abasement. This will cease only when they have reached the comparative security of Mahanaim. Like the other psalms in the sequence 56-60, 57 is an 'inscribed psalm', a *miḵtām*, with a refrain in which all can join: 'Be thou exalted, O God, above the heavens; Thy glory above all the earth' (vv. 5, 11). The references to Saul, and to the cave (1 Sam. 22, 24) are an unfortunate guess: only the fleeing was right.

57.1-3. In such a predicament the singer turns to God, his helper of last resort, with redoubled prayers for mercy. Here on the hilltop he has taken his refuge for the night, and he feels that that refuge is in God; he uses the perfect *ḥāsāyâ*. Indeed, the branches and leaves of the great terebinth trees will be the company's protection from the cold, clear October sky, and seem like the divine wings overshadowing and protecting them: they will continue to be his refuge, future *'eḥseh*, until the present devouring destruction (p. 72) has spent its force. God is supreme (*'elyôn*) over all the sons of men (v. 4), and he will answer the call and bring the ruin to an end—*gmr* means to end or complete (Pss. 7.9; 12.1; 138.8, intrans. and trans.) rather than RV's accomplish. He will send and deliver them from the surrounding rebels. The nightmare image is still before the psalmist's eyes of Shimei and his 'mighty men' panting along beside the tiring column, hurling abuse and stones and other missiles—'reproaching' in the way so vividly described in the Selah.

The Selah is the next section of 2 Samuel 16, following the encounter with Ziba (16.1-4; Ps. 55.19):

> And when king David came to Bahurim, behold, there came out thence a man of the family of the house of Saul, whose name was Shimei, the son of Gera: he came out, and cursed still as he came. And he cast stones at David, and at all the servants of king David: and all the people and all the mighty men were on his right hand and on his left... So David and his men went by the way: and Shimei went along the hillside over against him, and cursed as he went, and threw stones over against him, and cast dust. And (David) and all the people that were with him, came weary; and he refreshed himself there (2 Sam. 16.5f., 13f.).

The situation described in the Selah mirrors closely that presupposed by the psalm. David and his followers are marching 'by the way', the track, and Shimei and his Benjaminites are on the ridge (*ṣelaʿ*) of the hill above him. In 19.17 Shimei has 'a thousand' men, perhaps the standard regiment of around six hundred, but he need not have had so many living in Bahurim: he is not strong enough to challenge the royalists, but he can harass them from above, as the archers did in 55.18; 56.2 on the central spur of Olivet. David's column has finally shaken the bowmen off—perhaps they have run out of arrows—and its leading troops have entered Bahurim; the villagers have followed Shimei their elder out on to the ridge, from which they pelt the king with abuse and stones and dry clods. The psalmist's words for the scene are, 'He that panteth after me reproacheth'; and if his actual words were, 'Begone, begone, thou man of blood, and man of Belial' (2 Sam. 16.7), that would be entirely suitable for *ḥērēp̄ šōʾᵃp̄î*. The Passion Narrative says that David refreshed himself at Bahurim ('there', p. 110): that is, the troops commandeered all the food they could find in the place, and settled down for the night under the trees on the crest nearby.

57.3c-5. Standard translations have trouble with the way that the metre (which, as Gunkel says, is clearly shown) goes against the sense. Thus RV:

> 'My soul
> is among lions; I must lie
> among them that are set on fire, Even the sons of men,
> whose teeth are spears... '

I have kept the sense in line with the metre by taking *nap̄šî* as a vocative in v. 3c, like *k*ᵉ*ḇôḏî* in v. 8. Verse 5 can then open, 'Among lions will I lie'. The royalists are bedding down for the night by starlight. All round them they know that their enemies are encamping, and waiting for their blood in the morning; they are felt to be beasts of prey. They are not, however, real lions, as Delitzsch thought, but 'sons of men burning'. *lhṭ* is found only once elsewhere in the qal, Ps. 104.4, where it means to burn either intransitively ('flaming fire') or transitively ('consuming fire'). The common piel is transitive, and as no clear sense is given by the intransitive meaning, we may prefer the good sense given by the transitive. The 'lions' are sons of men burning fires, to keep away the night cold, and to cook their evening meal, the invariable scene at the end of an ancient day's campaigning. Our psalmist comforts his 'soul' that God will send forth his angels, his mercy and his truth (cf. 85.10f.); he prays that God will exalt himself in heaven and reveal his glory in a signal deliverance for the king on earth.

The Passion of David should probably be limited here to 2 Sam. 16.5f., 13f. It is an old tradition which has preserved Shimei's patronymic, and the king is 'David' in 5, 6 and 13, and 'king David' also in v. 6. In v. 14 'the king' may be editorial: it will stem from the Succession Narrator in vv. 9, 10. The latter will also be responsible for Yahweh in vv. 8 (x2), 9, 10, 11, 12 (x2). He will have expanded his Vorlage's 'cursed' with some lifelike obloquy (vv. 8f.), and supplied an edifying conversation between David and Abishai, demonstrating the king's humble piety (vv. 9-12; cf. 15.19f., 25f.). The picture of Abishai is the standard hot-headed son of Zeruiah (1 Sam. 26.8f.; 2 Sam. 19.21f.; Gunn, pp. 39f.). Thus vv. 7-12 look like the Succession Narrator's expansion of a basic Passion Narrative text, 16.5f.; 13f. Veijola, p. 33, suspects vv. 11f. of being an amplification, but for different reasons.[5]

The psalm presents commentators with problems from v. 3 on. Delitzsch and Kirkpatrick still held to the David tradition, with references to 1 Samuel 24, the cave. Gunkel, Kraus and most critics since have seen an individual Lament followed by an individual Thanksgiving, a faithful Israelite being slandered, and perhaps accused (Kraus, following H.H. Schmidt). Gunkel has him in the Diaspora in view of 'the peoples' (v. 9). Mowinckel, Eaton, Anderson and Dahood take a quite different approach, with a national, cultic setting, in which the king is praying for protection against the nation's lion-like enemies. The 'reproaching' of v. 3 is a difficulty for Gunkel ('zunächst unverständliche'), and Kraus similarly takes the text to be (considerably) 'verwirrt'; cf. NEB 'frustrate'. Kraus and others have the accused man incubating in the Temple, with his persecutors around him, praying for a theophany: the picture seems rather unreal. Rogerson and McKay have him 'lying down helplessly'. The lions and the fire of v. 4 are also a widespread puzzle. They are fiery foes with Kirkpatrick, and fire-breathing in Delitzsch and Eaton, man-eaters in the NEB: the metaphors seem rather bold for easy paralleling.

57.6 They have prepared a net for my steps;
He has bowed down my soul (*kāpap napšî*):
They have digged a pit before me;
They are fallen into the midst thereof themselves. (Selah
7 My heart is confirmed (*nāḵôn*), O God, my heart is confirmed:
I will sing, yea, I will chant to music (*ʾazammērâ*).
8 Awake up, my glory; awake, psaltery and harp:
I will awake the dawn.
9 I will give thanks unto thee, O Lord, among the peoples:
I will chant (*ʾazammerᵉḵā*) unto thee among the nations.
10 For thy mercy is great unto the heavens,
And thy truth unto the skies.
11 Be thou exalted, O God, above the heavens;
Thy glory above all the earth.

The dominant feature of 57 is the change of mood; from the 'cry' for 'mercy' amid the reproaches, lions, fire, sword, spears and arrows of vv. 1-4, and the net and pit of v. 6, to the song of triumph and thanks in vv. 7-11. The change comes at the end of v. 6, and it cannot but be a relief to find an explanation ready to hand from the Selah at that point. The passage next following the Shimei incident in 2 Samuel is in Absalom's court:

> And Absalom, and all the people the men of Israel, came to Jerusalem, and Ahi[ezer] with him. ... And the counsel of Ahi[ezer] which he counselled in those days, was as if a man enquired at the word of God; so was all the counsel of Ahi[ezer], both with David and with Absalom. Moreover Ahi[ezer] said unto Absalom, Let me now choose out twelve thousand men, and I will arise and pursue after David this night... And the saying pleased Absalom well, and all the elders of Israel (2 Sam. 16.15, 23; 17.1, 4).

The scene in Absalom's council, in which Hushai outwits Ahitophel, is clearly legendary (v. i.), and we have no alternative but to suppose something a little more probable. Since Ahiezer hanged himself, it is virtually certain that he suffered some humiliation worse than being outvoted; and the suggestion of the text is that he proposed an immediate attack on David's position, perhaps with a smaller force than twelve regiments ('thousands'). 2 Sam. 16.23 says that his influence was irresistible, so it seems likely that it will have been heeded, and the attack made. As David survived, it must have failed, and this will then have led to his disgrace, and suicide. Perhaps the Passion Narrative unit ended, 'But David and his men were bitter of soul; and it came to pass that he fell upon the men of Israel, and they fled' (cf. 17.8ff.), or something similar.

Such a course of events would cohere well with the change of tone in Ps. 57. 'They'—Absalom and his followers—have prepared a net for the king's steps (and the singer's), with their encampment by the Kidron crossing, and their archers and slingers on the hillside. 'He'—Shimei of v. 3, with his panting pursuit and his reproaches—has bowed down the king's soul: few experiences could be more demoralizing. They have digged a pit before him, and are fallen into the midst of it themselves: they have thought to compass the royalist force's destruction, but have themselves sustained heavy losses. The 'pit' could imply an ambush, a detachment being sent ahead to block the road eastwards; and this will then have been spotted and wiped out. The psalmist is speaking poetry, and I am turning it into prosaic military history. The detail is beyond us but the general impression fits satisfactorily with the probable state of affairs underlying 2 Samuel 16f.

RV supposes an intransitive meaning for *kāpap*, which is trans. elsewhere; others conjecture *kāp^{e}pû* following G, itself a *lectio facilior*. But a bigger problem is 'they are fallen': what is supposed to have happened? Gunkel and Kraus suppose a prophetic perfect, and Kraus then accounts for the triumphal tone of vv. 7-11 as arising from confidence that God will act in the morning. His psalmist is certainly a mercurial fellow; but cf. Kirkpatrick, '... convinced that God will manifest...' Others, as Rogerson and McKay, say 'the psalmist has escaped', without explaining how this has happened in mid-psalm; or, as Anderson, move over to 'The Thanksgiving' without comment. Duhm and Gunkel supposed that two psalms had been put together, and Jacquet follows this solution, with some further adjustment of the text. Mowinckel (Ps.st. I, 149, 153) supposed an oracle or cleansing ritual; but the relief and joy of vv. 7-11 do sound so *genuine*.

Cook,[6] Würthwein,[7] and Langlamet[8] concur in taking both the Hushai-Ahitophel debate and the concubines story as secondary matter, though for slightly different reasons; the latter two are properly criticized by Gunn,[9] who, however, himself believes the tales to be late and novelistic. For the concubines and the Succession Narrator's sexual interest, see above p. 82; the present passage suits his love of poetic justice ('The sword of the children of Ammon... the sword shall never depart...'). The Hushai-Ahitophel debate is his standard 'good story': it is remotely improbable that Absalom would trust a suspected traitor against the oracle voice of Ahiezer. The latter counselled attack in 17.1, and it is his counsel of attack which is reported to David in 17.21. He kills himself because David fought off his first attack, and slipped away before his second. David's forces were exhausted after the day's fighting (Pss. 53–57), and needed the night's rest. The Succession Narrator has fallen back into his normal 'the king' for David in 17.3, although Absalom is king now to Ahitophel. The passage is full of the Succession Narrator's beloved similes: 'as a bride comes home to her husband' (17.3G, RSV, NEB); 'as a bear robbed of her whelps in the field' (17.8); 'as the heart of a lion' (17.10); 'as the sand that is by the sea for multitude' (17.11); 'as the dew falleth on the ground' (17.12). We have his theological comment, 'For the LORD had ordained to defeat the good counsel of Ahitophel...' (17.14), as at 11.27; 12.24. It is he who has dramatized the role of Hushai with the whole fictitious debate. Hushai's historical part was to keep a low profile and say nothing, and by Jonathan and Ahimaaz to 'send unto me every thing that ye shall hear' (15.36).

57.7f. The thought—and in later years the reciting of the story—of the thwarted ambush evokes a paean of thankfulness, the more heartfelt because of the demoralization of the retreat earlier in the day. The singer's heart is confirmed, established (*nāḵôn*) in its faith, so often and so trembling expressed (52.1b, 6, 8, etc.). RV's 'fixed' fails to represent the reassurance that has come through the evening's military success. He will sing and chant to music (*'āšîrâ waᵃzammērâ*): Dahood aptly cites from an unpublished Ugaritic tablet RS 24.353:3-4, *dyšr wyḏmr bknr wṯlb*, 'who sings and chants with lyre and lute'. The *šîr* of our series is a song of triumph (65, 66, 67, 68), and the *mizmôr* (*zmr*) is a psalm sung to strummed music (62, 63, 64, 65, 66, 67, 68), expressive of hope and gladness. None of the psalms we have yet encountered aspires to the accompaniment of a stringed orchestra; 54, 55 and 61 permit limited (*nᵉgînōṯ*) or lone (*nᵉgînaṯ* stringed playing. Psalms 55–60 are Michtams, and 57–59 are 'Destroy Not' psalms, with ritual prostrations. It is only the thought of the minor victory which God has vouchsafed, which enables the psalmist to leave his minor key, and to bring in the strings. For *zmr* as singing accompanied by stringed music cf. Pss. 33.2; 71.22; 98.5; 147.7; 149.3; Kraus I, XIX. The singer calls on his soul, his 'glory', to awake; and even on their bleak retreat his priestly comrades have carried their harps and lyres, as the Oklahoma farmers took their guitars in 'The Grapes of Wrath'. His fears are gone (or nearly); he means to sing through the night and awaken the dawn.

57.9-11. The camp-fires of the enemy 'lions' (v. 4) are to be seen all round the copse where the royal column is laid up for the night, evidence of the presence of the feared Ishmaelite archers who have wrought so many casualties. But the psalmist will give his thanks to God 'among the peoples'/'among the nations'; even though surrounded by them he will sing his praises. For the *ḥesed̲* and *ᵉmet̲* of God, those two mighty extensions of the divine presence which were to be sent forth in v. 3, have now displayed their potency in the eyes of all. The refrain is taken up from v. 5: God is prayed to exalt himself *above* the heavens of v. 10, and above *all* the earth—that the deliverance of this evening may be repeated on the grand scale with the enemy's final defeat. The speaker was to see his prayer as granted in the battle of Zalmon (68.33-35).

The singing of praise 'among the nations' presents a puzzle to individual interpretations of the psalm. Gunkel has it sited among Diaspora Jews. Rogerson and McKay say the psalmist 'wishes the whole world could hear the praises' (cf. Weiser); which is not quite what the text says. National interpretations have the edge here. Anderson comments correctly that the refrain holds the psalm together, and makes composite theories implausible; but the text can always be amended to meet this difficulty (Gunkel).

Elation may endure for a night, but reality cometh in the morning.

58 For the Chief Musician. *'al-tašḥēt̲*. For (*lᵉ*) David: Michtam.

1 Do ye indeed speak righteousness, O ye gods?
Do ye judge uprightly the sons of men?

2 Nay (*'ap̄*), in heart ye work wickedness in the earth (diff.);
Ye weigh out the violence of your hands.

3 The wicked are estranged from the womb:
They go astray as soon as they be born, speaking lies.

4 Their poison is like the poison of a serpent:
They are like the deaf adder that stoppeth her ear;
5 Which hearkeneth not to the voice of enchanters,
Charming never so wisely.

The tone of 58 is different from its immediate neighbours (though it has been much misunderstood); but it takes its place in the Prayers sequence none the less. Its opening reproach to the *'ēlîm* for their failure to speak righteousness recalls the opening reproach to the *gibbôr* of 52 for his failure to speak righteousness (v. 3). The wicked here speak lies like snake-poison (vv. 3f.); in 52.2ff. deceit and wickedness like a whetted razor. The enemy of 57.4 were lions whose teeth were spears and arrows: the prayer of 58.6 is that God will break out the great teeth of the young lions. We have seen the menace represented by the enemy archers with their arrows earlier too, in 55.18 and 56.2; in 58.7 God is asked to frustrate the flight of 'his arrows'. 57.4 found the speaker surrounded by an enemy lighting fires: 58.9 (if emenders can be restrained) looks to God to blow the fires out before the food in the pots is cooked. The coming victory will enable the righteous to wash his feet in the blood of the wicked (58.10), a happy issue which comes to pass in 68.23. Even the estrangement of the wicked from the womb (58.3) has its parallel in David's 'Behold, I was shapen in iniquity; And in sin did my mother conceive me' (51.5).

For all the boost to morale that came from the successful skirmish of 57.6, the loyalists' situation remains perilous, and 58, like 57, is chanted to repeated prostrations (*'al tašḥēṯ*, see above, p. 117). They are nearly surrounded by an army much larger than their own; their food is limited to what they have carried and what they have looted in Bahurim; they are impeded by a large number of dependants, unable to fight and slowing their march; they are torn between hope that the rebellion will fizzle out (vv. 7f.), as the 1745 rising fizzled out at Derby, and reports of its popularity (2 Sam. 15.13) which would force them to withdraw to friendlier terrain. Their need of divine help remains urgent.

58.1f. It was an Israelite conviction, as late as Job and Daniel 10–12, and as early as the semi-polytheist times of Psalm 82, that events on earth were the mirror of events in heaven (cf. 1 Kgs 22): so the initial success of a rebellion against God's anointed king by traitors, with a professional foreign army, was a certain sign of similar treachery in the divine world. The psalmist begins therefore by upbraiding the *'ēlîm*, the gods of the nations whose armies so menace the royal encampment (57.9). Their task was to tell God the truth, and under his instruction to administer the provinces of his world for the ultimate benefit of his people Israel. But are they in fact telling him the truth? Are they administering their fiefs 'uprightly', that is with respect to Israel's primacy? Not in the least (*'ap̄*, Ps. 44.9). The lies told by Absalom to David, and the faithlessness of the Ishmaelite tribes, are the countersign of lies and faithlessness of the latter's presiding deities. To God's face they are all smoothness (cf. 55.21), but in their heart (*bᵉlēḇ*) they are working injustice on earth, and dispensing not peace but the violence of their hands. The symbol of 'weighing out' (*pillēs*) justice is also to be found in Job 31.6, and in the Prayers at 62.9; and on the roof of the Old Bailey.

Opinion remains divided as to whether the *'ēlîm* are 'gods' or 'mighty ones': Olshausen's conjecture that *'ēlîm* should be read for *'ēlem* ('silent') has carried the day. Delitzsch, Kirkpatrick, Dahood, Rogerson and McKay, Jacquet and NEB (text) prefer the human view: Kirkpatrick claims that the word is not used elsewhere in the plural of gods (cp. 82.1b, 6 *'ᵉlōhîm*), and Jacquet is bold to say that Israel never believed in their reality. Gunkel, Mowinckel,[10] Eaton, Kraus, Weiser and Anderson opt for 'gods'. This gives more force to 'in the earth' in v. 2, which belongs naturally as well as traditionally with the first colon; and much more force to the contrast with v. 11, 'Verily there is a God that judgeth in the earth'. There seems to be adequate parallel for the divine use in Exod. 15.11; Ps. 29.1; 89.7; 44.20; 81.9; and 82, as well; as 29 and 89, testifies to Israel's belief in such beings.

58.3-5. The opening verses reproached the gods for their injustice: the following verses describe in the third person the work of their minions, 'the wicked'. These are tactfully not specified. The thought is centrally of the mercenaries who are their worshippers; but the lies (*kāzāḇ*) which are their sole specified crime cannot but recall the deceit of Absalom also (52.1-4). The account of his career presented in the Succession Narrative certainly gives the impression of one 'estranged from the womb', 'gone astray as soon as he was born'; he is freely credited with murder (2 Sam. 13.28f.), revolution (15.7-12), rape (16.22) and arson (14.30). In a bitter moment the same might be held to be true of all who 'spoke lies', revoking their loyalty to the king; and nothing better was to be looked for from the non-Israelite tribesmen of the South whose oaths to keep the peace were spent breath. All of them *zōrû*, turned to hostility from the start, never recognized the Covenant between David and Yahweh.

Their deceit is potentially lethal, like snake-poison; and the image of the snake leads on to a second thought. One might watch a snake-charmer at work (Jer. 8.17; Eccl. 10.11) with his whisperings (*laḥēš*) and his spells (*ḥāḇar*); but sometimes, as these texts witness, the snake would not hearken, and the charmer was bitten. So were the traitors and their hirelings: God might declare his law to them all their days, but they have stopped (*'ṭm*, hiph.) their ears, and their fangs are poised now to kill his Anointed.

58.6 Break their teeth, O God, in their mouth:
Break out the great teeth of the young lions, O LORD.
7 Let them melt away as water that runs from them (*lāmô*):
When he aimeth his arrows, let them be as though they were cut off.
8 *Let them be* as a miscarriage (*šabb^{e}lûl*) which melteth and passeth away:
The untimely birth of a woman that hath not seen the sun.
9 Before your pots can feel the thorns,
Like a life, like a fire, he shall whirl them away (*k^{e}mô-ḥaî k^{e}mô-ḥārôn yiś'ārennû*).
10 The righteous shall rejoice when he seeth the vengeance:
He shall wash his feet in the blood of the wicked.
11 So that men shall say, Verily, there is a reward for the righteous:
Verily, there is a God that judgeth in the earth.

These verses are not personal maledictions but the prayers of a cornered loyalist, trusting that God will win him victory; they draw their meaning from the context which I have traced out, and are in no need of emendation. The enemy warriors are viewed as fierce and destructive lions, the standard image for 'him that is valiant, whose heart is as the heart of a lion' (2 Sam. 17.10), and which has already been used in the prayers at 57.4. The *k^{e}p̄îrîm* are usually thought of as young lions (Judg. 14.5), but may be used of a different kind of lion from the *l*ᵉ*ḇā'îm*. As the lion's destructive power lies in his teeth, so does the warrior's in his spear, sword and arrows: the singer prays for these to be neutralized—he does not mind whether the enemy is disarmed and captured or killed. The *maltᵉʿôṯ* are the incisors, for gnawing (*tlʿ*), and stand for his offensive weaponry. But the last thing the singer wishes is a bloodbath. He wants the rebel army to melt away (*mā'as*, niph.) like water which 'flows for them'. *hlk* is used of water flowing in Josh. 4.18; Eccl. 1.7, without any suggestion of its drying up (Gunkel, Anderson and most commentators)—exactly the reverse in Josh. 4.18: he is praying that the army may disappear in the same way that a soldier pours away water from his bowl. The same metaphor is used of the Philistine multitude which melted (*namûg*) in 1 Sam. 14.16, or of the inhabitants of the land in Josh. 2.9; we may compare, in not quite the same sense but nearly, 'And even he that is valiant, whose heart is as the heart of a lion, shall utterly melt' (2 Sam. 17.10, the present context, leading to panic and flight). What is in question is not personal malediction, but the desire for panic in the enemy ranks and the moment of victory. It is this moment that in time the women were to proclaim in the triumphant words, 'Kings of armies flee, they flee!' (68.12).

58.7b is not easy, but is best left unemended. *drk*, usually to march, is used occasionally with *qešeṯ* ('tread the bow'?), but in 64.3 as here is followed by *ḥēṣ*, an arrow, and clearly means 'aim' in both cases. We have seen what a threat the mercenary archers have been through the retreat so far (55.18; 56.2; 57.4), and it is they who have the power to decimate the royal forces as no stones or dust or bitter words have prospect of doing. The singer prays that the arrows (pl. Q, Targ. Syr.) may be blunted, as if their tips had been cut off (*mûl*, hithpo.)

58.8. The meaning of *šabbᵉlûl* is disputed. G.R. Driver[11] argued plausibly that in the only other instance in Hebrew or Aramaic, a discussion in the latter in jNidd. 59.3, it meant an 'effluxion', that is a miscarriage very early in pregnancy (ἔκρυσις). The embryo did not develop but melted (*temes*, root *mss*, another form of *m's* in v. 7) and went away (*hlk*, as in v. 7, but qal for hithpa.). In favour of this is the lack of syntactic link with v. 8b, 'the abortion of a woman which has not seen the sun'. *nēpel* is a more developed embryo (ἐκτρωμός), capable of 'falling' away, but the two words are used synonymously by the male singer. The imagery remains revolting, but it is a mistake to see it as conveying personal hatred. As in v. 7a, the thought is of the enemy forces melting away in flight and disappearing. We speak ourselves of a rebellion 'miscarrying' or being 'abortive'.

The alternative (Jastrow, ad voc.) is to take *šabbᵉlûl* as a slug, whose slimy trail made the ancients think, perhaps, that it was melting: the derivation for both views is from the shaphel of *bll*, confuse. The meaning of the image would not then be very different for the psalmist—he still wants the enemy to melt away.

58.9. Camp-fires were as normal a part of an ancient military campaign as they were of a 1970s strike: the soldiers slept between them for warmth (*šᵉpattāyîm*, 68.13), and they ringed the royal bivouac (57.4, q.v.), but their main purpose was the heating of the morning and evening meals. Absalom's troops will have stripped the numerous burnet bushes[12] of their dead-wood to make fires of thorn (*'āṭāḏ*). Their asses will be carrying water and pots, which are slung on a tripod like the jerry-can of more modern campaigns. These last are to 'perceive' (*yāḇînû*) the (heat of the) thorns, as Job said, 'Cannot my palate perceive disaster?' (6.30). But before your comfortable plans come to fruition, says the singer, God will whirl them away (*ś'r*). He will blow with a great gust of his storm-wind, and scatter wood and pot. This will be *kᵉmô-ḥaî*, like a live man, *kᵉmō ḥārôn*, like a fire, two instances of precious but unstable life, which can be extinguished in a moment by the overmastering force of the divine wind: 'thou takest away their breath, they die'. This is the second time that the psalmist has drawn on the imagery of 'the stormy wind and tempest' (55.8): we do well to remember that strong winds are not uncommon in October in Palestine, and to think that the retreat may have taken place in a gale.

The verse is difficult: most critics have recourse to emendation; Kraus despairs. It must be conceded that (1) *bîn* is not used elsewhere of other than sentient beings (Job 6.30 is the closest parallel I could find); (2) if *kᵉmô ḥaî* means 'like a live man' (which it most naturally does), the sense is very compressed, and rather obscure; (3) although *ḥārôn* is derived from the root *ḥārāh*, to burn, elsewhere it always means divine anger. But the general sense fits well into the context of the Prayers; and if we adopt the principle that liturgical texts like the Psalms will not have been corrupted easily these weaknesses may seem more supportable than the alternatives on offer.

58.10f. Weiser deplores the 'undisguised gloating and the cruel vindictiveness of an intolerant religious fanaticism'; but I think we may take a more understanding line. My friends and I danced in School Yard on V-E night: we rejoiced when we saw the vengeance—that is, the evils of Nazism receiving their deserts. It was not our custom actually to wash our feet in the blood of the wicked; but we used such an adjective of Goering and Ribbentrop, tried them as 'war-criminals', and were pleased when they were executed. The psalmist belonged to a more religious generation than ours, and the treachery and murderous intention of the rebels seemed to him equally a gross offence against God; indeed, it is difficult to see how the failure of the rising could have ended in anything else but the death of Absalom, Ahiezer and other leaders. It is in fact a remarkable testimony to David's mercifulness, or policy, that he spared the life of Amasa, the rebel general. The Israelites used to sacrifice some of the leading prisoners to Yahweh on such occasions (68.18) to restore the purity of the land (*ibid.*), and to dip their feet in the blood of the dead (68.23). We find the ceremony distasteful, but it was colourful, and the symbolism powerful; countries with a history of continual revolutions, like some in South America, might usefully adopt it 'pour encourager les autres'.

Psalm 58 is a Michtam, an inscribed psalm. It has no music, but a chanted response, here indicated by 'So that men shall say. . . ' The opening verse doubted whether the *'ēlîm* 'spoke *ṣeḏeq'*, or judged (*tišp*^{e}*ṭû*) the sons of men uprightly. No, came the answer, they did not; but now a happier issue is in view. With the coming victory it will be said, 'Verily there is fruit for the *ṣaddîq*; Verily there are *'elōhîm* judging (*šōp*^{e}*ṭîm*) in the earth'. The 'righteous' raise their voice in chorus to encourage heaven to its work. The *'elōhîm* have their participle in the plural: despite the perfidy of the *'ēlîm*, God and his faithful minions above will see justice done, we hope.

The psalm has presented a spiritual as well as a mental puzzle. Many commentators write of the sevenfold curse (not very suitably, for there are two prayers against the 'lions', followed by five curses) of spells and maledictions; these are always seen personally, and must be treated either apologetically (Anderson) or with square brackets (the 1928 Prayer Book). The setting from which the psalm has come is usually obscure. Delitzsch is warm, attributing it to David in Absalom's rebellion, but in the events of 2 Sam. 15.1-6. Kirkpatrick thought it belonged to later in Israelite history. Mowinckel[13] Eaton and Anderson take it as a National Lament; Weiser,

Dahood and Jacquet as an Individual Lament—Dahood thinks the 'lions' are slanderers, Jacquet that they are unjust magistrates. Gunkel for once is unspecific, and Kraus says that the situation is impossible to ascertain.

K. Seybold[14] describes a series of dissonances in the psalm: the opposition are sometimes divine, sometimes the wicked, and in the end the latter are punished but not the former; the style varies between cursing and didacticism; and the structure veers between an appeal to God and an appeal to the reader. The original poem was then a wisdom poem (vv. 1f., 4, 7ff., 11) from exilic times, asking whether the godly have their reward; and this was then corrected by the redactional addition of vv. 3, 5f., 10, with the stress moved from the gods to the wicked, in a dualistic expectation of Yahweh's judgment. Seybold's dissonances seem exaggerated. It is quite common in the Old Testament for Israel's enemies to be seen as agents of rebellious divine powers, e.g. in Psalm 46, and there also the nations see their weaponry go up in smoke, while the raging waters go unpunished. Nor is the tone of v. 6 very different from that of vv. 7ff.

59 For the Chief Musician; *'al-tašḥēṯ*. For (*l*ᵉ) David: Michtam: when Saul sent, and they watched the house to kill him.
1 Deliver me from mine enemies, O my God:
Set me on high from them that rise up against me.
2 Deliver me from the workers of iniquity,
And save me from the murderers (*'anšê ḏāmîm*).
3 For lo, they lie in wait for my soul;
The mighty encamp (*yāgûrû*) against me:
Not for my transgression, nor for my sin, O LORD.
4 They run and prepare themselves without *my* fault:
Awake thou to meet me, and behold.
5 Even thou, *Yahweh-'ᵉlōhîm Ṣᵉḇā'ôṯ*, God of Israel,
Arise to visit all the nations:
Be not merciful to any wicked transgressors.
(Selah

A number of features link 59 with its predecessors. The swords in the enemies' lips (59.7) recall the whetted knife of 52.2, the drawn swords of 55.21, the spears, arrows and sharp sword of 57.4 and the sword and arrows of 64.3. The nations who 'rise up against me' (59.1) remind us of the strangers who 'are risen up against me' in 54.3. There are 'men of blood' in 55.23 as in 59.2. They 'gather themselves' or encamp (*yāgûrû*) and wait/lie in wait 'for my soul' in 56.6 as in 59.3. There are 'workers of iniquity' in 53.4 as in 59.2. The prayer to bring the enemy down (to Sheol) in 59.11 recalls similar language in

55.23, 56.7. Eaton[15] has pointed to repeated terms implying a personal relation of the speaker to God ('my God', 'my strength', 'my high tower', 'my mercy'); he infers that it is the king speaking, though we may think rather of a highly placed priest—cf. also 'my people' (v. 11), and the nations of vv. 5, 8 whom God derides as in Psalm 2. It seems natural to interpret 59 in line with the sequence in which it stands, and to see the speaker as the royal priest-poet attending David in his time of weakness in the terebinth-wood by Bahurim (56 Heading).

The situation then will be that expounded in the previous psalms. The royalists, with their womenfolk and children, are surrounded in their wooded hilltop. They have needed the time to regroup; and perhaps they have hoped in vain that other loyalists would join forces with them. But their supplies of food are limited to what they have brought, and they cannot withstand a well-organized attack by the more numerous rebels. They are in acute peril, and 59, like 58 and 57, is accompanied by repeated prostrations (*'al-tašḥēṯ*, cf. p. 117). Its tone of weakness is reinforced by the absence of music, and by its being a Michtam, a psalm with an 'inscribed' refrain in vv. 6/14, 9/17. We may perhaps think of the priests as having written copies of these verses, and as joining in the chant at these points; while the people vow to 'watch for' God with prostrations following each chorus. The reference to Saul is an unlucky guess by a late commentator.

59.1f. The enemies are the rebels who have risen against David and his court (2 Sam. 18.31, 32); the speaker is in dire need of being 'delivered' from his present straits, and of being 'set up on high', that is, of removing to a fortified town on a hilltop, an acropolis capable of withstanding a more permanent siege (*śgb*, Deut. 2.36; Isa. 25.12). Psalm 59 is the first of a sequence of psalms in which God is pictured as 'my high-tower', 'my refuge', etc.; the image arises from the speaker's hope of deliverance depending upon such a literal stronghold. The thought has in fact already turned to Mahanaim, which had been Ishbaal's capital (2 Sam. 2.8). No doubt it was strongly defensible by nature; there would be stores of food and water in the town; and David had troops in Transjordan occupying Ammon (2 Sam. 12), Edom (2 Sam. 8.14) and lands further north (2 Sam. 8.6). The need immediately is to be 'delivered' and 'saved' from the rebels, who are quite reasonably spoken of of *pō'alê 'āwen*, workers of iniquity, that is traitors, and 'men of blood', that is murderers, in that they intend David's death (2 Sam. 17.2). Their most effective troops are the *gôyim*, the mercenaries from the Negeb whose archers have wrought such havoc (55.18; 56.2: 54.3); and it is against them, and against the actual conspirators, the *bōgᵉḏê 'āwen*, that the prayer is directed (v. 5).

59.3ff. The enemy 'lie in wait for my soul'; that is, they are encamped in companies around the royalists' wood, and are ready to cut off any sally, and to take the king's life. The 'mighty', that is the élite troops, gather (*yāgûrû*), or perhaps have set up their tents (cf. p. 114) against him. They 'run and prepare themselves': the royal look-outs can see that preparations are being made with expedition for what could be a major assault tomorrow. The speaker pleads the king's innocence, and God's consequent duty to intervene. Speaking in the king's name he says that the rebellion was quite without justification—'Not for my transgression, nor for my sin... without guilt' on the royal side. The royalists are in the right, as at 58.10, 11, and God should bestir himself (*'ûrâ*) and see what is afoot. He is called upon by a string of names which emphasize the crisis: he is Yahweh, God of Israel, who must be expected to act in face of the invasion of his land by the 'nations'; he is *'ᵉlōhîm*, the traditional divine name which dominates the Prayers; he is *Ṣᵉḇā'ôṯ*, (Heavenly) Hosts, the military name so often associated with the Ark.

There is a Selah after 59.5, and the next incident in the Passion of David narrative is the bringing of Hushai's message to David's camp:

> Then said Hushai unto Zadok and to Abiathar the priests, Thus and thus did Ahi[ezer] counsel Absalom and the elders of Israel... Now therefore send quickly, and tell David, saying, Lodge not this night at the margins (mlt MSS *'aḇᵉrôṯ* = 15.28) of the wilderness, but in any wise pass over; lest the king be swallowed up, and all the people that are with him. Now Jonathan and Ahimaaz stayed by En-rogel... And it came to pass that... they went and told king David; and they said unto David, Arise ye, and pass quickly over the water: for thus hath Ahi[ezer] counselled against you (2 Sam. 17.15ab, 16, 17a, 21).

The passage fits well with the situation we are supposing for 59. Ahiezer and Absalom are the enemies, those that rise against David, the workers of iniquity, the men of blood, the wicked transgressors, etc. Ahiezer has recommended a mass attack with twelve thousands against David's brigade of as many hundreds; and if this is allowed to happen, the royal forces will certainly be 'swallowed up'. The preparations for the attack are visible as the 'mighty' gather, run, prepare themselves, and so on; and the confirmation that the attack is coming is now brought by the intrepid priests' sons, who have made their way through the enemy lines. David's only hope is to break out at once, during the night. He must not stay where he is, encamped on the edge of the untilled land that stretches down the steep valleys to the Jordan; but 'in any wise pass over', *'āḇôr ta'aḇôr*, which we may render (cf. p. 82) 'sally forth and attack'. The besiegers are split into small units ringing the hilltop, guarding every avenue of escape: the royalists may hope to break through in the dark with impunity. They can then go by forced marches the twenty miles to the Jordan: once they are in Gilead they may hope to find support, and to make their way in safety to the *miśgāḇ* of Mahanaim.

Cook[16] pointed to he contradiction between 2 Sam. 17.21, where it is only said 'thus hath Ahitophel counselled against you', and where (consistently with this) there is urgent need to move, and 17.5-14, where Hushai's counsel is supposed to have overruled Ahitophel's, and there is no urgency. Veijola and Langlamet agree (see p. 122). I am supposing that both the Ahitophel-Hushai contest and the messengers-in-the-well story are part of the Succession Narrator's expansion; both exemplify his love of 'good stories'.[17] Both also lack the name 'David', which comes regularly in the Passion of David narrative (17.16, 21, 21): but the Succession Narrator has retained the true tradition that the messengers' peril was at Bahurim.

59.6 They return at evening, they snarl (*yeh*^{e}*mû*) like a
dog,
And go round about the city.
7 Behold, they belch out with their mouth;
Swords are in their lips:
For who, *say they*, doth hear?
8 But thou, O LORD, shalt laugh at them;
Thou shalt have all the nations in derision.
9 O my strength (MT *'uzzô*), I will wait upon thee:
For God is my high tower.

The royalists have brought with them three or four days' supply of food: the supply problem for the rebel army is much more acute—not only are there far more of them to feed, but they have come from much further, and any initial supplies must by now be exhausted. It is for this reason that they are to be seen during the day time circulating (*y^eśôḇ^eḇû*, cf. p. 102) round the city, buying up or commandeering supplies (cf. v. 15) from the farms around Jerusalem. They know that it would be hazardous for the royalists to try to force an exit in broad daylight, so they can send out foraging parties by day, and they then return to their units (*yāšûḇû*) with their takings in the evening. As they do so, they utter cat-calls, wolf-whistles and other aggressive cries, which our psalmist compares suitably to the snarls (murmurings, *hāmâ*) of a dog. They also shout pointed insults and cries of ridicule, which he describes as 'belchings', and as 'swords', following the imagery which he uses so often in the Prayers. This verbal violence is intended to weaken the defenders' soul, and his robust response is meant to counter any such sapping of morale.

They think that God is not listening (cf. 53.1); but, says our poet, He will be laughing at them in the end, and their ridicule will then seem less funny—especially the mercenaries ('nations'), who can expect less mercy than any misguided Israelites who have joined the rebellion. Their 'mighty men' (*'azzîm*, v. 3) are nothing beside God, 'my might' (*'uzzî*). The king and his followers mean to 'watch' (*'ešmōrâ*) upon Him: that is, tonight will be a night without sleep, as by God's help they break their way out of their encampment. He is 'my *miśgāḇ*': they will make their way to a fenced acropolis where they can withstand siege, whose defenders are the angels, and whose builder and maker is God.

Most Hebrew MSS read *'uzzô*, which is difficult. Some read *'uzzî*, as do G and the Targum, in agreement with v. 17. This is the preference of almost all critics, though Dahood postulates an old nominative form *'uzzu*; cf. also *ḥasdô* K in the next verse. We could conceivably think that in these verses the psalmist is speaking in his own name, and referring to God's covenant with David: God would then be 'his strength', and 'the God of his covenanted grace', sc. David's. David makes an unannounced entry elsewhere in the Prayers, e.g. at 53.5; 55.22; 68.23, 28.

59.10 My God with his mercy shall prevent me:
God shall make me look upon (*yar^e'ēnî*) them that lie in wait for me.
11 Slay them not, lest my people forget:
Make them to wander to and fro, and bring them down, O Lord our shield.

12 *For* the sin of their mouth, *and* the words of their lips,
Let them even be taken in their pride,
And for the perjury (*'ālâ*) and lying which they speak.
13 Consume them in wrath, consume them, that they be no more:
And let them know that God ruleth in Jacob,
Unto the ends of the land (*hā'āreṣ*). (Selah

The psalmist prays for an outcome which closely follows the future of the campaign. First he desires God to keep his promise to David (*ḥasdô*) and to lead (*yeqaddemēnî*, 'prevent') the royalist sally against the surrounding rebels. If God leads the assault, then there will be victory, and a break-out: cf. 60.9, 'Who hath led me unto Edom? Is it not thou, O God?'. The success of such a sally will also depend in practice upon accurate intelligence as to the posting of the besiegers: if God makes the royalists to look upon those who lie in wait for him (/those who have betrayed him, p. 95), then the element of surprise will be decisive, and the point of attack critical. He is not looking for an easy and complete victory now, such as would lull the people into complacency. Rather he would pray for a victory in battle ('O Lord our shield'), in which the enemy would flee (68.12), and wander in fear from village to village looking for asylum (*hanî'ēmô*). Only after this prolongued period of misery will they be brought down (to Sheol, cf. 55.23; 56.7).

59.12f. In the end they will be captured (*yillāḵedû*), in view of all the treasonable and arrogant things they have said (cf. vv. 6f., 'snarl', 'belched', 'swords'), which may be fairly described as pride, perjury and lying. Justice must be seen to be done, and in the victory parade they are to be 'consumed' in God's wrath; cf. 68.21, 'God shall smite through the head of his enemies'. In this way 'my people' (v. 11) will be duly impressed, and will not 'forget'; and the rebels themselves will know that God rules in Jacob, and is faithful to his royal covenant. 'To the ends of the *'āreṣ*' seems to be in apposition to 'in Jacob', and (against most critics) would most naturally mean the land of Israel (cf. 61.2). The speaker is looking to go to Mahanaim, near the Aramaean frontier, and he hopes to see God's rule vindicated there soon. The ceremonial slaughter of the prisoners, as in 58.10f., will be the seal of the divine imperium. The psalmist is no sentimentalist, and would have agreed with Clausewitz: 'In a matter so dangerous as war, the worst errors spring from a spirit of benevolence'.

The mention of the ends of the land leads the editor to insert here a second Selah; for the passage next following in the Passion of David records briefly the royalists' escape:

> Then David arose, and all the people that were with him, and they passed over Jordan: by the morning light there lacked not one of them that was not gone over Jordan. And when Ahi[ezer] saw that his plan was not put into action (*lō' ne'eś*^{e}*ṯâ 'aṣātô*), he saddled his ass, and arose, and got him home, unto his city, and set his house in order, and hanged himself; and he died, and was buried in the sepulchre of his father (2 Sam. 17.22ff.)

The Passion of David was clear that the royalists' preliminary camp had been at Bahurim, 'there' (2 Sam. 16.14), on the margins of the wilderness (15.28); the Succession Narrator is less clear about this, and has put David in the 'plains (*'ar*^{e}*ḇôṯ* for *'aḇ*^{e}*rôṯ*) of the wilderness' (17.16), near the Jordan. In fact David arose and 'passed over' in the military sense (p. 82). His Philistine guards moved down the slope eastwards as soon as it was dark, and overwhelmed the rebel post. The vanguard must then have defended the salient to north and south, while the womenfolk and the main body of the column poured through the gap and down the valley to Jericho. Counter-attack would have been impracticable in the dark, and the entire force escaped virtually intact. They 'watched to God' (Ps. 59.9) to good effect: in the twelve hours of the night they were able to cover the twenty miles to the Jordan. After the long summer the waters were low, and they could ford the river without difficulty. By sunrise they were on their way north to the Jabbok.

Their escape spelt disaster to the clear eyes of Ahiezer. He had tried to frustrate the royalists' withdrawal to the Distant Terebinths, and had failed (Ps. 57.6); he had planned a full-scale attack, and they were gone before it could be launched; there had again been casualties, and another skirmish had been lost. Confidence in his wisdom had ebbed, and there was no doubt talk of promoting Amasa already in his place. Even if he could maintain his position as counsellor, the chances of defeating the king were now much smaller, as we may see from the difference of the psalmist's tone in 60 and the psalms following, as against the depressed and often desperate 50's. He saw no hope, and took his own life.

In this way, dispensing with the Hushai-Ahitophel contest of counsel, we have a far more plausible sequence of events. Ahiezer takes his life not from pique at being outvoted, but because his plans have twice ended in failure. Hushai has a much lower and more believable profile as a royalist mole, sending warning of the coming attack. The tensions over the site of David's first encampment are resolved as being the Succession Narrator's misunderstanding of the Passion of David account. The motive for the night-time removal is now clear, and pressing, and the choice of Mahanaim as a defensible stronghold in royalist territory becomes explicable. The wording, 'when A. saw that his counsel was not done', can be seen to have meant originally, '. . . that his plan was frustrated', but to have been taken by the Succession Narrator to mean '. . . that not his plan (but Hushai's) was followed'. At every point the Prayers illuminate the Passion narrative.

The Hebrew of 59.10 is difficult: MT has *ᵉlōhê*, 'The God of his mercy shall prevent me'. Two MSS and G point *ᵉlōhaî*, and RV follows this; cf. Eaton, 'As for my God, his Fidelity will come to meet me'. Perhaps we should retain the harder MT and render, 'The God of [David's] covenanted love. . . ' (see on *'uzzô*, 59.9). RV renders *yarᵉ'ēnî* 'God shall let me see *my desire* upon. . . '; this is of doubtful justifiability (cf. p. 95), and the military context makes good sense of a plain translation as at 54.7—what matters is seeing where they are. Against most commentators, there is no contradiction between v. 11, 'Slay them not' and v. 13, 'Consume them'. They are not to be slain (*hrg*) in battle, but to wander (*nu'*) in flight, to be captured (*lkd*), and finally to be executed (*klh*, cf. 1 Sam. 15.18; 2 Sam. 21.5). In v. 12 RV gives 'for cursing and lying': but *'ālâ* properly means an oath, and it is linked with *kaḥaš* at Hos. 4.2 to mean a false oath. So here the psalmist accuses them of perjury and deceit: that is, they have sworn loyalty to the king, and gone back on it. 'Cursing' has been a popular alternative, doubtfully backed by Ps. 10.7, Job. 31.30, because it fits both the personal oppressor theory and the national lament theory, with foreign prophets at work cursing Israel.

59.14 And at evening let them return, let them snarl (*yehᵉmû*) like a dog,
And go round about the city.
15 They shall wander up and down for meat,
If they be not satisfied, and pass the night (*wayyālînû*).
16 But I will sing of thy strength,
Yea, I will sing aloud of thy mercy in the morning:
For thou hast been my high tower,
And a refuge in the day of my distress.

17 Unto thee, O my strength, will I sing praises:
For God is my high tower, the God of my mercy.

The sally is now determined upon, and God has been asked to lead it (v. 10); and the psalmist returns ironically to the besiegers. Let them do as they have been observed to (v. 6), foraging for food from farm to farm round Jerusalem; 'wandering up and down' (*nu'*) already, cf. v. 11, if they cannot find enough; returning at evening with their yowlings; and sleeping the night in their tents. They have a disappointment awaiting them. In the morning not a man of David's forces will be left on the West Bank; the birds will be flown. The psalmist will be hymning God's strength and his covenanted love, which he looks to to make safe the evacuation. The wooded hilltop where they have rested up for twenty-four hours and more has been a stronghold for them under the divine protection: God has indeed been a fortress and a refuge in the day of acute peril. The time of 'Do-not-destroy' prostrations is now ending, and there will be Songs (*šir*) and joyful singing (*rnn*) and chanting to stringed music (*zmr*). For God's word (*ḥsd*) has been shown to be his bond (*'uz*). For the third time the psalmist links God's power to his covenanted love (covenanted to David in 2 Sam. 7; cf. 60.6). God is indeed the royalists' stronghold, and he will see them safe on the acropolis of Mahanaim as he has in the Distant Terebinths.

Briggs found the psalm to be 'exceedingly difficult', and this is illustrated by the variety of interpretations, and the extent of emendations. Delitzsch still accepted the David-and-Saul context of the heading, and Kirkpatrick and Jacquet are sympathetic to this, though they suppose a later adaptation. Most opinion has rejected this as unworthy of serious consideration: the alternatives have then been a personal lament (Duhm, Gunkel, Rogerson and McKay, Weiser, Jacquet), or a national lament (Mowinckel,[18] Eaton,[19] Dahood). Anderson hesitates. For Duhm the enemies are Sadducees; for Gunkel the unhappy speaker lives among the Diaspora ('nations') who hound him with slanders in a pogrom-atmosphere; for Kraus this is a mistake—the mention of the Nations arises from a vision of Yahweh's universal authority. The *gôyim* can of course become *gē'îm*, proud (Mowinckel earlier, *Ps.st.* I, 71).

But it is not only the double reference to the nations (vv. 5, 8) and 'my people' (v. 11), and the chain of personal relations to God,[20] which are against the individual lament view: there is so much military language—enemies, those who rise up, men of blood, mighty ones, running, swords, stronghold (vv. 9, 16, 17), meeting ('as with an army of relief', Kirkpatrick), preceding, slaying, wandering, being captured, and so on. However, the concreteness of this language remains a puzzle even for those who see the Israelite king as the speaker, defying the sorceries of national enemies. There is the usual unsatisfactoriness of ritual vigils (v. 9) from the evening (vv. 6, 14), in expectation of some supposed divine response 'in the morning' (v. 16); and much of the natural force of the language has to be blunted—'they return in the evening', the foraging and spending the night (v. 15), the running, the 'going round' the city', the false oaths. The sequential context which I am proposing from the Passion of David commends itself in offering a concrete interpretation for each of these details to fit a given situation.

Chapter 6

THE SIEGE OF MAHANAIM (60–64)

60 For the Chief Musician. At (*'al*) the Lily of Testimony. Michtam for (l^e) David, to teach: when he strove with Aram-naharaim and with Aram-zobah, and Joab returned, and smote of Edom in the Valley of Salt twelve thousand.

1 O God, thou hast cast us off, thou hast broken us down;
Thou hast been angry; O restore us again.

2 Thou hast made the land to tremble; thou hast rent it:
Heal the breaches thereof; for it shaketh.

3 Thou hast showed thy people hard things:
Thou hast made us to drink the wine of staggering.

4 Thou hast given a banner to them that fear thee.
To which (l^e) they may flee from before the bow.
(Selah

Psalm 60 is different from its predecessors: in tone, in vocabulary, in the wealth of names and concrete detail. The only links that it has with the other Prayers are superficially of a minor kind: the prayer for restoration (v. 1, 53.6), 'those that fear thee' (v. 4; 61.5; 66.16), 'thou hast showed us' trouble (v. 3; 71.20). Nevertheless, there is no satisfying exegesis of the psalm without the context which is given to it, first by its place in the sequence of the Prayers, and second by the position which it occupies in the parallel Passion of David narrative.

Psalm 59 showed the royalist forces poised to break out of their camp on the Distant Terebinths; and the Passion narrative tells us that this move was a success—the whole column escaped down the valley to the Jordan in the night, and by morning was on its way north to Ishbaal's old stronghold at Mahanaim (2 Sam. 17.22-24). This was to be their fortress through the coming months, and their safe arrival brought an enormous lift of morale. There were to be no more 'Do-not-destroy' prostrations (57–59). This is the last of the Michtams in the Prayers (56–60). There is still not enough confidence for music (61, 'on a (single) stringed instrument'; 62–68 are Mizmors; 65–68 are 'Songs'); but the psalm has been composed with a conclusion that reflects its opening ('O God, thou hast cast us off. . . save with thy right hand'/'O God: thou hast cast us off. . . vain is the salvation of man'). Our best solution of the nature of a *miktām* is, following Delitzsch, to note the common feature of 56–60 as constituted by these echoes, and to suppose that the last verses have been inscribed (*ktm*) for use as a communal response.

Historically, 60–64 were composed during the Siege of Mahanaim, far to the northeast of the Terebinth wood; 65–67 were written during the advance to the West Bank and to the Forest of Ephraim; and 68 was the victory hymn after the suppression of the Rebellion, back in Jerusalem. The royal forces were thus involved in a campaign that took them in an enormous circuit, and back to the city, a mile or two southwest of the Distant Terebinths. When in later years this campaign was 'remembered' in an annual procession (as I am supposing, cf. pp. 247f.), it was impracticable to process to Mahanaim and back; it would be best to hypothesize that the procession moved *west* from the Terebinth wood and across the valley to Mt Scopus—they could thus enter Jerusalem from the north, as Joab and Ittai must have done after the battle of Zalmon. Here then will have been the third 'station', at *šûšan-'ēdût*, following those at Mahalath on Olivet, and the Terebinths by Bahurim. Israelite royal courts were decorated with fleurs-de-lys carved on the ashlars (1 Kgs 7.19, 22, 26[1]). Psalm 45, which celebrates the enthronement and marriage of the (northern) king[2], was recited *'al-šôšannîm*, that is at the royal courtyard in the city gate at Dan, where A. Biran has excavated the base of the royal throne[3] alongside 'ivory palaces' from whose windows 'stringed instruments make thee glad' (45.8). In our present series, Psalm 69 will bring the procession back to the palace at Jerusalem, after the victory parade of 68, and that also is marked *'al-šôšannîm*. Psalm 60 and its successors were not chanted at a permanent royal court, but there will have been a single symbolic Lily (*šûšān*), as perhaps there was also at Mahanaim, where the king gave his judgments as the divine law or testimony. For *'ēdût* is used from early times (Pss. 78.5; 81.5) in parallel with 'law', 'statute', 'ordinance', etc.: the royal throne was the place from which the divine (*ᵉlōhîm*) king held the sceptre of equity, and pronounced judgments of righteousness (Pss. 45.6f.), which were testimonies to the grace of God (45.2). The 'Lily of Testimony' will thus have been the site of a temporary royal court whence David dispensed justice, first perhaps in Mahanaim, later at a symbolic station on Mt Scopus (see Map 1, p. 88).

The references to Edom in the psalm have seduced the editor into the speculation that the psalm was composed before the Edomite campaign of 2 Samuel 8: a mistaken speculation, but not as mistaken as those of many more recent commentators. He also adds obscurely that it was *lᵉlammēḏ*, to teach; perhaps an echo of 2 Sam. 1.18.

60.1f. With the end of the prostrations and the change of station comes a big change of mood. Hitherto the royalists have been in dire straits, and the concentration has been sheerly on surviving—'there were they in great fear' (53.5), 'the terrors of death are fallen upon me' (55.4), 'my soul is among lions' (57.4), 'save me from the men of blood' (59.2). Now they have escaped, and a more responsible spirit prevails: what has befallen God's people, that they should have collapsed into a civil war? God has cast them off in anger—the standard theodicy that was to see them through the catastrophes of 732-722 (Pss. 42–44; cf. *PSK*, pp. 23-37, 85-98) and 586. But the significant image which the psalmist uses here is that of an earthquake. *ra'aš* means an earthquake (Amos 1.1; Zech. 14.5): God has made the land quake, he has burst us open (*prṣ*) as a barrel bursts open (Prov. 3.10), or as David once burst the Philistine defence at *Baal-pᵉrāṣîm* 'like a bursting flood' (2 Sam. 5.20). He is prayed to heal the broken pieces (*sᵉḇāreîhā*) for it is tottering (*māṭâ*); he has broken it open (*pṣm*), as one opens a hole in a wall for a window (Targ. Jer. 22.14). There could be no better image for a civil war; as we say ourselves, 'Charles I split the country'. There is no reference to a national defeat, and the civil war situation is in fact obvious from the psalmist's intention to 'divide' Shechem, one of the central Israelite cities. The country is divided, and vv. 7f. will describe the line-up. Essentially the division runs north and south, with Absalom broadly supported by the West Bank tribes and David by his garrisons on the East Bank, and by the nobles there; the determining feature, as we shall see, was the loyalty of the main northern tribes, Zebulon and Naphtali, to the king. So safe arrival in the clear, high air of Mahanaim has enabled the psalmist to adopt a more responsible line.

He is no longer anxious for his own skin. He feels the parlous state of the divided nation, due no doubt to the divine wrath; and he draws hope both from the recent escape (v. 4) and from God's oracular promise to David (v. 6).

60.3f. God has made his people to see, that is to experience, hard times. 'Thy people' are of course the loyalists only; and the preceding days have seen them driven from their homes, suffering severe casualities at the Kidron crossing, shot down, stoned and abused by the hour, regrouping in fear of their lives, and making a forced march in headlong flight. Small wonder if the sequence of events recalls the custom of making a defeated king drink a large bowl of mixed wine, so potent that he reels and staggers across the royal court to the jeers of his Israelite captors (Ps. 75.8). God's people has been similarly reeling from pillar to post. However they may now look for better things, for He has provided a *nēs* for them to flee to. The *nēs* was a standard set up, often on a hill, as a rallying point for an army (Isa. 5.26; 13.2); sometimes as a means of assembling a defeated and scattered people (Isa. 11.12). It is this last emphasis which is taken here. God has set up his standard at Mahanaim for the loyalists ('them that fear thee') to flee (to): they have fled (*hiṯnôsēs*) from the Terebinth wood, and God has given them a rallying point up the Jabbok Valley, whither other 'God-fearers' may join them in time. Very likely David raised an actual standard on Mahanaim height as a symbol that he would retreat no more. Once more the stress is laid on the bowmen who have been such a trial to the royal column. We heard of archers (*rabbîm*) at 55.18 and 56.2, and of arrows at 57.4; now we are told that they fled 'from before the bow'. *qōšeṭ* is not found elsewhere in Hebrew with this meaning, but most commentators have agreed with Gunkel that RV text's 'truth' (cf. *qōšṭ*, Prov. 22.21 only) gives no sense. Anderson draws a good parallel with Isa. 31.8, 'flee from before the sword', and follows the widely held suggestion that *qōšeṭ* is an Aramaic (I should say, early Hebrew) form of *qešeṯ*, a bow (rarely *qešeṭ* in Targums, cf. Palmyrene).

The verse ends with a Selah, and it is here that the celebrating community of later years inserted the next piece from the Passion of David to make clear the historical context:

> Then David came to Mahanaim. And Absalom passed over Jordan, he and all the men of Israel with him. And Absalom set Amasa over the host instead of Joab. Now Amasa was the son of a man whose

name was Ithra the Israelite, that went in to Abigal the daughter of Nahash, sister to Zeruiah, Joab's mother. And Israel and Absalom pitched in the land of Gilead. And it came to pass, when David was come to Mahanaim, that Shobi the son of Nahash of Rabbah of the children of Ammon, and Machir the son of Ammiel of Lo-debar, and Barzillai the Gileadite of Rogelim, brought beds, and basins, and earthen vessels, and wheat, and barley, and meal, and parched *corn*, and beans, and lentils, and parched *pulse*, and honey, and butter, and sheep, and cheese of kine, for David, and for the people that were with him, to eat: for they said, The people is hungry, and weary, and thirsty, in the wilderness (2 Sam. 17.24-29).

No doubt they were right: without these supplies the royalists could hardly have survived, let alone withstood a siege of months. 1 Chron. 2.17 calls Amasa's father 'Jether the Ishmaelite', which has appealed to many critics as more plausible than the plethoric 'Ithra the Israelite': and we should then have a satisfying link with the Ishmaelites, who, as professional men of 'the bow', and as inhabitants of the wastelands of the Negeb south of Hebron, are the most likely 'strangers' and 'nations' to whom the Prayers refer. But the Passion Narrator will not have David humbled by foreigners, and has Amasa an Israelite; indeed he suppresses the foreign element in the rebellion completely. He makes plain also how narrow was the circle of the command on both sides: Amasa was first cousin to Joab, and another nephew of David therefore.[4] Shobi is the son of Nahash, king of Ammon in Saul's time, and probably David's puppet put in after the Ammonite war (as Zedekiah was made puppet king in the room of his brother Jehoiachin at Jerusalem in 597). Machir son of Ammiel had looked after Meribbaal (2 Sam. 9.4); his estates, and those of Barzillai were southeast of the Sea of Galilee, an area much traversed by David's armies during the campaigns of 2 Samuel 8 in Aram and Edom. The steady reference to the king as 'David' suggests that all these verses were in the Passion Narrative.[5]

Mowinckel[6] suggests that the 'oracle' of 60.6ff. was uttered 'over' (*'al*) lilies, or other flowers placed on the ark or the altar of shewbread, and that these were known as the lily/-ies of revelation (*'ēḏûṯ*). Israelites, like Buddhists, used flowers in worship (Lev. 14 hyssop; 23.40 palm, willow, citron). The story of Aaron's rod suggests that oracles were given by cutting rods in bud, and then a bursting into leaf or flower would give a positive answer, but a withering the opposite, after a night in the Temple. This is a great man at his most fanciful. We *never* hear of flowers, let alone lilies being used in worship, only of various green twigs. Oracles were given by Urim and Thummim, which fortunately were available round the year, as is not the case with almond twigs. It is a strain to translate *'ēḏûṯ* 'revelation' as through an oracle. Psalm 45 is *'al šôšannîm*, and Mowinckel has difficulty finding an oracle in it,[7] while other of his oracle psalms, like 12, lack the Heading.

Gunkel points to a play on words between *qāšâ* and *hišqîṯānû*; and there is another between *nēs* and *hiṯnôsēs*; cf. our psalmist at 52.6 *w^{e}yir^{e}'û*... *w^{e}yîrā'û*.

60.5 That thy beloved ones may be delivered,
Save with thy right hand, and answer us.
6 God hath spoken in his holiness; I will exult:
I will divide Shechem, and mete out the valley of Succoth.
7 Gilead is mine, and Manasseh is mine;
Ephraim also is the defence of mine head;
Judah is my commander (*m^{e}ḥōq^{e}qî*).
8 Moab is my washpot;
Unto Edom do I cast (*'ašlîḵ*) my shoe:
Philistia, shout thou because of me.

God has been angry and split the land; he has provided his loyal troops a rallying point; now the prayer is that he will deliver (*ḥlṣ*) and save them, that is in the coming siege. The psalmist tactfully describes the motley defenders as *y^{e}ḏîḏeîḵā*, thy beloved ones; we may catch the overtone of the name of David, *dôḏ*, God's beloved, and perhaps of Solomon, whom David named *Y^{e}ḏiḏyāh*, Beloved of Yahweh (2 Sam. 12.25). No doubt Bathsheba, as David's Queen, was in the palace when the rebels struck, and no doubt she and her son, already Heir Presumptive, were among the women and children of the party.

60.6. Most critics take 'God hath spoken in his holiness/shrine' as the introduction to a reported oracle, 'I will exult... because of me': for the difficulties of this line of exegesis, see below. But a clear and satisfying exposition is possible if we take the 'I' of vv. 6-8 as being David. The psalmist asks that God will answer us (v. 5) in face of the coming contest; and he then comforts his hearers with two reflections—first God's famous oracle to David in 2 Samuel 7, and secondly his visible faithfulness in granting the king success so far. God had said, according to our text, that he would give David rest from all his enemies; that violent men should afflict Israel no more; that his offspring should succeed him; and that He would never take his covenanted love from David's house as he had from Saul's. However much of this is expansion, the concept of *ḥeseḏ* must have been there from the beginning, because we have had repeated references to it in the Prayers (52.1, 8; 57.3, 10; 59.10, 16, 17), and we have heard of God's word likewise (56.4, 10). So, says the speaker in David's name, God has spoken, and we may depend on his promise—we may prefer 'in his holiness' as emphasizing this dependability. The thought inspires the speaker, so lately delivered from imminent catastrophe, to feelings of exultation—*'lz* is almost always elsewhere used of the faithful exulting in God, e.g. Pss. 5.11; 9.2; 68.3. He will win the coming battle, and will divide as spoil/ measure out the lands of the cities of Shechem and Succoth.

As the royalists have had to flee the West Bank; and as Shechem was to be the centre of Israel's disaffection with the house of David in Rehoboam's time; and as the culminating battle of the campaign was fought in the Forest of Ephraim (2 Sam. 18.6) on Mt Zalmon (Ps. 68.14) just outside Shechem; and as the shrine of Dan on the peaked mountain of Bashan has to be warned in the same psalm not to look with jealousy at Mt Zion which is God's choice; it is perhaps not too perilous to reconstruct what lay behind this hitherto obscure threat. David had made Jerusalem his capital, and was planning to build a national temple there; he had accepted the old Jebusite priesthood, Zadok and his family, to preside, along with his faithful comrade of freebooting days, Abiathar. Where did this leave the traditional Israelite priesthoods of Shechem and Dan? It left them nowhere, without influence and, what was probably still more painful, without income. So of course they 'looked askance' at upstart Zion, and were the chief of Absalom's supporters; even Abiathar did not relish second place to a Jebusite, and backed Adonijah. Priesthoods were as regularly a threat to ancient monarchies as colonels are to modern Presidents. It is easily believable that when word came to David that the hearts of the men of Israel were after Absalom, it was said, 'and in particular the priests of Shechem are supporting him'. The valley of Succoth appears to be an East Bank link of the Shechemite priesthood. Jacob came to Penuel in Gen. 32.22-32 and to Shechem in Gen. 33.18, the next place mentioned. Jeroboam built both Shechem and Penuel in 1 Kgs 12.25. Gideon experienced disloyalty from the Ephraimites, and then the men of Succoth and Penuel in Judg. 8.1-17. It seems likely that the invading Ephraimites made settlements first at Penuel and in the Succoth valley, and advanced thence to Shechem; just as the men of Jabesh in Gilead seem to have stood in some blood-relation to the Benjaminites round Gibeah (1 Sam. 11; 31. 11ff.). So it would appear quite likely that Shechem and the Succoth valley towns were seen by the defenders of Mahanaim as the backbone of the rebellion; and it would be for this reason that the undoubtedly hostile 'dividing' and 'measuring' are threatened.

60.7. The psalmist is feeling more confident than he has at any time since the revolt began, and he describes the line-up between the two sides, a little optimistically. The land is divided (v. 2), but the East Bank is for the king. Shobi, Prince of Ammon, and Barzillai the Gileadite are staunch supporters, and may be said to constitute Gilead as being royalist. Machir is the name of a Manassite clan (Num. 32.39f.; Josh. 13.31; 17.1), and since he, and with him much of the area further north, where David had garrisons keeping the Aramaeans down, were loyal, it might be said that Manasseh was royalist too. At this stage the lines between East Bank tribes were probably not very firmly drawn, but eastern Manasseh might be held roughly to cover the area of Bashan north of the Yarmuk, while Gilead was mostly south of the Yarmuk and north of the Moabite frontier, the Arnon.[8] Since none of the Manassite and Gileadite princes are included in the roll of honour in Psalm 68, and since at least the valley of Succoth was conceded to have favoured the Revolt, we may wonder how well-founded was the psalmist's claim, 'Gilead is mine and Manasseh is mine': but then Ministers of Information in modern times have sometimes noted the force of arguments for presenting only the poetic truth, and have felt an especial responsibility for public morale.

Gilead and (eastern) Manasseh do not sound very impressive as a virtual half of Israel, so the psalmist does his best. The commander of the royal bodyguard, the Cherethites and Pelethites, was a man called Benaiah ben-Jehoiada (2 Sam. 8.18; 20.23); and he is likely to be the 'Benaiah of Pirathon', of David's Thirty in 2 Sam. 23.30. (There is a duplicate Benaiah from Kabzeel in 2 Sam. 23.20-23, to whom certain legendary achievements are attributed, and very likely a good Judaean home too.) Pirathon was in Ephraim (Judg. 12.15): hence 'Ephraim is the defence of mine head'. He is bracketed with Joab in 2 Sam. 20.23 as David's two senior lieutenants: 'Now Joab was over all the host of Israel; and Benaiah the son of Jehoiada was over the Cherethites and over the Pelethites'. Joab was a Judahite (1

Chron. 2.16): hence 'Judah is my commander'—*ḥōq* means a decree, or command, and the po'el part. *m^{e}hōqēq* means a commander or general in Deut. 33.21; Judg. 5.14; Isa. 33.22. So it is made to sound as if four of the most important tribes are on David's side, without actually saying anything untrue.

60.8. But even if the support in Ephraim and Judah was thus rather limited, the royalists really did have control of the southern East Bank, east of the Dead Sea. David had slaughtered a terrifying number of Moabites in 2 Sam. 8.2, two out of every three prisoners, and reduced the nation to tributaries: so he might well speak of the Moabite lake, the Dead Sea, as 'my washpot'. He had also (as the Heading recalls, roughly) massacred 18,000 Edomites in the Valley of Salt: 'and he put garrisons in Edom; throughout all Edom he put garrisons', and enslaved the whole people (2 Sam. 8.14). So there were soldiers within reach to relieve the royalists in Mahanaim; and no doubt messengers were sent to them while the column was withdrawing over the Jordan. David could certainly 'fling his shoe as far as Edom' (cf. Ruth 4.7). Finally, and by no means least, were David's faithful Philistines, who are now called upon to 'shout because of me'. *ru'* in the hithpo'el means to shout for joy (cf. Ps. 65.13 in the Prayers), and the trusty mercenaries are being bidden to cheer for the King. The improbability of such a command has scandalized many readers, beginning from Ps. 108.9, where the consonants are tactfully amended to 'Over Philistia will I shout'. But the text as it stands could hardly reflect David's predicament more truly. We are reminded once more of the highlanders of 1689:

> There are wild Dooniewassalls three thousand times three,
> Will cry Hoy! for the bonnet of bonnie Dundee.

The manifold detail presents standard commentators with a surd, and Weiser wisely concedes that there is no time in Israelite history which corresponds to it. It is often thought that the 'oracle' is from earlier than the psalm (e.g. Anderson, Jacquet), and the division of Shechem recalls to Kirkpatrick and others the distribution of the land under Joshua. However, few scholars today see an invasion in which Judah and Ephraim were partners as a historical likelihood; and in any case why Shechem and the valley of Succoth? One might have expected Jericho and Shechem, or perhaps Shechem and Ashtarot Karnaim on the evidence of the Hexateuch; and I can find no evidence for the often repeated claim that Shechem and Succoth *represent* the two Banks, or stand as *pars pro toto* (Kraus). Delitzsch,

Rogerson and McKay and others take the Edomite War setting seriously (see Mowinckel,[9] Eaton, Dahood, Weiser). But not only is there no evidence at all that Edom or Moab had invaded central Israel and captured Shechem and Succoth, but even if they had, surely we should expect 'I will *restore* Shechem...'. not the hostile 'I will divide...' Mowinckel also considered the possibility of a setting in Joram's reign[10] (2 Kgs 8.16-22); but we then have the difficulty of an oracle which both regards Ephraim as God's helmet and also means to divide up the land of Shechem. To accommodate the hostility to Shechem and Succoth, Gunkel, Kraus and Anderson site the psalm after 722: but then 'Gilead is mine...' has to mean '... mine by right', and so far from being God's helmet Ephraim was effectively exiled to the river of Gozan and the cities of the Medes; nor was Judah very often in a position to undertake a war against Edom; nor did the Philistines shout with joy very often for Yahweh. If anything Duhm makes a better case for Maccabaean times; but happily this is not so seriously regarded today.

60.9 Who will bring me into the strong city?
Who hath led me (RV text) unto Edom?
10 Wilt not thou, O God, which hast cast us off?
And goest not forth, O God, with our hosts?
11 Give us help against the adversary:
For vain is the salvation of man.
12 Through God we shall do valiantly:
For it is he that shall tread down our adversaries.

Most critics identify the strong city (*māṣôr*, ramparted; cf. Zech. 9.3; 2 Chron. 8.5; or perhaps proleptically, besieged; cf. BDB, 848f.) with Petra in Edom, or Bosra (Ps. 108.11 *mibṣār*); but the text of the psalm suggests that it is Shechem which is ultimately to be attacked. Just as God was prayed to go before the royalists in their escape from the Terebinth wood (59.10), so now the psalmist desires Him to do the same in the campaign which will 'divide Shechem'. There is a change of tenses in the two verbs of v. 9 *yōḇilēnî/nāḥanî* in the MT, and it is natural to follow this in the translation—'Who will bring me to Shechem? Who led me to Edom? Is it not thou, O God?' God saw us to a crushing victory in the Valley of Salt, and He will do the same for us on Mt Zalmon when it comes to it. Although the disasters of the Revolt show that God has recently cast us off in anger, and has not been going forth with our forces on the retreat up Olivet, yet we may turn to him in confidence in view of his 'word' to David. With his help we shall do mighty deeds (*ḥāyil*, Num. 24.18; 1 Sam. 14.48) and trample down our adversaries: human force alone would not succeed.

Thus did the priest-prince survey his prospects from the walls of Mahanaim that October day. Humanly speaking, the odds looked far more evenly balanced than at any time so far: the East Bank was with the king, the West Bank with the rebels. Religiously speaking, the cards were stacked in his favour: the sure mercies of David were with him, and the promises of God were without repentance, even if from time to time His unpredictable anger might issue in unaccountable periods of rejection and trouble. But poise has been regained. The prayers are no longer for survival, but for national healing.

Gunkel reads *yan*^{e}*ḥēnî* in v. 9, following GS, and justifying by the parallel; but this looks like the easier reading. He sees the 'me' as a general or prince, where Mowinckel, Eaton and others opt for the king. The general willingness to see the alternation I/we as the sign of a royal, and even a Davidic setting is encouraging. It is a puzzle why this key has not been turned in the lock, to reveal a consistent background for the 'oracle'; whose altered 3 + 3 + 3 rhythm betokens not a different source but a different and more joyful mood.

61 For the Chief Musician; on a stringed instrument. For (*l*^{e}) David.
1 Hear my cry, O God;
Attend unto my prayer.
2 From the end of the land (*hā'āreṣ*) call I (*'eqrā'*) unto thee, when my heart fainteth:
Lead me to the rock (RV text) that is too high for me.
3 For thou hast been a refuge for me,
A strong tower from the enemy.
4 I will dwell in thy tent for ever:
I will take refuge in the covert of thy wings.
(Selah

The mood of sudden optimism which characterized 60 has matured in 61: on the one hand there is a yearning homesickness for the familiar shrine on Zion, with its 'tent', its seraphim with outstretched wings, and its daily offerings—and a confidence that a return is coming; but on the other hand there is a realistic awareness that the royalist forces on their own are quite inadequate to the task.

The psalm has much in common with other psalms in the Prayers sequence. 'Attend to my prayer' recalls 55.1, 2. 'The end of the land/

earth' echoes 59.13. The God who is the psalmist's refuge, rock and strong tower, spiritually and literally, is a leitmotif of this part of the series: 59.9, 16, 17; 62.2, 6, 7, 8; 71.3, 7. The covering of the divine wings recurs in 57.1 and 63.7. The temple on Zion is referred to in 52.8; 53.6; 63.2; 65.1; 68.24, 29. Vows of praise and thank-offerings have been a feature already in 51.19; 52.9; 56.12, and will come again in 65.1; 66.13, 15; 69.30f.; 71.8, 14f., 17f., 24. Prayer for the king recurs in 63.12; 65.4. The twin angelic powers, *ḥeseḏ* and *ᵉmeṯ*, were sent to protect the speaker/king in 57.3, 10, and *ḥeseḏ* was similarly paired with *ʿōz* in 59.9f., 16, 17.

61.1-2a. The psalmist is well aware of the royalists' limitations, and of their need for divine assistance (cf. 60.11f.); but his Prayer is marked with a certain hopefulness, and even serenity. He dispenses with the musicless sequence of Michtams, and accompanies his petition on a single instrument, or perhaps a single string; Delitzsch defends *nᵉgînaṯ* as the original Semitic feminine termination, and Dahood supports this as the harder reading, against the easily amended form *-ôṯ* found in many MSS and versions. There will be more strings in 62–68 as confidence rises.

The speaker calls, and cries, and prays; and his heart faints as he looks out over his timber defences. *ʿṭp* is used elsewhere of *physical* fainting: 'Children who faint for hunger' (Lam. 2.19), 'for the spirit would faint from before me (God)' (Isa. 57.26; cf. Gen. 30.42; Ps. 102 Heading). We may think that physical weakness is sapping the speaker's heart here also. Mahanaim is not certainly identified as a site, but it may not have been very large. The arrival of an additional two thousand mouths must have put some strain upon the foodstores as soon as the besieging army under Amasa cut off any further import. Generous supplies from Shobi, Machir and Barzillai (2 Sam. 17.27ff.) would not last long, and rationing will have begun. The prayer is *miqᵉṣeh hāʾāreṣ*, which following Kirkpatrick, we may render 'from the end of the land': Mahanaim was close to the Aramaean frontier. In passages which speak clearly of 'the ends of the earth', the plural *qᵉṣôṯ hāʾāreṣ* is usually used (Isa. 40.28; 41.5, 9; Job 28.24); where the singular is used, as in Ps. 46.10; Deut. 28.49, 'the frontier of the land' is an admissible translation. Ps. 59.13 spoke of God as ruling 'in Jacob, to the *ʾapsê-hāʾāreṣ*'.

61.2b-4. God has been a refuge for the speaker, and a strong tower from the enemy: Judg. 9.51 shows what a *migdal-'ōz* was, an acropolis within a fortified town, often the earliest point of settlement, and the inhabitants' ultimate refuge, as at Thebez. Such there was at Mahanaim, and such was the psalmist's home from home, and a symbol to him of the divine protection. But this is past history now (*hāyîṯā*): his present prayer is for God to bring him back to Zion. God had gone before the royalists in the breakout from the Terebinth wood (59.10), and he had led them (*nāḥanî*) as far as Edom (60.9): 60.9 asked God to bring them to the fortified city of Shechem, and now he is prayed, 'Lead me (*tanḥēnî*) to the rock that is too high for me'. It is hard to remember that as recently as 1743 British kings led their armies into battle: the courage, strength and skill of the ancient leader was often displayed to good effect before his troops (Judg. 5.14; 1 Macc. 3.23). The rock to which God is to lead must from v. 4 be Zion, where the Dome of the Rock now stands: mount Zion which cannot be moved (Ps. 125.1). As he remembers the daunting fight up Olivet a few weeks back, he knows that rock to be 'high(er) than I (can manage unaided)': he could not, as things stand, force his way up. But as God has helped him to Mahanaim, so will he be led, he confides, to God's 'tent', the temporary abode of his presence (Ps. 132.5), and to the protective wings of the seraphim; which we must think to have been the focal symbol of the divine presence in the Jebusite temple, described by the D-historian as 'the house of Yahweh' (2 Sam. 12.20).[11]

After v. 4 we have a Selah; and here we find for the first time our thread of Ariadne broken. From 2 Sam. 15.7 where the Passion Narrative began ('And it came to pass at the end of forty years. . . '), we have had a continuous narrative taking us from the raising of the Revolt to the Siege of Mahanaim; and this breaks into a ten-part story, each section of which has found an appropriate echo in the succession of ten Selah's in Pss. 52–60. I have set out a Table of these on p. 46. There continued to be incidents to the end of the campaign, and as the psalmist reacted to them, so did those who edited his work for processional use continue to insert 'Selah' at suitable moments. But the station on Mt Scopus was but an artificial symbol for the realities of Mahanaim and on: the Succession Narrator had no interest in the minima of military history, and he has erased the whole. Once the environs of Jerusalem are left behind (and so the route of the procession), he tells us nothing more. Even the great battle is reduced to the human incidents of Absalom's death and David's response thereto. So (aside from one or two heavily overwritten passages) our Passion of David story is at an end. We can but conjecture from the text of each Psalm what little incident has affected the writer. Here the rise in confidence ('thou, O God, hast heard my vows...') may suggest to us that word has come of the approach of a relief column, or of the loyal support of the northern tribes for the king. Hitherto we have been able to interpret one text by another; henceforth we can but infer and speculate.

61.5 For thou, O God, hast heard my vows:
Thou hast given an heritage unto those that fear thy name.
6 Thou wilt prolong the king's life:
His years shall be as many generations.
7 He shall be enthroned (*yēšēḇ*) before God for ever:
O prepare loving kindness and truth, that they may preserve him.
8 So will I sing praise unto thy name for ever,
That I may daily perform my vows.

The good news reported in the Selah, whatever it may have been, is an encouragement to all. God has hearkened to the psalmist's vows, and the victory is coming which will enable them to be paid—and paid daily. He has also thereby opened the way to a share-out of the lands of the defeated among the loyal soldiery: literally, 'Thou hast given the heritage of those that fear thy name', sc. to them. It was until comparatively modern times the obvious, and the only practicable way of paying off a victorious army. Alexander gave his soldiers fields in the lands they had conquered for him, and Caesar, and other Roman generals, established *coloniae* similarly for their veterans. Cromwell in the same sort of way paid off his New Model army with land in Ireland. So here: the psalmist has already been exulting in the thought of dividing Shechem, and measuring out the valley of Succoth. These are the places where the deserving Philistines, who have saved the sum of things for pay, can now expect to end their days in wealth and contentment, each in his own *y^eruššâ*.

61.6f. But the centrepiece of all the hopes in Mahanaim town is the King himself. He is the pivot of all that happens: those who are not for him are against him. So now the psalmist sees a happy vision of years to come. God will add days to the days of David's life, which would indeed have been near completion but for the deliverances of the last weeks (2 Sam. 17.12). A suitable vagueness of hyperbole is allowed to veil the question whether David himself will reign for another century, or whether his successors will be enthroned 'for ever', as in 2 Sam. 7.16.

God was to send forth his *ḥeseḏ* and his *ᵉmeṯ* to deliver the psalmist in 57.3, 10, and the recurrence of the same pair of angelic extensions of the divine presence is the more striking because we have three times had a similar use of *ḥeseḏ* and *ʿōz* in Ps. 59 (vv. 9f., 16, 17). Later Jewish (cabbalistic) imagination saw strength (*gᵉḇûrâ*) as the right hand and *ḥeseḏ* as the left hand of the divine throne;[12] and we should probably be right to think that *ḥeseḏ* and *ᵉmeṯ/ʿōz* are the names of the two seraphim under whose wings the speaker looked to take refuge. The two central wings touched, and were thought of as providing the seat of God's throne in the Debir at Jerusalem.[13] The (four) cherubim on the ephod at Dan seem to have been named Mercy and Truth, Righteousness and Peace (Ps. 85.10-13, *PSK* pp. 112ff.). Jerusalem had absorbed the northern cherubic tradition by Ezekiel's day (Ezek. 1), but it is likely that the earlier twofold seraphic symbolism of Isaiah 6 carried the same ideology of named hypostatic Powers. Solomon's two Temple pillars were similarly named.

The change of person, from 'me' to 'the king', has been a problem to critics. Gunkel and Jacquet suppose an adaptation of an earlier Lament for the king's use by the insertion of vv. 6f.; Kraus takes intercession for the king to be a normal part of a pilgrim's prayer. The matter is more easily handled by those who see 61 as a national psalm. Mowinckel has it spoken by the king on campaign, far from Zion;[14] Dahood and Eaton[15] see him as on the edge of the underworld, and metaphorically far from God. All three see the change of person as natural, between the king as a person and as an office, comparing Jer. 38.5 and Ugaritic texts. Eaton points to a number of features as standard for the king: long life, God his fortress, daily sacrifice, access to God's 'tent' and his 'wings'. I should not wish to exclude the king as speaker; indeed in many passages in the Prayers I see the Chief Musician as a kind of speech-writer for the king (e.g. 51). But in other psalms he addresses the king as 'thou' (53.5; 55.22; 68.23, 28), and in these he is clearly distinguished from the king. Furthermore most of Eaton's points—access to God's tent and his wings, daily sacrifice, God as fortress—apply as much to the priests as to the king; and since David's sons were priests (2 Sam. 8.18), the best solution must lie in supposing the speaker to be a prince-priest. This has the additional advantage of giving a natural reading to 61.6f. The only biblical parallel offered seems to be Jer. 38.5, and there the king refers to himself in the third person, but there is no change from the first person: the distinction between the king as person and as office seems rather fine.

61.8. The psalmist has been making promises and vows from early in the sequence: 51.19, sacrifices of righteousness, when the walls of Jerusalem were finished; 52.8 thanks/thank-offerings for ever; 53.6, rejoicing and gladness, when God restores his people; 54.6, sacrifice with a freewill offering; 56.12, 'Thy vows are upon me, O God'; 59.16f., the singing of praises. In some cases these praises are associated with Yahweh's name (52.9, 54.6), as they are here. But we notice now the sharp rise in confidence: God is going to extend the king's life, and the concrete 'daily' performance of the vows is becoming a real expectation. In 65.1, 'Unto thee shall the vow be performed', the expectation is more real still, and is charged with joy.

Interpretations of 61 divide on what are now familiar lines. Faithful Delitzsch boldly credits the psalm to David in the time of the Mahanaim siege, and Kirkpatrick follows him with caution—if it is by David, then it is from the time of Mahanaim. Jacquet also thinks the main poem goes back to David. Duhm as usual sees it at home in the days of the Maccabees. For Gunkel, Kraus and Anderson it (or most of it) is an individual lament; in view of the more relaxed last verses, Weiser calls it an individual thanksgiving. The speaker is variously envisaged as a pious Jew in the Diaspora, as a pilgrim to the festival, or as a man surrounded by enemies and at the boundaries of this life. Mowinckel, Eaton and Dahood have the king as speaker, with real enemies, and (for Mowinckel) a real distance from Zion. The individual theories have trouble with the prayer for the king; and all theories but Delitzsch's have trouble with 'the end of the earth'—Dahood's interpretation of *'ereṣ* as Sheol depends upon an idiosyncratic exegesis of Jer. 10.11f. The 'heritage of those that fear thy name' is also a difficulty: many, like NEB, emend to *ᵃrešeṯ*, desire (cf. 21.2); Weiser postulates a setting in the septennial liturgy of the redistribution of land, of which we do not hear much elsewhere.

The fragile moment of confidence which we have seen in 60–61 has received a severe shaking in 62:

62 For the Chief Musician; after the manner of Jeduthun.
A Psalm for (*lᵉ*) David.
1 My soul is silent unto God alone:
From him *cometh* my salvation.

2 He only is my rock and my salvation:
He is my high tower; I shall not be greatly moved.
3 How long will ye set upon a man,
That ye may shatter *him* (*t^eraṣṣ^eḥû*) all of you,
Like a bowing wall, like the breached defence (*gāḏēr hadd^eḥûyâ*)?
4 They only consult to thrust him down from his excellency;
They delight in lies:
They bless with their mouth, but they curse inwardly.
(Selah

Later use accompanied the psalm with strings (*mizmôr*); perhaps reflecting the last verse of 61 *ᵓazamm^erâ*, and in any case providing a climax—four Maschils (52–55), five Michtams (56–60), one on a single string (61), three with full strings, Mizmors (62–64), four with full orchestra, Songs (65–68). But the text of 62 is less joyful than 60 or 61, and may be accurately reflecting the obscure comment, 'after the manner of Jeduthun'. Jeduthun is the junior of the three Davidic musical guilds (2 Chron. 5.12, etc.); but the significance of the note can be gleaned only by noting similarities with the other two Jeduthun psalms in the psalter, 39 and 77. Ps. 39.2 has 'I was dumb with silence (*dûmîyâ*), I held my peace', and 39.9 has 'I was dumb, I opened not my mouth'. Ps. 77.6 has 'I commune with mine own heart', and 77.12, 'I will meditate also upon all thy work, And muse on thy doings'. Thus 39 at least offers a striking parallel to 62.1, 'My soul is silent (*dûmiyâ*)', and 62.5, 'My soul, be thou silent (*dômmî*) unto God', especially in view of the surprising noun *dûmiyâ* ('My soul is silent submission', Delitzsch); and although there is no clear evidence of silence in 77, it may certainly be implied. It seems best therefore to think that Jeduthun specialized in a psalmody in which there was a short period or two of silence; and that this was used in moments of crisis like the present.

62.1ff. For there has indeed been a crisis, and one that the royalists have only just survived. The psalmist turns once more to his favourite images—the rock (62.2,6, 7; 61.2), my refuge (62.7; 61.3), the 'high tower' (*miśgaḇ*, 62.2, 6; 59.9, 16, 17; cf. 61.3), my strength (62.6; 59.9, 17)—and well he may. He owes his life (his 'salvation') to the broad rampart and the well-built walls of the acropolis at Mahanaim, which have withstood the assault of the rebels' battering-rams. The images are best seen as deriving their force from reality. God is seen as the speaker's rock, salvation and fortress (*miśgāḇ*) because the rocky eminence at Mahanaim has saved his life, and he feels God to have willed this. The rebels are seen as 'setting upon' David (*t^eĥôṯ^eṯû*, Delitzsch: 'press upon so as to intimidate') that they may 'shatter' him (reading *t^eraṣṣ^eḥû* with ben Naphtali GV; Delitzsch: 'break him down', contundere) like a bowing wall, a curtain-wall (*gāḏēr*), the one that has been pushed in (*hadd^eḥûyâ*). They are thought of as *like* hooligans beating up an old man in the street, because in reality they filled the ditch with earth and built a ramp, and rammed the defence-wall at its weakest point, and made it bow (*nāṭûi*) and breached it, and so nearly brought the king to his death. But a breached wall is not a captured fortress, as Henry V knew at Harfleur, and the faithful and formidable Philistines were able to fight them off. The narrow margin by which catastrophe has been avoided is eloquently expressed by the adverb: 'I shall not be *greatly* moved'.

The Hebrew of vv. 2f. is not easy. *t^ehôṯ^eṯû* is a hapax: BDB follow Delitzsch in a derivation from *hut*, to shout, with a Damascene text implying 'to rush upon with shouts and raised fists'; the Greek ἐπιτίθεσθε would be close to this. Köhler and Baumgartner derive from *htt*, suggesting 'overwhelm with reproaches'. *t^eraṣṣ^eḥû* is an alternative reading to *t^eroṣṣ^eḥû* given by ben Asher, from the pual of *rṣḥ*, 'you shall be slain' rather than the piel. *rṣḥ* normally means kill, murder,[16] but BDB give an Aramaic cognate meaning 'bruise','crush', and this gives the best sense here. Without it, Gunkel and Kraus amend to a form from *ruṣ*, to run upon; and they also delete *rabbâ* to agree with v. 7. The article with *d^eḥûyâ* has also seemed scandalous, and has often been transferred to the preceding noun, to form *g^eḏērâ*. But we may retain the Massoretic pointing, and explain the article as ostensive: they set upon David as upon a wall, indeed as upon the city wall of Mahanaim there, which we see breached.

62.4. The mention of *ḵāzāḇ* suggests that the assault was preceded by a truce and parley. Amasa knew that the acropolis was held in strength, and that storming it would be perilous: so he proposed a parley—perhaps the royalists would surrender on terms he could later interpret, and in any case time was for the moment on his side, and he might get a better idea of the defences. Their plan all along was (*'aḵ yā'aṣû*) to thrust David down (*ndḥ*, hiph.) from his eminence (*ś^e'ēṯ*, Gen. 49.3; Job 13.11): they delight in deception.

They bless with his mouth (*pîw*, that is Amasa's, or whoever was the chief spokesman): they said 'May God bless my lord the king', or some similar formula, but in their heart they cursed him, they intended to depose him. The psalm has a Selah at this point; we may conjecture that the Passion Narrative gave some account here of the truce and negotiation, without which v. 4 is difficult to understand.

62.5 My soul, be thou silent unto God;
For my expectation is from him.
6 He only is my rock and my salvation:
He is my high tower; I shall not be moved.
7 With God is my salvation and my glory:
The rock of my strength, and my refuge, is in God.
8 Trust in him at all times, ye people;
Pour out your heart before him:
God is a refuge for us.
(Selah

62.5f. are close to being a restatement of vv. 1f.; perhaps Jeduthun's mode included two breaks in the psalm, and an element of refrain, since both 39 and 62 share both these features, the breaks being marked in each case by two Selahs. 77 also has two Selahs, but no refrain. It would look as if 39 and 62 both had periods of silence at the breaks, and perhaps before and after the psalm. The silence has helped to restore the psalmist's confidence, as so often. Before it, God was 'my salvation': his thought was for his life, so lately in peril. Now it is for the future: God is his expectation. Before it, he would not be greatly moved: now he will not be moved at all. He is even able to look forward with v. 7 to his coming glory, that is the honour and richness of his position at Jerusalem; that is with God too. But underneath all remain the defensive images which I have noted above: rock, salvation, fortress, strength, refuge. He is still really thinking of the rebels' frustrated attack on the walls, and no doubt the Selah will have told the tale with the Passion narrator's laconic accuracy.

Ps. 62.3 turned on the rebels, demanding how long they meant to set on the king. Now *62.8* addresses 'ye people', originally David's army; all through the Passion Narrative the royalists were 'David and the people that were with him'. In later years *'ām* will be the faithful Israelites on procession. In face of present disloyalties the psalmist does his best to ensure that similar things do not happen again; like the Christian hymn-writer who has watched one generation melt away, and teaches the next to sing 'Grant us grace to persevere'. The 'people' are to 'trust in God', that is to be faithful royalists, since God has made a covenant with David (and his house, in the later version, 2 Sam. 7). They are to do that 'at all times', i.e. especially when rebellions and coups are in the air. They are to 'pour out their heart before him'; that is, as Kraus says, to be fully open to Yahweh—no blessing the king with the mouth and inwardly cursing him. God is a refuge for us; he looks after his own. But, as the last verses go on to stress, Big Brother is also watching those who do not trust in him, and they will get their deserts.

62.9 Surely men of low degree are a breath, and men of high degree are a lie:
In the balances they will go up;
They are together lighter than a breath.
10 Trust not in violence (*'ōšeq*),
And become not vain with force (*gāzēl*):
If power (*ḥayil*) increase, set not your heart *thereon*.
11 God hath spoken once,
Twice have I heard this;
That strength (*'ōz*) belongeth unto God:
12 Also unto thee, O Lord, belongeth lovingkindness (*ḥesed̲*):
For thou renderest to everyman according to his work.

62.9f. The force of the combination 'sons of *'ād̲ām*'/'sons of *'îš*'is not quite plain: RV takes it to correspond to the British presupposition, 'officers and other ranks', but J. van der Ploeg[17] concludes that there is no substantial difference, but rather a contrast between men and God. Such is the situation, it seems, underlying Ps. 49.2, where the sons of *'ād̲ām* and of *'îš* are the 'peoples' of 'the world' (49.1) who have invaded Israel, and who will be overthrown by 'the upright' in battle (v. 14); like the opposition here, they trust in their *ḥayil* (49.6)—cf. *PSK*, pp. 181-95. On the other hand, 49.13 does contain a contrast between the boastful speakers and 'those that follow them', so it may be that the officers-and-men view is justified. But in any case the parallel with 49 is helpful. The contrast is basically between God's *'ām*, who have followed the king, and the sons of men who have not. The latter are men without any principle, men of straw, of no weight, of such levity that if you put them on one side of the scales it will be sure to go up. They put their trust not in God and his promises, but in *'ōšeq*, which should be given its neutral meaning, violence, as in Job 40.23, 'if a river be violent': 'extortion' and 'oppression' presuppose a position of authority which does not obtain here. *gāzēl* similarly has the primary meaning of force rather than robbery; cf. Job 24.9, 'those who snatch (*gzl*) the fatherless child from the breast'; 2 Sam. 23.21, 'snatched (*gzl*) the spear from the Egyptian's hand'. *ḥayil* again means power before it means wealth, though it is easy to see the connection: cf. BDB, *ad voc.* 1, 2. The real power (*'ōz*, v. 11) is with God, and it is futile to trust in earthly power in the way that Absalom and Amasa have. Violence and force may succeed for a short while, but God will have the last laugh.

*62.11*f. In interpreting 'God hath spoken once...', appeal is usually made to an oracle; and we may agree with this proposal, specifying it as the oracle behind 2 Samuel 7, God's original promise to David, which has underlain so many references to *ḥesed̲* and to God's word in the Prayers. We have also heard at least twice of the combination of God's *ḥesed̲* and his *'ōz* (59.9f., 16, 17; 61.3, 7). The double truth which the psalmist has laid to heart (*šāmā'tî*) is to be derived entirely from this revelation. First (ultimate) power rests with God, and not with the violence and force of any rebels (vv. 11f.); and secondly he will be true to his promise (*ḥesed̲*). Everyone will get the reward of their deeds: those who have stood by the king will receive their 'heritage' from confiscated lands round Shechem and Succoth (61.5; 60.6); those who have been faithless will have their heads beaten in following the victory parade (68.21). What is so satisfactory is that everything turned out exactly in line with the psalmist's confident predictions.

Interpretation has followed the now familiar divisions. Delitzsch, followed by a more hesitant Kirkpatrick ('If David...'), and an optimistic Jacquet ('Why not David?'), sites the psalm in David's days, and during Absalom's rebellion; but they do not think of an assault on Mahanaim. Mainstream interpretation (even Smend, p. 51; Gunkel, Kraus, Weiser, Dahood, Anderson, Rogerson and McKay) has seen the speaker as a pious Jew persecuted by his erstwhile friends. He has taken asylum in the Temple, and received an oracle which has given him serene confidence in God; and has now become the leader of a godly party, whom he addresses in the assembly. This implausible scenario involves reducing *śᵉʾēṯ* from 'eminence' to 'respect' (Weiser), or emendation (Gunkel, Kraus); the psalmist seems to be rather a simpleton, all of whose doubts and bitter experiences are laid aside on the strength of a personal 'oracle'. But then it is precisely this 'trust in God' which is so appealing to the pietist commentator. The later Mowinckel[18] and Eaton[19] carry more conviction with a picture of the king leading worship on a day of prayer; oracles are given by prophets for the nation; the accumulation of personal epithets ('my rock', etc.) and the alternation with the first person plural ('a refuge for us') forcibly suggest a leader of the people (v. 8) in the liturgy. We may applaud this as far as it goes; but perhaps Eaton is rather cautious in attributing so much to 'traditional features', and nothing to 'particular circumstances'. The links with the other Prayers forcibly suggest a place in a sequential psalmody, with the echoes of many particular circumstances.

Assault and battery are not the only ways of reducing a fortress, and 63 is the reflection of a slower method.

63 A Psalm for (*lᵉ*) David, when he was in the wilderness of Judah.
1 O God, thou art my God; early do I seek thee (*ʾᵃšaḥᵃreḵā*):
In a dry and weary land, where no water is.
2 So have I looked upon thee in the sanctuary,
To see thy power and thy glory.
3 For thy lovingkindness is better than life;
My lips shall praise thee.
4 So will I bless thee while I live:
I will lift up my hands in thy name.
5 My soul shall be satisfied as with marrow and fatness;
And my mouth shall praise thee with joyful lips.
6 If I have remembered thee on my pallet (*ʾim-zᵉḵartîḵā ʿal-yᵉṣûʿāi*)
I will meditate (*ʾehgeh*) on thee in the night watches.
7 For thou hast been my help,
And in the shadow of thy wings will I rejoice.
8 My soul hath followed hard (*dāḇᵉqâ*) after thee:
Thy right hand hath upheld (*tāmᵉḵâ*) me.

Many commentators have seen 61–63 as a sequence (cf. Delitzsch, Kirkpatrick), and some themes are obviously in common: the longing for worship on Zion (61.2; 63.3ff.), from which the speaker is at present separated (61.2; 63.1), with its tent/sanctuary (61.4; 63.2) and the covert/shadow of the divine wings (61.4; 63.7; cf. 57.1); the promise of lasting praise there (61.8; 63.4) to the God who has been his rock, refuge, help, etc. (61.3; 62.3, 6f.; 63.7); the prolongation of the king's life (61.6f.; 63.11), and the destruction of his enemies (62.12; 63.9ff.). The thirsting and longing of 63.1, in a dry and weary land, recall the fainting of 61.2 at the end of the land. More generally, the appeal to God's *ḥeseḏ* (v. 3), the praise of his name (v. 4), and the fate of 'those that seek my soul' (v. 9), have been recurrent topics through the Prayers.

Delitzsch and Kirkpatrick still saw the psalm as Davidic; and they sited it correctly during Absalom's rebellion. But just as the early commentator seized on the 'dry and weary land' as a basis for putting it 'when David was in the wilderness of Judah', i.e. in Saul's time, so they have too hopefully aligned the *'āyēp̄* of v. 1 with the *ᵃyēp̄îm* of 2 Sam. 16.14, and seen the occasion of the psalm as by the Jordan. We do better to take 63 as arising from the plight of the royalists besieged in Mahanaim, chronologically after the investment of the town in 60–61, and the repulse of the rebels in 62. Later use knew that all was to turn out happily, and accompanied the psalm with music (*mizmôr*); but at the time, the end of the water and food supplies was facing the defenders with disaster. The revolt had taken place at harvest festival time, and Ziba had brought David grapes (2 Sam. 16.1). October had become November, and still there had been no rain; and Mahanaim enjoyed in any case only half the annual rainfall of Jerusalem.[20] The view from the battlements will have been of unrelieved brownness: 'a land of aridity and weariness, without water'. The psalmist is thirsty (*ṣāmᵉ'â*) and hungry (his flesh faints, pales, *kāmah*): the mood is as in Londonderry before the Boyne, but with the addition of the standard peril of Israelite sieges, water failure.

Our speaker is a religious man, and he views his privations as in relation to God, *ᵉlōhîm*, the *'ēl* who has covenanted to David and his house (*'ēlî*). The thirst and hunger are not just for the slaking of physical need, but for the rich life in God's shrine; we may think of the pilgrims of 42.1f.; 84.2, processing through the parched valleys of northern Israel (84.6) to the cataracts of the land of Jordan at Dan (42.6f.), where the living God (42.2, 8) continuously pours forth water for all.[21] Back in Zion the olive trees are green round the year

(52.8), and the imagination of thirst and hunger plays over the delights of that happy world. But he is also doing what he can to move God to action: he has been at prayer as the sun rises. This seems to be the primary meaning of *šiḥar*, to seek early (with the dawn, *šahar*), and it is best suited to the present context (*pace* Gunkel), because of the references to keeping vigil in v. 6. The repeated *kēn* (vv. 2, 4) gives the drift of the psalm. The speaker remembers the glories of worship at Zion (v. 2), and has been carrying the same on as best he may in dire circumstances (vv. 1, 6a): he promises to do the same with the same devotion (*kēn*) when he is restored to Zion (vv. 3b, 5b, 6b, 7b). The dawn prayer is a regular feature of life now (impf.): so (*kēn*) was it at Jerusalem before, when he would gaze (perf.) through the morning twilight in the sanctuary for God's invisible presence, to catch first sight of the Ark, God's strength (Pss. 132.8; 78.61a) and his glory (Pss. 78.61b; 24.7; 1 Sam. 4.21). For (v. 3) to have God's favour (*ḥesed̲*) is the highest privilege a man can have, better than life, he says hyperbolically: when he is back there, his lips will laud Him.

63.4-8. With such sustained devotion (*kēn* again) will the psalmist bless God all his days with uplifted hands. He will enjoy 'a meal of well-fed, lusty animals' (Delitzsch) on many a day, and he will know the deep satisfaction of soul that goes with it. Mowinckel and Eaton are right to see in the 'marrow and fatness' the hint of coming thank-offerings (cf. 56.12; 61.8), in which, as communion sacrifices, he himself will have a share. The restrictive rulings of Lev. 3.10; 7.23, 25, whereby the fat belonged to God alone, will hardly have been in place so early. A rather believable picture emerges of the man of God wiping the fat from his lips before uttering a fulsome grace, reminiscent of the banquet of a pious sheikh of modern times.

63.6ff. Many critics have found v. 6 a problem; we do best to take the changing tenses seriously. The psalmist used to be up with the lark in Jerusalem, gazing on the ark (*ḥ^{a}zîṯîkā*, perf., v. 2), and he has made a practice of meditative vigil (*z^{e}ḵartîḵā*, perf., v. 6): if he has done this faithfully now, God may depend he will meditate (*'ehgeh* impf.) through the night-watches similarly (understand *kēn*) in future. *'im* with the perfect naturally carries this meaning, BDB *ad voc*. a. (4), e.g. Judg. 9.16ff., 'if ye have done honestly. . . '; 1 Sam. 26.19, 'if it be the LORD that hath stirred thee up'. Israelite vigils did not involve nights of total sleeplessness. The devotee slept in the Temple on his *yāṣûa'*, a padded bedroll (*yāṣa'*, to spread), and rose at the watches to pray; cf. 119.62, 'At midnight I will rise to give thanks unto thee'; v. 147, 'I prevented the dawning of the morning, and cried'; v. 148, 'Mine eyes prevented the night-watches, That I might meditate in thy word'; v. 164, 'Seven times a day do I praise thee'. Prayer was said 'on the bedrolls' (*miškāḇ*, 149.5), perhaps with prostrations. Our psalmist gladly promises such devotion because (*kî*, v. 7) God has been his ally; he will know sheer joy when he is back under the protection of the seraphim wings. He has followed God closely to the divine stronghold at Mahanaim, just as Jeremiah foretold that the feared famine would follow the Judaean refugees closely (*dāḇaq 'aḥ^{a}rê*, 42.16) to Egypt; but in every crisis God's right hand has held firmly on to him. God has been a refuge for him at Mahanaim, a strong tower against the enemy (61.2), and will lead him back to Zion (61.2); He is not thought of as resident in Zion only.

63.9 But those that seek my soul shall be destroyed:
They shall go into the lower parts of the earth.
10 They shall be given over to the power of the sword:
They shall be a portion for jackals.
11 But the king shall rejoice in God:
Every one that sweareth by him shall glory;
For the mouth of them that speak treason (*šāqer*) shall be stopped.

The prince-poet speaks half for himself and half for his father. The rebels who seek both their lives (supply relative, Dahood) are for destruction. They will go down to Sheol (cf. the pit of destruction, 55.23); God ('they', divine plural) will pour him out (*ngr*, hiph.) at the hand of the sword—*him* (*-hû*), the unspeakable Absalom; they shall lie out, a portion for the jackals. A battle is clearly in mind, and we should probably see the comment in 2 Sam. 18.8, 'the forest devoured more people than the sword devoured', as a reflection of the psalmist's prophecy. Many Israelites lay wounded in the woods, and were preyed upon alive by the jackals; Joab and his armour-bearers stabbed Absalom to death. But David will rejoice in God, as indeed he does, broken-heartedly, in 68. All those who who take their oaths in loyalty to David will join in his triumph; we may remember Uriah's faithful words, 'As you live, and as your soul lives, I will not do this thing' (2 Sam. 11.11; cf. 15.21). Those on the other hand who speak deceit (*šeqer*), that is who have sworn by the life of Absalom (cf. 52.3), will have a less happy part in the celebrations. Their mouths will be stopped as God smites through their hairy scalps by the hand of his prophets (68.21).

It is these last verses which test the commentator. Gunkel, Kraus, Weiser, Anderson, Rogerson and McKay, Jacquet have the pious Israelite taking asylum in the Temple, pursued by enemies, a paradigm of godly trust, comforted by a theophany, etc.: but then what is to be done with the king and the battle? Gunkel and Jacquet have the king in v. 12 as a later liturgical insertion; for the former the battle scene becomes execution and unburied exposure to the animals, and so too for Weiser. But Weiser has the king present to vindicate the speaker, and the enemies are thus national enemies too. Eaton takes these proposals apart with a kindly effectiveness,[22] and expounds the use of privileged language to argue for the royal 'I'.[23] But even he finds the 'sequence' difficult,[24] and spiritualizes—'The king and his people endure an absence of divine salvation which afflicts their whole existence like an absolute drought'. The sequence problem solves itself if we see the psalmist as really thirsty and fainting, in a really waterless land; in fact in some such situation as the heading suggests for David—only it is King David (v. 12), so we are better off in Mahanaim.

64 For the Chief Musician. A Psalm for (*l*^{e}) David.
1 Hear my voice, O God, in my complaint:
Preserve my life from fear of the enemy.
2 Hide me from the secret counsel of evil-doers;
From the throng of workers of iniquity:
3 Who have whet their tongue like a sword,
And have aimed their arrows, even bitter words:
4 That they may shoot in secret places at the perfect (one):
Suddenly do they shoot at him, and fear not.
5 They resolve upon (*y*^{e}*ḥazz*^{e}*qû-lāmô*) an evil purpose;
They commune of laying snares privily;
They say, Who shall see them?
6 They plan (*yaḥp*^{e}*śû*) iniquities;
They have accomplished (*tām*^{e}*nû*) a well-planned plan (*ḥēpeś m*^{e}*ḥuppāś*):
And the inward thought of everyone, and the heart, is deep.

For the numerous links of style and language with the other Prayers, see pp. 20f. It is such links which suggest taking the Prayers as a unity;

and a sequential context then provides a setting for what are otherwise puzzling details.

It is notorious that the problems of besiegers are often as debilitating as those of the besieged. Amasa had more soldiers to feed and water than David had. The cisterns might be running low in Mahanaim, but there were no cisterns at all outside. The harvest had been gathered into the town: corn outside had to be carried from Succoth, and villages beyond. If morale sagged within the walls, there was nowhere to desert to: if things looked bad without, one could always melt away in the night, and there was work to do on everyone's farm at home. The troops were mostly Israelite volunteers, who had joined up in the hope of a quick coup. Furthermore, the failure of the assault on the walls, implied in 62, was sure to have given the defenders a fillip, and to have discouraged the attackers; and we cannot tell whether word may have reached Absalom's camp either of a relieving column on the way, or (more probably) of a threatened direct march on Shechem. Whatever the precise balance of considerations, Amasa decided to raise the siege and withdraw; and it is the preparations for this which so worry the psalmist.

64.1-4. The rebels are not going to force the breach again; but before they go, they will try their hand at creating alarm and despondency. Trotsky believed that if the Russian and the German other ranks might fraternize, the latter would join arms with the former in the great class struggle of 1917; and we have seen how often 'words' and 'tongues', whetted like swords and arrows, have caused anxiety to our singer (Pss. 52, 55, 56, 58, 59). They have aimed their arrows (if so we may translate *dārᵉḵû*), even bitter words, shooting in secret places: that is, they have crept up behind outcrops of rock, or trees, and called out demoralizing slogans and questions. The substance of these may be inferred from the defensiveness of the adjective *tām*, used of David (cf. 'a man', 62.3; 'the man whom thou choosest', 65.4); for this is a stress which we have had before—'Not for my transgression, nor for my sin, O LORD', 59.3—and we shall hear protests of innocence again (65.3; 66.18; 69.5), and of expiation fulfilled (69.19ff.). The rebel Haw-Haws cried out, 'David is a sinner!', 'God has cursed him for a murderer and adulterer', 'Nathan pronounced God's judgment on him', 'There will be no water till Uriah's blood is purged', and similar comments. These could indeed be extremely effective: 'suddenly do they shoot at him, and fear not

(God)'. For the religion of the time was certainly on the rebels' side as much as on David's, and the royalists' hands would indeed be weakened if they listened to such propaganda. The stress on David's 'perfection', i.e. as having atoned for his sin, as earlier on the divine 'word' and *ḥesed̲*, are the best the psalmist can do to reassure his doubtful comrades.

64.5f. But there is a second phenomenon which also raises his anxiety level. From his towered eminence the royal look-out can descry the enemy dispositions; he can see foregatherings in Absalom's tent, 'the secret council/counsel of evil-doers'; he notices unwonted comings and goings, 'the throng of workers of iniquity'. The question is what these betoken. He would like to think (what was in fact the case, cf. 65) that the siege was about to be raised; but, like Pepys, he was slow to believe what might be to his own advantage. They will have 'strengthened for themselves', i.e. resolved upon (BDB), some evil purpose: very likely an ambush—*liṭmôn môqᵉšîm*, to conceal snares. Any such stratagem would be undetectable: 'they say, Who will look on them?' They are sure to be devising (*yaḥpᵉśû*) some beastly thing (*'ôlōt̲*): 'they have accomplished' (if *tāmᵉnû* can mean that, cf. Lam. 3.22) 'they have concealed' (if we may read *ṭāmᵉnû* with many MS) 'a devised device'—that is, they have a well-planned strategy. They are inscrutable (v. 6c), and they strike fear (v. 1b) into the psalmist's heart. He feels like Laocoon watching the Greek ships leaving Troy: 'quidquid id est, timeo Danaos'.

The Hebrew of 64 is not straightforward. Dahood points to the recurrent plays on words, *tastîrēnî* (v. 2) with *mistārîm* (v. 4), *yōruhû* with *yîrā'û* and *yir'eh* (vv. 4f.), three forms of the *ḥpś* root in v. 6; we may compare the Maschils in 52–55, or 52.6 in the Prayers. He also gives ground for thinking that *mār* was used for the poison in which arrowheads were dipped (cf. Kirkpatrick). Eaton and Kraus take *yᵉsappᵉrû* to imply reciting spells. 'They say, Who shall see *lāmô*?' is not easy. It is often taken as an indirect reference to the speakers—who shall look on them (Delitzsch). Or it could be a weak dat. commodi. Anderson suggests helpfully, 'Who will see (the ambushes)?' *tamnû* is similarly problematic. With MT's pathach it should be 1st pl. of the perf. qal of *tmm*/*tm*. So RV, supplying 'they say': but *tmm* almost always means 'be complete, finished', and BDB describe the active usage as 'very strange'. With qames it could be the 3rd pl. of the related verb *tmn* also occurring at Lam. 3.22; but these would be the only two uses. Or many MSS have *ṭāmᵉnû*, they have concealed. I have opted for the second as being less easy than the third, and less suspect than the first. A play with *liṭmôn* is probable in any case.

64.7 But God hath shot at them with an arrow
(*wayyōrēm ʾᵉlōhîm ḥēṣ*);
Sudden have been their wounds
(*pitʾôm hāyû makkôṯām*).
8 And they against whom their tongue was have made
him to stumble (*wayyakšîlûhû*):
All that see them wag the head (*yitnōdᵃdû*).
9 And every man fears (*wayyîrᵉʾû*)
And declares (*wayyaggîḏû*) the work of God,
And they wisely consider (*hiśkîlû*) of his doing.
10 The righteous shall be glad in the LORD and shall take
refuge (*wᵉḥāsâ*) in him;
And all the upright in heart shall glory.

This is one of the most difficult passages in the Prayers. The tenses are mostly perf. or *wᵉ*-consec. +impf. One may take the standard view that these represent perfects of confidence: God will do these things, so he has (virtually) done them already. This coheres with the prayer of vv. 1f., 'Hear my prayer... Preserve... Hide me...', and it is really the only interpretation available for the (normal) personal, or (occasional) national, view of the psalm's setting. I have translated the tenses literally, and rather hesitantly offer a literal exegesis; but a prophetic perfect sequence would suit my Davidic theory equally well.

64.7-10. The rebels have shot at God's perfect one with their verbal arrows, and made sudden hits; but God has given them in exchange real arrows, and sudden wounds—either during the assault on the walls (cf. 62), when they must have suffered considerable casualties, or perhaps their *mistārîm* (v. 4) were not quite sniper-proof. The royalists have had to endure much abuse and shouting ('against them their tongue'), but they have brought Absalom to the verge of ruin ('they have made him to stumble'). As in 52, or at 63.10, it seems politic to leave the pretender nameless. All that see them wag the head: most critics prefer a derivation from *nod*, to wag, whether in excitement or in scorn (Jer. 48.27), rather than *ndd*, to flee. 'All that see them' will then be the royalist defenders on the Mahanaim battlements, who will have stood cheering and jeering, like the Maltese on the quayside when the Italian suicide torpedo-boats were blown out of the water in the raid in 1942. I have rendered with presents in v. 9, as the time reference becomes increasingly vague.

The further minor success brings an access of religious thankfulness: all the defenders fear (God), and attribute the flight of their arrows to Him, and 'wisely consider' his providential goodness, as in the days of National Thanksgiving after Dunkirk in England. Perhaps they have just done so; no doubt they will do so even more after the final victory. Then (v. 10a is straight future) the righteous (that is, the royalists) will rejoice in Yahweh and will take refuge in Him: they will conduct a triumphal march to his shrine on Zion (Ps. 68), and all the upright in heart (the pro-David among the people) will cry out their Hallelujahs. *w*^{e}*yiṯhal*^{e}*lû* warns us against any confidence over the tenses: it may well be that God's arrows, the wounds, the stumbling and the nodding are all in the future, after the battle that is to come.

With so little clarity, most critics see 64 as an individual Lament: even Kirkpatrick, and Dahood. But it is hard not to see God's arrows as real arrows, and the wounds inflicted as real wounds: God does not trifle with mere words. In which case the enemies are being punished in a real battle, and we are better with a national situation (Eaton, Mowinckel, 'a protective psalm',[25] Anderson).

Chapter 7

THE STORM (65-67)

God was soon to show the two armies which side He was on.

65 For the Chief Musician. A Psalm. A Song for (*l^e*) David.

1 Praise is due (rd. *dōmiyyâ*) to thee, O God in Zion:
And unto thee shall the vow be performed.

2 O thou that hearest prayer,
Unto thee shall all flesh come.

3 Accusations (*dib̲rê*) of iniquities prevailed (*gāb̲^{e}rû*) against me:
Our transgressions, thou purgest them away (*t^{e}k̲app^{e}rēm*).

4 Blessed is the man whom thou choosest, and causest to approach *unto thee*,
That he may dwell in thy courts:
We shall be satisfied with the goodness of thy house,
The holy place of thy temple.

5 By terrible things dost thou answer us (*ta'anēnû*) in righteousness,
O God of our salvation;
Thou that art the confidence of all the ends of the earth,
And of the sea, afar off:

6 Which by his strength setteth fast the mountains;
Being girded about with might:

7 Which stilleth the roaring of the seas, the roaring of their waves,
And the tumult of the peoples.

8 They also that dwell in the uttermost parts are afraid at thy tokens:
Thou makest the outgoings of the morning and evening to rejoice.

There has been a total change of atmosphere from the preceding psalms, 52–64. In them vows have been made, of sacrifices and hymns (52.9; 56.12; 61.5, 8): now the vows are to be paid. Many of them called on God to hear prayer: now he is addressed as 'thou that hearest prayer'. In some of them the speaker seemed to be far from Zion (52.6; 61.2ff.; 63.1-7): now he speaks with confidence of the joyful praise which is to come in Zion. Earlier psalms have been chanted in silence (52f.; 56–60), or to strings (54f., 61–64): 65 is not accompanied with strings only (*mizmôr*), but is a *šîr*, like the three psalms following. *šîr* was accompanied by music of all kinds, brass and woodwind, percussion and dancing (68.4, 24f.; 149.1, 3; 150; cf. Isa. 30.29; Amos 8.3), and was a joyful Song: as Amos says, the *šîrôṯ* of the palace shall become howlings on the day of Yahweh.

What has brought about this enormous access of confidence? The ancient world was more religious than ours, and God's presence and concern went without saying: the only question was whether it was in blessing or in judgment. God has just made it clear, in the plainest possible terms, that he is with the royalists in blessings; for he has unleashed an impressive thunderstorm. 'Thou hast visited (*pāqaḏtā*) the earth. . . ' (v. 9) introduces a most detailed and loving description of the fructification of the ground, which owes nothing to an innocent enjoyment of nature. What has happened is that the long drought is broken; the barren and dry land where no water is overflows with the infinite water from the canal of heaven. There is going to be food next year: God is establishing corn for his people, and the valleys are going to be covered with it. The third strophe of the psalm (vv. 9-13) is bursting with happiness at the prospect.

The splendid thing about a thunderstorm is that it not only guarantees next year's food supply (almost); it is also a naked demonstraton of our God's almighty power. 'By terrible things (*nôrā'ôṯ*) dost thou answer us in righteousness, O God of our salvation' (v. 5). A thunderstorm is an awesome (*yr'*) event, and an answer to prayer. God provides it 'in righteousness': he has promised to bless king and people, and he is keeping his word. He is the God of our salvation: we were in need and he has supplied our want. This experience leads directly into the ancient mythology which we find exemplified at Ugarit, and which is so widespread. It is our God who has set the mountains from which he sends his bolts; the raging sea is in rebellion against him, and is quelled by his voice; the whole world can hear his thunder, and must tremble, and ultimately worship. The second strophe of the psalm (vv. 5-8) is full of the wonder of divine power and of its universality.

But why is the storm so significant in our Davidic context? It is an answer to prayer; 'by terrible things thou answerest us'. But its meaning is made much clearer by v. 3: 'Words of iniquities prevailed against me: Our transgressions, thou forgivest them'. We have heard so much of the words and lies and deceit of the enemy throughout the Prayers, the swords and arrows, even bitter words, that it is difficult to think there is no connection. In 64 the psalmist replied to such words that the king was perfect (*tām*) whom they were hitting; and this itself suggests that the rebels drew the same theological conclusion as the Succession Narrator—David was an adulterer and murderer, and God was punishing him. We have no adequate explanation for the popularity of the Revolt. People do not rebel because justice is administered inefficiently (2 Sam. 15.1-6), nor because they fancied Absalom (15.13), nor only because they have to pay taxes. David had driven out the Philistines, united the nation, and subjugated all the surrounding peoples. There must have been an enormous reservoir of goodwill towards him, and he had nothing to fear from a few jealous priests in Shechem and Dan. There must be a better explanation for the success of the Revolt than this. We have one suggested to us in the setting of the Succession story: it had its origin in the simple providentialism of the time, or to use a harsh word, its superstition.

In Israelite belief murder could be expiated only by the death of the murderer. 'So ye shall not pollute the land wherein ye are: for blood, it polluteth the land: and no expiation can be made for the land for the blood that is shed therein, but by the blood of him that shed it' (Num. 35.33; cf. Deut. 19.12f., 21.1-9). Solomon bid Benaiah kill Joab, 'that thou mayest take away the blood, which Joab shed without cause, from me and from my father's house' (1 Kgs 2.31); and Ps. 68.18 will see the rebel leaders ceremonially killed 'that the God Jah might dwell' (in his Temple). Israelite thought also gave a special position to the king: he especially was the funnel of divine grace, and any sin in him must be a unique pollutant to the land—hence the ease with which unsuccessful kings were deposed and murdered. So by his notorious sin with Bathsheba and (much more) with Uriah (since it was in Uriah that blood was involved), David had exposed himself to great weakness. He might make a nominal expiation by accepting the whip and the hyssop (51.7f.), but everyone knew that this was not the law: all eyes were fixed on Yahweh, whether he had accepted so light an affliction, or whether he would regard the land as polluted. The vital test was the rain. The first year that there was a poor harvest would stir speculation; the second would make it clear that God had indeed remembered David's sin, and would send no more blessing until that sin was expiated in his blood. No king of Israel could undertake that the rain would fall regularly; and the first succession of two poor harvests would be the moment of opportunity for ambitious princes and envious priesthoods. In such circumstances, a rebellion was inevitable: the only question (as we would put it) was how long the royal luck would hold.

The royal luck gave out in the year of the Revolt; and the postponement of the autumn rains, which we have seen reflected in the drought at Mahanaim, lent force to the rebels' providentialism. Small wonder if they sought to save lives in combat by constantly shooting their verbal arrows, so likely to corrupt the loyalty of the equally superstitious defenders: 'Why is there no rain? Why has God cursed the land? Is it not for the king's sin? There will be no blessing on the land till the blood of Uriah is purged'. Small wonder if the psalmist harps nervously on their 'words'. But the royal luck turned in the nick of time; and there are few things so impressive as a really heavy thunderstorm, and when fertility is in question, few things so decisive as enough rainfall to overflow the furrows and beat down their ridges. 'Charges of iniquity prevailed against me', says the psalmist in the king's name; but lo, all is well, 'our transgressions, thou coverest them'. Well, God seems to have covered them for now; but we have not yet reached the end of the tale (cf. Ps. 69).

A modern providentialist might take heart at the raising of the siege, but to our singer this was no clear sign: the rebels might be planning a mock withdrawal and an ambush (64.5). The storm was no mockery: this was God, and none other. Its impressiveness continues to fill the following psalms. God's deeds are *nôrā'* at 66.3 and 5; the earth yields its increase at 67.6; and there is a full description in 68.7-10:

> O God, when thou wentest forth before thy people,
> When thou didst march through the wilderness;
> The earth trembled, the heavens also dropped at the presence of
> God...
> Thou, O God, didst send a plentiful rain,
> Thou didst confirm thine inheritance when it was weary...

The psalmist of 68 saw the thunderstorm as a good augury for victory in the battle.

One final point may occur to us about the rainstorm. Most of Israel sided with the rebels: the Succession narrator regularly calls them 'Israel', and the Passion narrator 'the men of Israel' (2 Sam. 16.15; 17.24). There can be little doubt that this included Judah; and it was Israel and Judah generally that will have suffered the drought and bad harvest. The East Bank was loyal for the most part, but that was *force majeure*: David had his garrisons there. The day at the battle of Zalmon was turned, as we shall see, by the tribesmen from Zebulun and Naphtali, who were free agents. Now it is in well-watered Galilee, in Zebulun and Naphtali, that the rain is heaviest in Israel; and so a light rainfall in any one year will be less disastrous there than further south. So perhaps the paean of gratitude over the storm suggests an explanation for the Galilaeans' loyalty too.

65.1-4. Delitzsch and others loyal to MT read *dûmiyyâ*, translating 'Unto thee is resignation as praise': but this seems forced (Anderson), and most critics read *dōmiyyâ* as fem. part. qal *dmh* I, to be like, fitting, which is the understanding of LXX πρέπει, Syr. Vg. This yields excellent sense: the royalists have only been able to approach God from the ends of the land, but now praise is due in Zion, and the royal vow will be paid there. By his dramatic intervention in the storm, God has shown himself to be a God who listens to prayer; and flesh cannot resist such power. 'All flesh', that is (as normally) all mankind (cf. vv. 5-7), will be driven to bow their heads and come to Zion to worship the all-powerful God of Israel; in particular the warlike Ishmaelites who have been the spearhead of the Revolt will be awed into subjection. As 66.2 will put it, 'How terrible (*nôrâ'*) are thy works! Through the greatness of thy power shall thine enemies cringe unto thee'.

The delight in so evident a revelation of divine blessing is increased by the contrast with affairs before the storm. The connection between sin and drought is made expressly in Solomon's Consecration prayer for the Temple: 'When heaven is shut up and there is no rain because they have sinned against thee, if they pray. . ., then hear thou in heaven and forgive the sin of thy servants' (1 Kgs 8.35f.). *dāḇār* is a normal Hebrew word for a charge or accusation (Deut. 22.14, 17, 20, etc.; 1 Sam. 22.15). *gāḇᵉrû* is perfect, and refers to a state of affairs which is over: with *min* it means 'to be stronger than' in David's Lament (1 Sam. 1.23), and often 'to prevail' as with enemies in Exodus 17, or the waters in Genesis 7. The charges were too much for king and speaker—but now, our transgressions, thou forgivest them. The 'our' is tactful: of course not only the king's supposed shortcomings were in question—none of us is perfect. The rain shows dramatically that God has put all that away, and will go on doing so.

The evident forgiveness of David's sin leads on to a word of blessing for him; for David is the man whom God chooses (*bḥr* is used especially of him, 1 Sam. 16.8, 9, 10, etc.), and admits to permanent (*yiškōn*) residence in his Temple courts, as being king. In later times the combination *bḥr/qrb* was used of the priests (Num. 16.5), and 'dwelling' on Zion might be the privilege of any pious Israelite (Ps. 15.1); but here it is David whose sins are forgiven, and who is now to return to the happy sacrificial atmosphere of his sanctuary in perpetuity. With him goes the priest-poet who has been his faithful spokesman. He looks forward in his hunger to being satiated with the great Temple communion-offerings—Anderson is surely right to say that sacrificial meals are in mind, not just spiritual delights.

65.5-8 now expands the universal claims adumbrated in v. 2b. Lightning is seen by all and thunder is heard by all; and this awesome spectacle, the answer to the psalmist's prayers and the salvation of his community, must surely win the faith of the ends of the world, and beyond on the seas. We have come a long way from 55, where the speaker so feared for his life, and 60, where he could pit the loyal East Bank against the rebel West Bank: now the whole world must be for God. The thought goes back to Creation for a moment, with God like a giant setting the mountains in place, his loins clad in *g*ᵉ*ḇûrâ*, his extension, Strength. Ps. 68.8, 17 suggest that Yahweh set out from Mount Sinai on his storm- and war-path (whether by the psalmist or his editor). It is from such a mountain fastness that Yahweh, like Baal from Saphon, asserts his dominion over the sea and its rebel waves, and over their counterpart, the multitude of the peoples. We should not, with Mowinckel and Kraus, excise the last *metri causa*: they are the enemies who are brought to cringe by God's awesome acts in 66.2, and the psalmist is much more concerned with them than he is with the Eastern Mediterranean. Indeed, he says, people everywhere are in awe at God's 'signs', his thunder and lightning: the east and the west exult in his power.

65.9 Thou hast visited the earth and given it abundance
(pâqaḏta hâ'âreṣ watt^ešōq^eqehā),
Thou greatly enrichest it;
The river of God is full of water:
Thou providest them corn, for so preparest thou her.
10 Thou waterest her furrows abundantly;
Thou lowerest the ridges thereof:
Thou makest it soft with showers;
Thou blessest the springing thereof.
11 Thou hast crowned (*'iṭṭartā*) the year of thy goodness;
And thy paths drop fatness.
12 They drop upon the pastures of the wilderness:
And the hills are girded with joy.
13 The pastures are clothed with flocks;
The valleys also are covered over with corn;
They shout for joy, they also sing.

There are three verbs in the perfect, *pāqaḏtā*, *'iṭṭartā*, *lāḇ^ešû*, as testimonies to the awesome thing which God has done, the sign which he has given in answer to prayer: he has visited the land of Israel with his rainstorm, he has crowned the year of blessing, and he has clothed the pastures with flocks. It is December, or perhaps January, for the rains have been very late. The land has been ploughed and sown (or perhaps sown and ploughed: the order varied); this was sowing time according to the Gezer calendar.[2] Now, suddenly, the land has been soaked: not just showers, inches of rain. God has visited the earth and given it *abundance*—the po'lel of *šuq*, to be abundant. He has *greatly* enriched it. As the farmer irrigates his land with channel or conduit (*peleg*), so has God an enormous canal of water in heaven, which he has sent cascading down. He is making ready his people's ('their') corn, for with this teeming rain ('so') he is making the earth ('her') ready. He *drenches* the furrows (*rawwēh*, inf. abs., to saturate); he *beats down* (*naḥēṯ*, inf. abs. piel, to press down) the ridges or clods; he *melts* the earth with the rain (*mug*, po'lel); he gives life to ('blesses') the young shoots. This was not a light drizzle which refreshed the tops: it was a massive downpour.

65.11ff. A more sceptical mind might hardly speak of the psalmist's recent experiences as 'the year of thy goodness'; and in another mood he will say, 'Thou hast tried us, as silver is tried' (66.10). But the religious man's sense of gratitude is commonly increased by afflictions; and the singer sees himself as repeatedly delivered from death. However this last blessing is by far the greatest: God has crowned it all with his transparent public endorsement of the king's righteousness. He is thought of as on expedition from Sinai through the wilderness (68.7f.), attended by twenty thousand angelic chariots (68.17); wherever the divine army passes overhead, fruitfulness pours down in its tracks (*ma'gāleîḵā*). Not just the fields, but the uncultivated areas beyond, the hilltops, are included in the divine bounty: they are girded with joy, as God was with strength. The sheep which had been under threat from the drought are everywhere: there is now grass for them to crop on the hillsides, which seem to wear them like a fleece. The valleys beneath are similarly covered with the green corn as with a garment (*'ṭp*); they cheer, like the Philistines in 60.8, and sing (*šîr*) with the psalmist.

Psalm 65 has deeply divided commentators. Delitzsch and Kirkpatrick scent a military victory as well as an abundant harvest, and find the two in 699 BC (Isa. 37.30). Gunkel and Kraus see a public liturgy of thanksgiving in vv. 1-8, to which a personal thanksgiving for harvest has been attached, in a different metre (vv. 9-13); Jacquet has two attached fragments, in two different metres. Mowinckel[3] views the psalm as a harvest thanksgiving at the New Year festival, combining the themes of forgiveness, creation and harvest blessing. Dahood takes the perfects as precative, and understands the psalm as a prayer for rain; and Eaton similarly stresses the elements of anticipation and petition. Weiser thinks the detail suggests spring rather than autumn, and opts for a Passover thanksgiving, perhaps in Josiah's reign (Kirkpatrick thought of Passover too). Anderson sees it more as a Thanksgiving for the averting of a drought.

It is not a sound argument to take a change of metre as the basis for a supposed change of author. Hebrew poetry is not governed by strict metrical rules as Greek poetry was, and we have seen a change of mood reflected in a change of metre in 60.6-8 (tricola for bicola) without Gunkel insisting on a fragments hypothesis (cf. on 45, 53, 57). There is no sign that the last verses are personal. But the detail of the psalm does not correspond well with an Autumn Festival setting. The concentration is on an exceptionally heavy rainfall averting a drought, as Anderson says; and the furrows and young growth (*ṣimḥāh*) suggest winter—but there is no regular festival in winter. A Davidic setting accounts for the plainly felt link between the awesome rainfall which is an answer to prayer (vv. 5-13) and the king's change of status from loaded with guilt to demonstrably innocent (vv. 2-4). It also sharpens the motive for including the world in the resultant worship; the 'strong note of anticipation' (Eaton) of worship at Zion; and the recurrence of the rainstorm theme in the next three psalms.

66 For the Chief Musician. A Song, a Psalm.
1 Make a joyful noise unto God, all the earth:
2 Sing forth the glory of his name:
Make his praise glorious.
3 Say unto God, How terrible are thy works!
Through the greatness of thy power shall thine enemies cringe (*yᵉḵaḥᵃšû*) unto thee.
4 All the earth shall worship thee, And shall sing unto thee;
They shall sing to thy name.
(Selah

For the first time in the Prayers, the name of David is missing from the Heading; and this is true of 67 and 71 also. Psalm 71 is less of a problem, as many MSS treat it as a unity with 70, whose tone and content are markedly similar; but this is not true of 66 and 67, and we have to decide whether 'For David' has dropped out, or whether the two psalms are later insertions in the series.

The former alternative is to be preferred: 66 and 67 were integral parts of the David sequence, and David's name has been dropped because, unlike so many of the other Prayers, they seem to have no reference to David's life of persecution and battle. But a more significant feature is their similarity of tone and content to 65, and more generally to the Prayers. There is an emphasis on the awesome display of divine power (66.3 *nôrā'*; 66.5 *nôrā'*) as in 65.5 *nôrā'ôṯ*; and this leads on to God's blessing of the harvest in 67.6 as in 65.9-13. Associated with this is the coming worship of the nations in 66.1-4 and 67.2-7 as in 65.2-5, 7f.: these two themes dominate 65 and 67, and the opening part of 66, and recur in 68.7-10 (rainstorm providing food for 'the poor') and 68.28-32 (forced worship of the nations), as well as 72. In 66.13f. the psalmist promises to pay his vows as in 65.1, and these are sacrifices (66.15) as in 65.4: we have often had hints of these vowed sacrifices in earlier Prayers. Our psalmist protests his purity from sin in 66.18, and this is again a theme which we had in 65.3, 64.4 ('the perfect one'),and which I have argued to be hanging over the whole sequence since 51. A contrast with the earlier Prayers is that they often called upon God to hear the speaker's prayer, but in 66.19f. as in 65.2, 5 it is triumphantly asserted that God has heard prayer. Thus both psalms seem to belong integrally to the Prayers, and more particularly in the happier context of 65–68, where God's rainstorm leads to expectations of further blessing.

66.1-4. The opening verses develop the universalist claims of 65. The whole world is to praise God under 'his name', Yahweh, with joyful shouting (*ha̱rî'û*), chanting to stringed music (*zammerû*), cries of praise ('Say unto God...'), prostrations (*yištaḥawû*), and the payment of tribute (*yeḵaḥašû*). 'Thine enemies' and 'all the earth' are treated as effectively the same. *kḥš* implies an element of deception, and there is no hoping that the worship offered by 'the peoples' will be genuine. But the first thing is that they should be found 'humbly bringing pieces of silver', and the scene is painted in clearer colours in 68.29-34.

The thing that will force the peoples to their knees is 'thy works', 'the greatness of thy power'; and (despite much learned opinion) this bears no relation to their having heard the amazing tale of Israel's deliverance from Egypt. The psalms are normally quite realistic documents, written by intelligent people. What will finally bring the peoples to Zion is the greatness of God's power exerted on the battlefield: when the fight is won, the psalmist will say, 'Thy (David's) God hath commanded thy strength'. But in the meantime he appeals to God's awesome works, which in 65.4 meant the thunderstorm; and again in 68 the kingdoms of the earth are to sing unto God whose strength is in the skies—'Lo, he uttereth his voice, and that a mighty voice'. Such an appeal might seem to be simple-minded and parochial at first blush; for the people of Ugarit worshipped Baal-Hadad as a thunder-god on Mt Saphon, and the Israelites can hardly have been so ignorant as not to know that many neighbouring peoples similarly ascribed such powers to their own god. But the point is that 'thine enemies' in the present campaign are not Syrians: they are Ishmaelites from the desert-lands south of the Negev, where the annual rainfall is less than 100mm.,[4] and where thunderstorms are virtually unknown. A point is made of this in 68.29-34: Egypt, and 'the calves of the peoples', the frontier tribes, and Cush further south still, worship gods who command no thunder and bring no rain—they are to ascribe strength to the God of Israel who utters his mighty voice in the thunder, and does deliver the rain. We have the same appeal, but before the battle, in 66.1-8. Just as the rebels had used theology to tempt the royalists to desert (since God was plainly withholding the rain for the king's sin), so does our psalmist use theology to tempt the Ishmaelites to desert, since God has so plainly shown his support for the king in the storm. The editor has added the Selah at this point: no doubt the Passion narrative spoke of the rain.

66.5 Come, and see the works of God;
He is terrible in his doing toward the children of men.
6 He turned the sea into dry land:
They went through the river on foot:
There let us rejoice.
7 He ruleth by his might for ever;
His eyes observe the nations:
Let not the rebels exalt themselves.
(Selah

The standard Red Sea/Jordan interpretation is ringed with difficulties. The peoples are asked to 'come and see the works of God': what are they to come and see? In 46.8f., the only close parallel, they were to come and behold a huge bonfire of their captured muniments.[5] Verse 6ab is supposed to refer to two different events: 'He turned the sea into dry land' to Exodus 14, 'They went through the river on foot' to Joshua 3. These are indeed linked in Psalm 114, but what is coupled there is the double miracle, the fleeing of the sea, the driving back of Jordan: here the language corresponds to what is normal after any prolongued drought—the Jordan is reduced to a fordable meander, and the north end of the Dead Sea to a dry waste. Especial problems are posed by v. 6c *šām niśmeḥā-bô*, of which the natural translation, with RVmg, is 'there let us rejoice in him'. Where? At the Red Sea? Or at Gilgal? Many opt for a doubtful translation, 'There did we rejoice in him', e.g. Delitzsch (who indeed substitutes 'Then...'), on the ground that ''*'āz* with the imperfect takes the signification of a aorist', and that the cohortative does 'occasionally, at least' have the same meaning. This has the ring of special pleading: the rejoicing is much more conveniently that of the Israelites in Exodus 15. But even this is suspect, for how is the change of person to be explained, 'They went through...There did we...'? A first person plural 'solidarity' including the present generation with the fathers, is extremely rare in early texts (cf. Pss. 114, 78, 105-106). Delitzsch offers Josh. 5. lK; Hos. 12.5 as support.

66.9-12 gives an account of *recent* perils and deliverances as a basis for the peoples to praise God (v. 8), and it is easy to take vv. 5-7 in the same sense; more especially as 68.22 has God promise, 'I will bring again from Bashan, I will bring again *from the depths of the sea*,

That thou mayest dip thy foot in blood. . . ' The peoples are to come and behold God's works, a source of awe to sons of men such as them (cf. 62.9 *b^e^nê 'āḏām*): the royalist army which left Jerusalem in such straits, has now recrossed the Jordan (v. 6b) and been brought out into a land of abundance (v. 12). This was done in God's usual majestic way (*mip'alôṯ*, v. 5). When Joab's forces came down the Jabbok, the heavy rain had made the river impassable without horses. They therefore pressed on southwards, and were able to ford the river on foot (no mention of their being dryshod): G. Adam Smith[6] reports the fording of the Jordan three feet deep after rain as high as Beisan, and the Jordan is broader (90ft) and shallower near the Dead Sea. The river is still within its banks, and there is dry land where soon the Dead Sea will extend once more. The prince-poet has remained with David in Mahanaim ('*They* went through. . . '), but he means (*niśm^e^ḥâ*, cohort.) to join in thanksgiving with the expedition on the site of God's further manifest deliverance ('There shall we rejoice in him') when the time comes. God always has the last word, for his power is supreme (v. 7a); he has his eye on the Ishmaelites (v. 7b), who would do well to join the royalists now (v. 8); and the rebels should keep their heads down. This is the first time that the psalmist has faced the uncomfortable reality that the royalists are not just up against a foreign invasion of 'strangers', 'the nations', 'the peoples', trying to impose a puppet government under Absalom. Beside them are *sôr^e^rîm*, rebels, whom we shall meet again in 68.6, 18. The actual fighting has been mainly with the mercenaries; but as the armies muster for the decisive battle, there is no denying that thousands of Israelites have sided with Absalom. They are bidden not to exalt themselves.

In this way we have a natural reading of the Hebrew, and an explanation of the text in terms of current military realities, answering to our overall context. The second Selah will have been inserted after v. 7 to explain to later generations how Joab's forces contrived to cross the barrier of the Jordan and reach the West Bank. Like Fr Choblay in A. Grimble's *A Pattern of Islands*,[7] their God had turned up trumps again.

66.8 O bless our God, ye peoples.
And make the voice of his praise to be heard:
9 Which putteth our soul in life,
And suffereth not our feet to be moved.

10 For thou, O God, hast proved us:
Thou hast tried us, as silver is tried.
11 Thou broughtest us into the net;
Thou layedst anguish (*mûʿāqâ*) upon our loins.
12 Thou hast caused men to ride over our heads;
We went through fire and through water;
But thou broughtest us out into abundance.

The peoples, and especially the Ishmaelite mercenaries, are called upon to join in praising Yahweh for his delivering of the royalists. They had been very close to death (55.4f.), but God has now set them securely among the living; they had been close to stumbling and falling, but now their feet are firmly standing. The siege of Mahanaim is raised, and the battle is now transferred to the West Bank. God had surely put his loyal ones to the test, in the evacuation of Zion, the fight to cross the Kidron, the withdrawal up Olivet, and the trials of the siege. He has smelted them, as silver is smelted. The psalmist adds two further metaphors to cover the anguish of the last months. They have been like a wild animal fallen into the hunter's net, and struggling to get out (*mᵉṣûḏâ*, cf. Ezek. 12.13; 17.20); God has put anguish (*mûʿāqâ*, what makes one cry out, *ʿiq*)[8] in their loins, the seat of such emotion (Isa 21.3; Nah. 2.10). They have been like prisoners of war exposed to the disagreeable custom of being forced to lie down in rows for the victors to drive their chariots over (Isa. 51.23). They have been like the same subjected to a double ordeal by fire and by water (Isa. 43.2). But now all this is over. Word has come to Mahanaim that Joab is across the Jordan, brought out by God to 'saturation' (*rᵉwāyâ*, cf. 65.10 *rawwêh*). His men are soaked but happy, for they know what the rain means too.

66.13 I will come into thy house with burnt offerings,
I will pay thee my vows,
14 Which my lips have uttered,
And my mouth hath spoken when I was in distress.
15 I will offer thee burnt offerings of fatlings,
With incense of rams;
I will offer bullocks with goats. (Selah)
16 Come, and hear, all ye that fear God,
And I will declare what he hath done for my soul.
17 I cried unto him with my mouth,
And high praise was under my tongue.

18 If I had regarded iniquity in my heart,
The Lord would not hear:
19 But verily God hath heard;
He hath attended to the voice of my prayer.
20 Blessed be God,
Which hath not turned away my prayer,
Nor his mercy from me.

66.13-15. The change of person from 'we' to 'I' has caused many to stumble, but Delitzsch already saw it as the people's representative, the high priest, and Birkeland,[9] Mowinckel,[10] and Eaton speak of the king. We have had a similar move at 52.8, 'But as for me, I am like a green olive tree. . . ', and 60.9, 'Who will bring me into the strong city. . .?' I am combining Delitzsch and Birkeland: the speaker is the king's son whom he has appointed priest, and he will offer the sacrifices in the Temple ('thy house') in the king's name, just as he is now offering praise in the king's name. He vowed to give thank(-offering)s for ever at the end of 52, and at the end of 56 said, 'Thy vows are upon me, O God: I will render thank-offerings unto thee' (56.12). At the end of 61 he is able to say, 'For thou, O God, hast heard my vows. . . that I may daily perform my vows' (61.5, 8); and we have seen him looking forward to a share in the sacrifices in 63.5 and 65.4. Pss. 65.1 and 66.13-15 show a renewed enthusiasm, in which the offerings are thought of as imminent. We can testify to the speaker's truthfulness in his having uttered such vows in trouble, and his genuineness in wishing to pay them is transparent. The scale of the sacrifices is plainly large—even Gunkel, who thought the speaker a private citizen, conceded that he must be wealthy. But the vows were not only large but to be performed daily (61.8), for ever (52.9); and that must imply royalty.

We have a third Selah after v. 15; perhaps giving some account of how David and his retinue came not to be present at the battle. We have a fragment of the Passion Narrative at 2 Sam. 18.1f.:

> And David numbered the people that were with him, and set captains of thousands and captains of hundreds over them. And David sent forth the people, a third part under the hand of Joab, and a third part under the hand of Abishai the son of Zeruiah, and a third part under the hand of Ittai the Gittite.

'David', and the simple factuality, suggest that this is the Passion narrator; but the piece probably belongs with the 66.7 Selah, celebrating Joab's march. The following verses, 2 Sam. 18.3ff., use 'the king', and speak of the people's loyalty, David's courage and his care for Absalom: all matters close to the heart of the Succession Narrator. But it is something of this which is needed at Ps. 66.15 too.

66.16-20. The psalmist frames his last lines as David's personal confession to his followers; in time it will become his own personal confession to the annual procession celebrating the events—'all ye that fear God'. We have listened to his cry, his Prayers through the 'distress' of 52–64. There could be no exalted praise (*rômam*) during these trials, but it was 'under his tongue', waiting to be expressed (Eaton). We have often heard of the wicked lying in wait for his soul, or hunting it: now he will declare in the liturgy what God has done for his soul (v. 9, 'our soul', which God set in life). Only a national figure can be imagined as giving such testimony ever, let alone regularly, as the liturgical use of the psalm implies. But all has turned, as we have so often heard, on the king's purity (v. 18). Was Uriah's death a constructive murder? If so, he had 'looked on iniquity in his heart', and God would never have been able to forgive him; the pollution of the land must have followed inevitably, and a lasting drought. But 'verily God hath heard', and the downpour is the transparent evidence that he has. So Uriah's death had been a manslaughter. David had admitted his complicity ('Deliver me from bloodguiltiness', 51.14), but kings must often involve themselves in matters of life and death. He had expiated his guilt with a whipping, a draught of bitters, and a ritual bath, and God had accepted this (51.7-9). God has now sent both the rain and the expectation of victory. The psalmist blesses him for so evidently hearing his prayer, and for not withdrawing his *ḥeseḏ*, his promised favour.

The use of 'we' in vv. 1-12, and of 'I' in vv. 13-20, has posed a problem from the last century. It would be easy to see two psalms combined (Kraus, Duhm), the first a national hymn-and-lament, the second a personal thanksgiving; but the first lacks a convincing end, and the second a suitable opening, and many have attempted to find a setting for the two together—Gunkel as a rich man's thanksgiving to which he has prefixed a more general community hymn, Weiser as an annual liturgical hymn, to which an individual has added his personal testimony, etc.—so Anderson, Rogerson and McKay, Jacquet; more vaguely Dahood). Birkeland, Mowinckel and Eaton continue the view of Delitzsch and Kirkpatrick that there is a basic unity to the psalm, with the national leader in the second half expressing representatively the national thanksgiving of the first. Kirkpatrick offered Hezekiah as the speaker, in 701. The confidence of both sides is a cause of anxiety: Mowinckel[11] thought the representative view obvious, while Anderson thinks the personal individual view obvious. But the scale of the offerings in v. 15 contrasts with the simplicity of the votive sacrifices for individuals in Lev. 22.18f., and are hardly to be written off as poetic hyperbole. Eaton[12] properly stresses too the situation implied by an address to 'All you who fear God': this should be the community leader.

Almost all exegetes take v. 6 to refer to the Exodus; Dahood and Kraus (apparently) to the Exodus only, taking *hannāhār* as the Red Sea also, on the basis of Ugaritic parallels. Kraus offers a plausible explanation for *šām*:[13] the peoples are to come and see Israel's annual celebration of the crossing of 'the river' in the spring festival at Gilgal. But there is no mention of Gilgal in this psalm, nor any reference to the Exodus experiences anywhere in the Prayers, not even in 68, where Egypt and perhaps Sinai have their place. Otherwise critics have been reduced to emending *šām* (say to *šimᵉᶜû*, Gunkel), or giving it curious meanings ('Behold!', Dahood); and to taking the cohortative as a perfect ('There did we rejoice', Delitzsch and many).

It is also almost invariable to understand *sôrᵉrîm* in v. 7c as identical with *gôyim* in v. 7b. This is unwary. Not only is *srr* used elsewhere of *Israel's* stubborn rebellion against Yahweh (Hos. 4.16; Isa. 30.1; Neh. 9.29: the fundamental image is of a son in rebellion against his parents, Deut. 21.18); but 68 shows that the two are treated differently. The nations there are humbly to bring their pieces of silver, God having scattered them in their delight in war (68.30); they are to be glad and rejoice before the God who judges them (67.4). Gentiles are always welcome at Israel's festivals, bringing tribute. But the *sôrᵉrîm* are not welcome; they are rebels and traitors. If they are lucky they will have their lands confiscated and be sent to farm the desert (68.6). Their leaders will be paraded in chains, and will be sacrificed as 'gifts among men'; they will have their hairy scalps beaten in (68.18-23).

67 For the Chief Musician; on stringed instruments. A Psalm. A Song.
1 God be merciful unto us, and bless us,
And cause his face to shine with us; (Selah
2 That thy way may be known upon earth,
Thy victory (*yᵉšû'āṯeḵā*) among all nations.
3 Let the peoples praise thee, O God;
Let all the peoples praise thee.
4 O let the nations be glad and sing for joy:
For thou shalt judge the peoples with equity,
And lead the nations upon earth
(Selah

5 Let the peoples praise thee, O God;
Let all the peoples praise thee.
6 The earth hath yielded her increase:
God, even our own God, shall bless us.
7 God shall bless us;
And all the ends of the earth shall fear him.

Psalm 67 is often taken to be a Harvest Thanksgiving, suited to the celebration of Tabernacles; but, as Kraus says, this is far from clear, and Gunkel is only able to turn it into the Harvest Thanksgiving by re-writing the first line, and other phrases. In fact the produce of the land is mentioned only in three words in v. 6a. Most of the psalm is not thanksgiving at all, but petition for God's blessing, and for the nations to fear him and join in his praise.

The psalm is best understood in the context of the series in which tradition has set it. Psalm 65 saw God as drenching the furrows with his thunderstorm, beating down their ridges and blessing the new growth (*ṣimḥāh*, v. 10). This was an awesome sight (v. 5), and might be hoped to bring 'all flesh' to come to God (v. 2); 'all the ends of the earth' would come to trust in him (v. 5), and 'they that dwell in the uttermost parts' would fear his tokens (v. 8). Such worship would not come easily: God has to still 'the tumult of the peoples' first (v. 7). Similarly in 66 'all the earth' is called upon to make a joyful noise to God, sing forth Yahweh's glory, make his praise glorious, worship and sing to him, etc. (vv. 1f., 4). But it is not expected that the nations will do such a thing willingly: it is his awesome works which will compel their submission (vv. 3, 5)—'Through the greatness of thy power shall thine enemies cringe unto thee'. In 68 similarly God begins the battle by going before his people, making the heavens drip, sending a plentiful rain and preparing of his goodness (food) for the poor (vv. 7-10). Then in v. 12 the kings flee, and in v. 29 they are seen bringing tribute to God for his temple at Jerusalem.

This linked complex of ideas comes frequently in the Old Testament: when Israel is obedient, or forgiven (65.3), then God will bless the land, and defeat her enemies, who will then offer tribute, and join in Yahweh's worship. So Lev. 26.3-12: (a) 'If ye walk in my statutes, and keep my commandments, and do them; then (b) I will give your rains in their season, and the land shall yield her increase (*w*^{e}*nâṯ*^{e}*nâ hā'āreṣ y*^{e}*ḇûlāh*, = 67.6a)..., and (c) I will give peace in the land... And ye shall chase your enemies, and they shall fall before you by the sword...' Deut. 28.1-14: '(a) if thou shalt hearken diligently unto the voice of the LORD thy God... (b) Blessed shalt thou be in the city, and blessed shalt thou be in the field... (c) The LORD shall cause thine enemies that rise up against thee to be smitten before thee... And all the peoples of the earth shall see that thou art called by the name of the LORD; and they shall be afraid of thee'. Ezek. 34.24-31: (a) 'I the LORD will be their God, and my servant David prince among them... (b) I will cause the shower to come down in its season; there shall be showers of blessing... and the earth shall yield her increase (*w*e*hā'āreṣ tittēn y*e*bûlāh*)... (c) and they shall know that I am the LORD, when I have... delivered them from the hand of those that made bondmen of them'. The somewhat surprising collocation of the peoples' defeat and their praise of Yahweh is well seen in Psalm 47: God is the great King over all the earth, who subdues the peoples under us and the nations under our feet (vv. 2f.). They are then called upon to worship him gladly: 'O clap your hands, all ye peoples; Shout unto God with the voice of triumph... Sing praises unto God, sing praises... ' (vv. 1, 6). The explanation of this is that with the conquest the peoples are co-opted into the Israelite empire: 'The princes of the peoples are gathered together as the people of the God of Abraham' (v. 9, *PSK*, pp. 153-59). The British felt much the same in the last century. The Ashanti and the Zulu must be conquered first, and if possible Christianized; and they can then be expected to send delegations to take part in the Diamond Jubilee of the Great White Queen.

67.1. So Psalm 67 is not a Harvest Thanksgiving at all: it is a prayer for God's blessing in bringing the nations to fear him (v. 7), and so to worship him; that is, in the first place in defeating them. The land's giving of its increase is merely incidental to this, and is mentioned only incidentally, as a sign that all is well between us and God; it is a reason for confidence in expecting the divine *b*e*rākâ*. Prayer is made first for God to be merciful to us (*y*e*ḥonnēnû*), the opening imperative of 56 and 57, also battle prayers: everything depends on God's continuing to cover our sins (65.3). He is to 'cause his face to shine with us', a phrase used elsewhere in psalms looking towards battles. In Psalm 31 'thou hast not shut me up into the hand of the enemy' (v. 8), and they devise to take away the speaker's life (v. 13); he prays, 'Deliver me from the hand of mine enemies, and from them that persecute me. Make thy face to shine upon thy servant'. Even more clearly is Psalm 80 a national lament: God is angry with his people, and Israel/Joseph, whose branches had spread out to the Sea and the River, is burnt with fire and cut down. Three times the psalmist asks: 'Turn us again, O (LORD) God (of hosts): (And) cause thy face to shine, and we shall be saved' (vv. 3, 7, 19). The phrase occurs also in the priestly blessing (Num. 6.25), which must often have been used before battles; but the variant in 67.1, '... shine *with* us' may especially stress 'on our side, and against the enemy'.

67.2. God is asked to act so that his 'way' may be known upon earth, his *y^ešû'â* among all nations. Gunkel comments optimistically: 'Wenn die Heiden von all dem Gute hören, was Israel von Jahve empfängt, sollen sie sagen: was ist das für ein Gott, der so freundlich schenken kann!' But I do not think that those who gathered in the enormous bounty of the Nile or the Euphrates would have been much impressed with the product of Israel's marginal hill-terraces; and the Israelites were only too aware of the comparative wealth of their oppressive neighbours (Pss. 49; 73). What the psalmist does expect to strike the nations is the victories which he grants over them in battle 'by the greatness of his power' (66.3): for *y^ešû'â* is a standard word for victory. The overthrow of the Egyptians was a *y^ešû'â* at Exod. 14.13; 15.2; and the same word is used for the defeat of the Philistines in 1 Sam. 14.45 and of Judah's neighbours in 2 Chron. 20.17. BDB give it as the closest meaning for four texts in Isaiah and eleven in the Psalter, including 68.19. So God's 'way' may be interpreted by the parallel ('power', Anderson). It is his habitual custom to give victory to his people, and the heathen are more likely to have said, 'What sort of a God is that, who wins every battle against us!' It is that which will bring them cringing with their tribute, to join in the national, now indeed to be the international, thanksgiving.

67.4-7. The nations' rejoicing is to be on the basis of God's 'judging them with equity', and leading them. We are not to think, even so early, of Birkeland's 'fanatical nationalism',[14] or at least not in any narrow sense. There is something of the dignity of the French 'mission civilisative', of Vergil's vision of the vocation of Rome, 'et totum sub leges mitteret orbem'. When the peoples had given up their pretensions to independence, they would enjoy true peace in observing the laws of the God of the whole world. He, in person of his chosen king, would judge their affairs and direct them, leading them like a shepherd (Ps. 23.3). They would attend his festivals with thanks. It is a fine pipe-dream.

Commentators are divided over the force of the perfect *nāṯ^e^nâ* in v. 6a: Dahood, followed by Anderson, takes it as a precative perfect, and thus a prayer for rain, in view of the parallel *y^e^ḇār^e^ḵēnû*; Eaton translates, 'the earth shall yield. . . ' But I think it best to take it as a true perfect, with the majority. *y^e^ḇûlāh*, 'its increase', however, does not have to refer to the final harvest: in Ps. 78.46 it is the growing corn, 'He gave also their increase (*y^e^ḇûlām*) to the caterpillar'. In this way it will be parallel to *ṣimḥāh* in 65.10: there the springing growth of the furrows was the earnest that 'Thou providest them corn', and in 68.10 the 'plentiful rain' was a sign that 'Thou, O God, didst prepare of thy goodness for the poor'. So here 'the land has given its increase', and the springing green tells the psalmist that 'The valleys also are covered over with corn' (65.13). All is well: 'our transgressions, thou coverest them'; God will bless us in the coming battle, and all the ends of the earth shall fear him.

The Harvest Festival interpretation—so probable in an agricultural community like Israel, so mysteriously almost absent from the Psalter (65?; 67?)—has attracted most exegetes: Delitzsch, Kirkpatrick, Gunkel, Mowinckel,[15] Weiser, Rogerson and McKay, Jacquet. But its difficulties are stressed by Kraus; and Dahood and Anderson say correctly that 67 is much more prayer than thanksgiving. The centrality of the Gentiles' worship of God is clearly seen by Weiser, Rogerson and McKay and Jacquet, but a slightly unreal air pervades their comments ('worldwide conversion', Rogerson; 'recognition of divine salvation granted to all the nations', Weiser), as if the psalmist were the precursor of the White Fathers or the Church Missionary Society. Only Eaton brings a touch of reality: the nations' praise is anticipatory, and depends upon Israel's victory, and dominion over the world. The church of England has thought the psalm suitable for the Marriage Service; but that great English Christian warrior, Oliver Cromwell, was nearer the mark when he sent his soldiers into battle chanting these psalms. H.G. Jefferson[16] gives links with Canaanite poetry covering many of the words in the psalm, and suggests that it is ancient.

Chapter 8

THE BITTERS OF VICTORY (68)

Psalm 68 is the victory hymn of the royalists after the defeat of Absalom's rebellion at Zalmon in the forest of Ephraim. It describes the flight of the kings (later implied to be from the Egyptian frontier), and the expropriation or execution of the rebels: Absalom's army had consisted of both, as we have often seen. God's promise that David would return from Bashan (the East Bank) is seen as fulfilled. The greater part of the psalm is a description of the liturgy at which the singer was present, and it gives us a magnificent insight into the detail of the rites and the feelings of those present. The psalmist was not present at the battle, for he was part of King David's retinue, and had stayed with the king in Mahanaim; he speaks of Joab's force in the third person at 66.6, 'They went through the river on foot', and all references to the advance and the battle in 68 are in the third person also. His account of the battle therefore is somewhat schematic; but he shared to the full in the emotions of those who had taken part in the fighting, and there is no doubting his power of expressing them.

68 For the Chief Musician. A Psalm for (*l*^{e}) David. A Song.
1 God arises (*yāqûm*), his enemies are scattered (*yāpûṣû*);
They also that hate him flee (*yānûsû*) before him.
2 As smoke is driven away, so dost thou drive them away (*tindōp*):
As wax melteth before the fire,
So do the wicked perish (*yō'ḇ*^{e}*ḏû*) at the presence of God.
3 But the righteous are glad (*yiśm*^{e}*ḥû*); they exult (*ya'al*^{e}*ṣû*) before God:
Yea, they rejoice (*yāśîśû*) with gladness.
4 Sing unto God, sing praises unto his name:

Chant (*sōllû*) to him that rideth on the clouds (*bāʿarāḇôṯ*);
His name is JAH; and exult ye before him.
5 A father of the fatherless, and a judge of the widows,
Is God in his holy habitation.
6 God maketh those cut off (*yeḥîḏîm*) to dwell in their home (*baîṯâ*),
He bringeth out the prisoners into prosperity:
But the rebels (*sôrarîm*) dwell in a parched land.

In the original celebration David returned from the East Bank cautiously (2 Sam. 19) and nursing a broken heart. The ark had been kept in Jersulaem, and no victory celebration would have been possible for some weeks, until the beaten rebels, and in particular the Jerusalem garrison, had accepted the king. Such a passage of time is implied in 2 Sam. 19.40-43, behind the Succession Narrator's loyal distortion of the facts. The victory procession would then have gone up to the sanctuary (v. 24), beginning perhaps from the house of Obed-Edom (2 Sam. 6.10; cf. Ps. 84 Heading *haggittîṯ*). In subsequent years the national procession will be setting out from *Šûšan ʿēḏûṯ*, representing Mahanaim (see p. 142), on the fourth leg of its journey: it has been on Mt Scopus since Psalm 60, and, as would be expected, no new name of location is given. The psalm is a song of triumph, and is accompanied by minstrels and girls with tambourines (v. 25)—it is a *mizmôr šîr*.

68.1-4. The Yahwist reports that whenever the ark set out Moses would say, 'Arise, O Yahweh, and let thine enemies be scattered; and let them that hate thee flee before thee'. As Mowinckel says,[1] he was familiar with processions which began with the ark being lifted to the opening line of Psalm 68; and he has turned the words from a future to an imperative jussive prayer, with the address to Yahweh rather than Elohim. God has in fact just dramatically scattered his king's enemies and put them to flight; and the psalmist's claim is that this state of affairs is permanent. As the ark is lifted for the procession, the choir begins, 'God arises, his enemies are scattered. . . ': the same faith which took the ark from Shiloh to Aphek, 'that he may save us from the power of our enemies' (1 Sam. 4.3), is still potent. God drives them away like the drift of smoke: they perish like the melting of wax (cf. Ps. 58.8). The 'wicked' are both the Ishmaelite auxiliaries (who do not even recognize God's laws) and any rebels such as the last months have shown to be lurking among God's people. But the righteous—those who have been faithful to their oath to the king—rejoice, they exult before God. The psalmist calls on them to 'lift up' their voice (the same meaning of *sll* as we have had so many times with Selah (*sōllâ*), a cantillation or chant) as they sing to the music (*šîrû*) and strings (*zammᵉrû*). The God they are honouring is He who rides his chariot on (*bā-*) the clouds, and so has brought the fruitfulness of the rains in 65, to which return is made in vv. 7-10. The raising of their voices was not at first by joining in the psalm (whose words they did not know), but in cries of Hallelujah—'in (*bᵉ*) Yah his name'.

The Hebrew is not very easy. The verbs in vv. 1-3 are futures rather than jussives (*yāqûm*, not *yāqom* or *yāqum*), and it seems better to take them so with Mowinckel and Kirkpatrick; the easier jussive, 'Let God arise...', is allowed by RV, Kraus and Anderson, and we cannot be dogmatic with such small differences in such early Hebrew. The same is true of MT's *hindōp* for which BHS commends the niph. inf. *hinnāḏēp*, cf. *tindōp*; fortunately no substantial difference of meaning is involved. Critics are divided over *sōllû* in v. 4, with NEB, Eaton and others preferring the traditional 'cast up' (a way, as in Isa. 57.14; 62.10); but it is quite unclear what action would then be expected of the psalmist's audience, who are in a real, liturgical situation and not a prophetic, eschatological situation. Most modern critics take *rōḵēḇ bā'arāḇôṯ* as 'riding on the clouds' in view of the standard Ugaritic epithet for Baal, *rkb 'rpt*, but NEB follows the traditional 'deserts'. Yahweh certainly did traverse deserts on his way from Sinai (Deut. 33.2) and found Israel in the desert (Deut. 32.10); but 65.11, 'thy paths drop fatness...', gives a picture of God's chariot fructifying the fields and pastures of Israel from the clouds, and 68.7, 'When thou didst march through the wilderness' seems to envisage God at the head of his army ('before thy people'), i.e. going from Mahanaim to Zalmon through the unsown hill-country.

68.5f. On David's return to Zion, his first duty would be to set matters to rights. Some hundreds of his soldiers have been killed in the campaign, and he must see to the support of their widows and orphaned children. God is a father to the fatherless and a judge for such widows in the abode of his holiness; and the king must take his throne in this sanctuary, and administer his justice. They must in fact be given land, and we know where this land is to come from: it will come from dividing Shechem and meting out the valley of Succoth (60.6). The same note of high joy that the future is secure dominates both passages—'I will exult' (60.6), 'exult before him' (68.4). At the same time other injustices wrought by the usurpers must be undone. Some loyalists were cut off (*yᵉḥîḏîm*), isolated from their families by the fighting; they are now restored to their homes and loved ones. Others who were known supporters of David have been in chains (*ʾᵃsîrîm*), and these can now be released to prosperity (*kôšārôṯ*)—that is, with a reward for their loyalty and suffering. No doubt Zadok and Abiathar were in one or other of these categories. But the rebels (have been sent to) dwell in the glaring desert (*ṣᵉḥîḥâ*). They have been deprived of their rich farms around Shechem or on the Jabbok, and despatched to eke out their poverty where they can find some marginal land.

In this way a historical setting gives force to vv. 5f.: the king has been giving such judgments from early morning before the procession began, and the psalmist calls on the people to exult in God's faithfulness to his character, that he has thus vindicated his own. Without such a setting we are left with the lack of context of which so many commentators complain. God was defeating the army of the wicked in vv. 2f., and riding on the clouds in vv. 4, 7-10: what has that to do with widows, the 'solitary' and rebels? Mowinckel[2] gives Cain and Hagar as instances of *yᵉḥîḏîm*: but how do they come in? So he, and most critics, suppose that the author has Israel's history in mind. God's fathering of the orphans and widows is an echo of the Exodus, now to be repeated in a cultic celebration at the autumn festival (Mowinckel), or awaiting its ultimate fulfilment in post-exilic times (Gunkel). The rebels' dwelling in the desert recalls the rebellions of the book of Numbers, and God's judgment that they should not enter the land. But the evidence for such references is flimsy. The Israelites who came out of Egypt are never spoken of as widows and orphans: they were six hundred thousand men, beside women and children. Israel was not fatherless in Hos. 11.1, but God's son. Deutero-Isaiah pictures Israel in exile under the image of a widow, but never speaks of the people as consisting of widows, orphans and 'solitaries'. The rebels in the desert are normally destroyed (Pss. 78.31; 106.17f., 26; Exod. 32.35; Num. 11.33), or else condemned to travel through the lands; at all events they do not settle (*škn*) there.

68.7 O God, when thou wentest forth before thy people,
When thou didst march through the wilderness; (Selah
8 The earth trembled,
The heavens also dropped at the presence of God,
(om. *zeh Sînaî*)
At the presence of God, the God of Israel.

9 Thou, O God, didst send a plentiful rain,
Thou didst confirm thine inheritance, when it was weary.
10 Thy army hath made its dwelling (*ḥayyāṯᵉḵā yāšᵉḇû*) therein:
Thou, O God, didst of thy goodness prepare for the poor.

We have met this thunderstorm before: it was the awesome answer to the psalmist's prayer of 65.2, 5, when God visited the earth and watered its furrows and beat down their ridges (65.9-13), when he prepared (*tāḵîn*) corn for his people, for so he prepared the earth (*tᵉḵînehā*, 65.9). It was the first of God's awesome works in 66.3, 5, and the earth's giving of its increase was the earnest of God's blessing in 67.6. Now we have an actual description of it—no doubt given in some detail by the Passion Narrator in the Selah. The storm took place after the raising of the siege of Mahanaim, for God 'went forth before his people', he led them on their march westwards in the downpour. The march (*ṣā'aḏ*) was in fact through the wilderness, *yᵉšîmôn*, the standard word used in 1 Samuel 23; 26 for the area of eastern Judah sloping down to the Jordan and the Dead Sea, where the soil was too poor for agriculture.

It was here that Joab led the royal forces to cross the river on foot (66.6), marching them south to 'the depths of the sea' (68.22). The thunderstorm is described in traditional language (Judg. 5.4f.): the earth trembles, the heavens 'distil'. Dahood compares the trembling, sweating and micturition of the gods at the presence of Baal in the Ugaritic tablets. God broadcasts (*tānîp̄*) the rain (*gešem*) in sheets (*nᵉḏāḇôṯ*), so establishing (*kônantāh*) the land (cf. 65.9d), his inheritance, for its harvest. In 63.1 the land was dry and tired (*'āyēp̄*); now it is weary (*nil'â*). God's force, his armed community (cf. 2 Sam. 23.13), has now taken up its dwelling in this refreshed, life-giving land: the rare word *ḥayyâ*, usually an animal, is used for the Davidic army, as God is thought of as populating his renewed land with living creatures. They have settled (*yāšᵉḇû*) in the land, because the king has allotted confiscated estates to all his loyal followers. After the deprivations of the last weeks—the wounds inflicted by enemy archers, the forced marches, the siege with its shortages of food and water—the royal troops were lean and ragged, *'ānî*, like the desert-stained Eighth Army in the victory parade at Tunis. But God has with his bounty (*ṭôḇâ*) prepared (*tākîn*, as in 65.9) for them, and they will now be fed and wealthy.

The language of these verses is close to that of Judg. 5.4f.:

> LORD, *when thou wentest forth* out of Seir,
> *When thou marchedst* out of the field of Edom,
> *The earth trembled, the heavens* also *dropped*,
> Yea, the clouds dropped water.
> The mountains quaked *at the presence of* the LORD,
> *Even yon Sinai, at the presence of* the LORD, *the God of Israel.*

God's domicile is now left vague, not specified as in the southeast; and the quaking of the mountains is not stressed. But the framework of the wording is virtually unaltered otherwise, *ᵉlōhîm* being as usual preferred to Yahweh. Our psalmist has followed the Song of Deborah because this is a classic victory hymn, composed to celebrate a real historical battle, and opening similarly with the good omen of a rainstorm. At Tabor the river Kishon swept the kings away, that ancient river, the river Kishon (Judg. 5.21), which it surely would not have done in the dry season. In the present campaign the coming of the rains has been even more significant.

The giving of Psalm 65 to the celebration of the rainstorm, and its understanding there as a sign of forgiveness for 'our transgressions', gives a satisfactory explanation for the mention of the rainstorm in 68.7-10: once the psalms are understood as a sequence, the two storms are the same, and initiate the royal victory. Without this connection exegetes are thrown back on the hypothesis that the psalm is a reflection of Israel's *Heilsgeschichte*; and all the commentators whom I am following take this general position. The present strophe then presents a dilemma. God goes forth before his people in the Exodus, leading them in the pillar of cloud and fire; he marches before them through the deserts of Shur and Sin; the earth trembles at the theophany of 'yon Sinai'. So far so good: but what about the plentiful rain? It would seem as if the heavens' distillation in v. 8b were the same as the plentiful rain, and as if both fell at Sinai, or at least in the Wilderness. Gunkel takes it therefore as a rain of manna and quails, and is followed in this by Jacquet. He translates *gešem nᵉḏāḇôṯ* as 'a rain of gifts'. Verses 9b and 10a are emended: *naḥᵃlāṯᵉḵā*, your inheritance, becomes *naḥᵉlâ*, weak. Jacquet and others retain the text at this last point, and understand God's inheritance to be the people; but von Rad argues that the land is normally Yahweh's inheritance.[3] Most critics take the rain to be standard water, and the inheritance to be the land which was weary and is now established: but then it appeared that the rain was falling on Sinai, or in the desert; and there is in any case no reference in the *Heilsgeschichte* to rain in connection with Joshua. So we have with Mowinckel a kind of overlap: part of the text refers to Israel in the desert, and part to the annual gift of rain, which is associated with Creation. Unfortunately the only clear echo of Israel's history is with the Song of Deborah, which comes too early in the psalm, and has nothing to do with the Exodus.

The Exodus-Wilderness view has a further problem over *zeh Sînaî*, which is absent from some MSS and is deleted by Mowinckel and Kraus. The MT yields a literal English version: 'The heavens also dropped at the presence of God—this (is) Sinai—at the presence of God, the God of Israel'. This is so clumsy as to suggest an early gloss: either the copyist thought God was going forth from Sinai as in Deut. 33.2, and causing the earth to tremble; or that Israel had reached Sinai, amid the theophany of Exodus 19. I could retain the words on the view that the author thought the divine march began from Sinai; but they seem to me to be obviously a gloss, from Judg. 5.5. Dahood and others accept the words, translating 'the One of Sinai'. v. 17.

68.11 The Lord giveth the word:
The women that publish the tidings are a great host.
12 Kings of armies flee, they flee:
And she that dwells in the house (*n^{e}waṯ bayiṯ*) divideth the spoil.
13 Though (*'im*) ye lie between the campfires (*ḇên š^{e}paṯtāyîm*).
The dove's wings (*kan^{e}p̄ê yônâ*) are covered with silver,
And her pinions with yellow gold.
14 When the Almighty scattered kings therein,
It snowed in Zalmon.

The psalmist's mind moves from high point to high point of the campaign; from the drama of the thunderstorm to the drama of the battle. In both the initiative is with God: he utters his decree now, *'ōmer*, 'always weighty language' (Delitzsch), *^{a}ḏōnāî* because he has the course of history in his hand. The decree is for a royalist victory, and the enemy kings, the chieftains of Absalom's desert mercenaries, turn at the divine word and run. They were formidable foes too, kings of armies—the Succession Narrator thought the battle was on an enormous scale, with twenty thousand casualties (2 Sam. 18.7)—but 'they flee, they flee': the repetition enhances the drama, as in Judg. 5.22.

Commentators usually think of the women as safely at home in their towns and villages; 'publishing the tidings' in chant down the streets as they did for Saul and David (1 Sam. 18.6f.) or Jephthah (Judg. 11.34); dividing the spoil as Sisera's wife did for her wise ladies (Judg. 5.30). But our text suggests a more direct involvement. The women proclaiming the tidings are a great *ṣāḇā'*, like the *ṣ^{e}ḇā'ôt* commanded by the fleeing kings. The flight of the kings in v. 12a leads straight on into the dividing of the spoil by the women in v. 12b. The supposed parallel in Judg 5.30 does not say that Sisera's wife divided the spoil: the wise ladies say, 'Have they (sc. the men) not found, have they not divided the spoil?' Sisera is expected to bring home a damsel or two, and various fine embroideries, which *he* will distribute, if he wishes, to his womenfolk. The dividing of the spoil in 68.12b is not only done by the women, but the psalmist's thought is still on the battlefield through v. 13 and into v. 14.

It looks therefore as if we should rather think of the women as present at the battle. Sisera's 'a damsel, two damsels to every man' might suggest that this was often the case: in the present campaign the Succession narrator tells us that all David's household but ten concubines went after him from Jerusalem (2 Sam. 15.16), and that the Philistine troops were accompanied by their 'little ones' (15.22); this must imply that their womenfolk went too—indeed they had no protection but their husbands, and what befell the concubines might well be expected to happen to them too. So it is likely that Joab's army would have been accompanied by a considerable *ṣāḇā'* of women, camp-followers as they were called at Bannockburn. They would gather wood and cook for the men; they would watch the issue of the battle discreetly, crying out 'They flee, they flee', or fleeing themselves as the case may be; in the present happy event they would be after the men, stripping the dead and wounded of clothes and finery. Ancient Near Eastern armies consecrated themselves for battle, putting on bracelets and ear-rings of precious metal (Judg. 8.21-27): in a world of first-come first-served, a man might be glad to have his faithful wife pick up a few such trinkets in his wake. So it might come to pass on this occasion that the women, not the men, divided the spoil; and the irony strikes the psalmist that kings of armies, men of power, are in flight, while a great army of humble housewives, dwellers in the house, split their splendour between them.

68.13. šᵉpattāyim is an uncommon word, occurring in this form here only, in the related form *mišpᵉtayim* at Judg. 5.16; Gen. 49.14. BDB derive from *šph* II, to set a kettle-pot on a tripod, cf. *'ašpōṯ*, an ash-heap; and this derivation would mean camp-fires. This seems to yield good sense in all three passages. Joab's army has had a tough life even since leaving Mahanaim, camping without tents in the sub-zero nights of January/February. The troops have lit camp-fires and slept huddled together between them. Reuben is reproved by Deborah for his 'great searchings of the heart': 'why did you tarry between the camp-fires, to hear the piping for the flocks?' They had waited around in the warmth between the fires in the morning, discussing whether to march or not, while the shepherds led out their sheep. Issachar was 'a strong ass couching down between the camp-fires': Jacob reproves him for his love of comfort ('he saw a resting place that was good') and willingness to submit to slavery, and compares him to a powerful ass lying in the warm while others prepare to make him work. The alternative translation 'sheepfolds' is weak because it is difficult to see why people should lie, sit or couch between two of them. KB take it as = *mišpᵉṭayim*, the saddle-bags of a donkey: cf. Eaton, Anderson for difficult sense.

The psalmist is drawing a contrast between the rigours of the past and the glories of the present. Although things have been so bleak, yet 'the wings of the dove have been covered with silver' and gold. We have seen the royalists twice compared to a dove. During the ascent of Olivet the psalmist said, 'Oh that I had wings like a dove' (55.6), and their camp by Bahurim was called 'The Dove of the Distant Terebinths': the symbolism of the bird which is able fly away into the wilderness and later to return to its home, is taken up by Hosea, 'they shall come... like doves from the land of Assyria, and I will return them to their homes' (Hos. 11.11; cf. Ps. 74.19). So now has the dove escaped and returned; and returned furthermore with the arms of its members glittering with captured silver and gold bracelets and earrings, which sparkle in the light with movement like the wings of a bird in flight. Golden earrings were a speciality of Ishmaelites (Judg. 8.24). The precious metal on the victorious soldiers' wrists in the procession is as much a testimony to their courage and skill as any MC proudly displayed on a modern warrior's breast marching past the Cenotaph. Even the quality of the gold is a concern to the psalmist: his eye can pick out the high-carat mined gold (*ḥārûṣ*) gleaming with the authentic light of fresh olive oil (*yᵉraqraq*, like Solomon's *šemen tûraq*, Cant. 1.3).

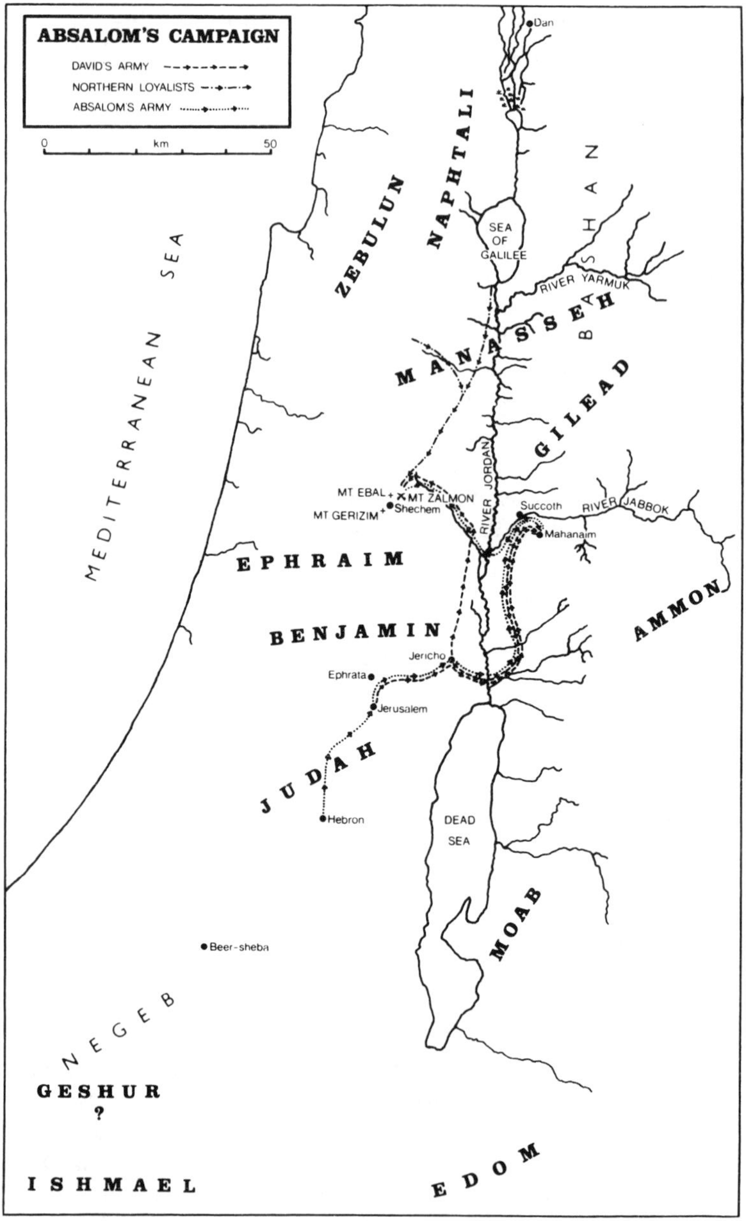

ABSALOM'S CAMPAIGN
DAVID'S ARMY
NORTHERN LOYALISTS
ABSALOM'S ARMY
0
km
50
Dan
NAPHTALI
ZEBULUN
BASHAN
SEA OF GALILEE
MEDITERRANEAN SEA
RIVER YARMUK
MANASSEH
GILEAD
RIVER JORDAN
MT EBAL
MT ZALMON
MT GERIZIM
Shechem
Succoth
RIVER JABBOK
Mahanaim
EPHRAIM
AMMON
BENJAMIN
Jericho
Ephrata
Jerusalem
JUDAH
Hebron
DEAD SEA
MOAB
Beer-sheba
NEGEB
GESHUR
?
ISHMAEL
EDOM

68.14. Zalmon, mentioned here as the scene of the battle in which God scattered the enemy kings, occurs also in Judg. 9.48. Abimelech has destroyed Shechem, and the men of 'the tower of Shechem', that is the acropolis above, have withdrawn into their wooden hold. Abimelech 'gat him up to mount Zalmon', and took an axe, and cut down a bough from the trees, telling his followers, 'What ye have seen me do, make haste, and do as I have done'. So a great pile of wood was laid to the defences, and the defenders were all burnt to death, about a thousand people. So Zalmon is the name of a mountain close to Shechem; it was covered in woods, hence perhaps its name, the Dark Mountain, Monte Negro. E. Nielsen,[4] suggests that it is another name for Mt Ebal.

Many commentators, even Kirkpatrick, say that no known battle took place here, but it must occur to us that the battle which put down Absalom's rebellion was fought in 'the forest of Ephraim' (2 Sam. 18.6), which cannot be far away. Shechem is on the border of Ephraim and Manasseh, and both contexts mention a forest. Furthermore, we know from Ps. 60.6 that Shechem was the centre of the rebellion in the psalmist's eyes, and this enables us to account for the fact that the battle was fought, according to the Succession Narrator, on the *west* bank, since Ephraim is entirely on the west bank. The varied details, from the Prayers and from 2 Samuel, thus suggest the following reconstruction of the military movements.

David withdrew from Jerusalem to Mahanaim (2 Sam. 17.24), where he was besieged by Amasa (17.26), and withstood a direct attack with battering rams (Ps. 62.3) and a water shortage (Ps. 63.1). His troops' morale was high once Mahanaim was reached (Ps. 60.4-12), because there were royal garrisons in Gilead/Aram (Ps. 60.7; 2 Sam. 8.6), and in Edom (Ps. 60.8; 2 Sam. 8.14), to which word was sent. There was strongly loyalist support for David in Zebulon and Naphtali (Ps. 68.27), and the clan-leaders of these tribes, with or without the northern garrisons, marched direct on Shechem, which was the centre of the Revolt (Ps. 60.6; cf. 1 Kgs 12). This forced Amasa to withdraw from Gilead to defend his base, and Joab, Abishai and Ittai led three battalions from Mahanaim (2 Sam. 18.1f.), probably with reinforcements from Edom. They set off in heavy rain (Ps. 65.9-13; 68.7-10), and were pleased to be able to ford the Jordan on foot (66.6) near the Dead Sea (68.22). The northerners delayed the battle until they were joined by the Mahanaim force with its experienced commanders, and especially Joab (2 Sam. 18.16): the latter were advancing from the south, so they joined forces south of Shechem in the forest of Ephraim (2 Sam. 18.6)—north of Shechem it is Manasseh. It was here that the battle was fought on Mt Zalmon (Ps. 68.14), which is a wooded hill near Shechem, perhaps a spur of Mt Ebal, which is to its north. The campaign took about four months in all, from October, when Ziba brought David grapes (2 Sam. 16.1), through a delayed thunderstorm (Ps. 68.8, December?), to January or February when there was snow (68.14, *tašlēg*). The scene comes to us vivid across three millennia—the women's cries, the kings fleeing through the snow like the driven flakes about them, the stripping of the bracelets from the wounded and dying, the chaos amid the trees.

The *Heilsgeschichte* hypothesis is in further difficulties here. The kings are to Gunkel the leaders of Exod. 15.14, or Sihon and Og; to Anderson, Jabin, etc., in Canaan; to Jacquet, also the kings who fled before Gideon. Mowinckel and Kraus think of ancient material from Mt Tabor, with the Deborah echoes, and Zebulon and Naphtali not far away, and the rare 'Shaddai' for God. F.M. Cross[5] derives the name from Ugar. *ṯd* = mountain + *-ai*, one of, cf. Pidray: 'the one from the mountain'. About the 'sheepfolds' there are great searchings of heart, but no clear solution: cf. Kirkpatrick for three attempted solutions. The dove is often taken to be a captured work of art (Gunkel), an image of Astarte (Kraus). Zalmon is almost aways correctly identified from Judges 9, but the evidence is then refused in favour of the Jebel Hauran, the supposed mountains of Bashan of vv. 15f. The latter identification goes back to Wetzstein, who is cited by Delitzsch: '(Zalmon, dark,) would suit the mountains of Hauran, among which Ptolemaeus[6] mentions a mountain ᾿Ασαλμανος (according to one of the various readings)'. The understanding of the dove as Israel is Mowinckel's,[7] though he bases it either on the dove's plangent moaning, or better as Yahweh's Beloved (cf. Cant. *passim*): he sees also that the silver and gold are the spoils of battle (so too Eaton), but an extensive rewriting of the text enables him to remove the signs of a real battle at a real place, Zalmon, fought in real snow. The snow is often reduced to an image (e.g. PBV): kings fleeing *like* snowflakes (Kirkpatrick), bodies and munitions lying like snow (Mowinckel), bleached bones, etc.

68.15 A mountain of God is the mountain of Bashan;
A mountain of summits is the mountain of Bashan.
16 Why look ye askance, ye high mountains,
At the mountain which God hath desired for his abode?
Yea, the LORD will dwell *in it* for ever.

17 The chariots of God are twenty thousand, even thousands upon thousands:
The LORD is come from (rd. *ḇ ā' mis-*). Sinai to the sanctuary.
18 Thou hast ascended on high, thou hast led *thy* captivity captive;
Thou hast received offerings consisting of men (*mattānôṯ bā'āḏām*),
Yea, even the rebels (*w*^{e}*'ap̄ sôr*^{e}*rîm*), that the God Yah might dwell *there*.

There were many local shrines in pre-monarchic Israel, but the later tenth century showed that two were of dominant importance, Bethel in southern Ephraim, and Dan on the northern frontier of the land (1 Kgs 12.26-33). These, and more especially Dan,[8] became the centres of official worship in Israel. Shechem still had some traditional appeal (1 Kgs 12.1), but it may well have been destroyed by David, for Jeroboam 'built' it (1 Kgs 12.25), and Penuel too, and it never regained its former importance: it is quite likely that the Shechem priesthood was expropriated by David, and that it took refuge in Bethel.[9] But while Ps. 60.6 and the site of the battle at Zalmon strongly suggest the association of Shechem with the revolt, we have here an interesting reflection on Dan. The mountain of Bashan is Mt Hermon: 'so we took the land... beyond the Jordan, from the valley of the Arnon to Mount Hermon... all the cities of the tableland and all Gilead and all Bashan' (Deut. 3.8ff.). Hermon is an enormous mountain 10,000 ft high, four times the height of Zion; it has three peaks of nearly equal height, Hermon, Senir and Baal-hermon (1 Chron. 5.23), and so may be spoken of as *har(îm) gaḇnunnîm*, mountain(s) of peaks. It is from Hermon that the Jordan rises, and at its main source stands the sanctuary of Dan: cf. Ps. 42.6, 'Therefore do I remember thee from the land of Jordan, And the Hermons, from the little hill'. Our psalmist is aware of resentment among the Danite priests, the sons of Korah,[10] and he does not want further trouble, so he takes up an irenic if nervous approach. Hermon is a mountain of God, no doubt, and impressively high; but it just happens that God has set his heart on Zion for his abode, so there is no point in sulking about it. This is a permanency, so the best policy is to submit, and to join in the national worship at Jerusalem. As the revolt was followed by a further rebellion in a matter of months under Sheba (2 Sam. 20), which ended at Abel-Beth-Maacah in Dan, our speaker's anxieties were probably well-grounded. We should remember that a good proportion of the loyalist troops were from Zebulon and Naphtali, which had no major sanctuary in their territory, but might naturally turn to Dan in their neighbourhood; in the legend, Dan and Naphtali belong together as the sons of Bilhah. So an irenic and nervous olive branch was most appropriate.

68.18. The thought of Hermon's transcendent height prompts the thought of two countervailing considerations. First, however strong Hermon is in height, God's chariotry is numberless. Above and round about the divine presence in the ark are the myriads of his angels, invisible to mortal sight (2 Kgs 6.17): twenty thousand, perhaps, or multiplied myriads (Delitzsch), thousands reduplicated. Second—if we accept the standard emendation *bā' missînaî* for *bām sînaî* (BHS compares Deut. 33.2)—the Lord has come from his well-known mountain home on Sinai to the sanctuary of Zion, and Sinai is a mountain even more prestigious than Hermon.

RV mg translates the MT 'Sinai is in the sanctuary', which gives questionable sense: *baqqōḏeš* recurs in v. 24, where it clearly means the sanctuary on Zion—how can Sinai be in Zion? Anderson follows Johnson,[11] 'The Lord is amid them, the God of Sinai is in the sanctuary', which puts some pressure on the Hebrew. One feels forced to agree with Gunkel that 'Sinai' yields no sense as it stands. 'The Lord has come from Sinai' is close to the MT and gives a suitable counter to claims from Dan; it could have been changed by a Levite who thought God resided not on Sinai but on Zion, as in v. 16c.

68.18. But the best answer of all to Danite pretensions is the ark, and possession is nine tenths of the law. God has been here before our eyes this day, leading the procession up the hill to his sanctuary on the high place. Behind this awesome mysterious presence, this divine chariot, are led the prisoners in chains: they have been consecrated to him, and come next in order behind him. On arrival at the sanctuary God has received them, offerings in men, human sacrifices, yes, the rebels themselves. God had taken Absalom in the battle, and David spared Amasa from motives of policy: but there will have been other rebel leaders without Amasa's influence, and who would make suitable offerings. For without shedding of blood is no remission of sin. Rebellion is as witchcraft, and the deaths consequent upon it pollute the land. For blood, it polluteth the land: and no expiation can be made for the land for the blood that is shed therein, but by the blood of him that shed it (Num. 35.33). Only if Israel walked in his statutes would God set his tabernacle among them (Lev. 26.11); and Ezekiel would in the end see the divine presence in its chariot leaving the Temple. So if the God Yah is to dwell—sc. in his holy place, as in v. 16c—expiation there must be by the blood of him that caused so much to be shed.

mattānôṯ normally means offerings, sacrifices. *bā'āḏām* might mean one of three things: (1) sacrifices consisting in men, the *beth essentiae*. Such a view was common in the last century (cf. BDB), though the suggestion was often that they were offered to be Temple servants, Nethinim. (2) Delitzsch translates *inter homines*, and this is normal, cf. Kirkpatrick, in person of the king. But if so, the phrase seems plethoric. (3) Anderson justifies 'from men' by Ugaritic parallels. I have not seen the grim but obvious solution expounded (cf. vv. 19-23), though Eaton writes 'in human kind' and may intend it. Without it v. 18c leaves critics in perplexity.

68.19 Blessed be the Lord, who daily beareth our burden,
Even the God who is our salvation. (Selah
20 God is unto us a God of deliverances;
And unto Yahweh the Lord are goings forth (*tôṣā'ôṯ*) to death.
21 Verily (*'aḵ*) God smiteth (*yimḥaṣ*) through the head of his enemies,
The hairy scalp of him that goeth (*miṯhallēḵ*) in his guiltiness.
22 The Lord said, I will bring again from Bashan,
I will bring again from the depths of the sea,
23 That thou mayest wash (rd. *tirḥaṣ*) thy foot in blood,
That the tongue of thy dogs may have its portion from the enemy.

RV leaves a space after v. 18, and many commentators hail a second half to the psalm; but in fact the sense runs straight on. God has accepted the sacrifice of the rebels, and will in consequence continue to dwell in his cleansed sanctuary (v. 18): the cry of thanksgiving goes up to the Lord who day by day bears for us—*ya'amās*, sc. bears away our load of guilt (v. 19). He is the God who gives us victory (*yᵉšû'āṯēnû*), and that is the principal cause of the day's rejoicing: the editor has inserted a Selah at this point to give some account of the battle, which the Succession Narrator has suppressed in favour of his drama of Absalom's death. But God does not provide victories *yôm yôm*, nor would *'ms*, to carry a load, be a suitable verb for them: what does come daily is pollution, which only God can take away as we offer the prescribed sacrifices. Each side does its own part: God delivers us, and we give him his due in animal or human life. *lānû*, for us, is balanced by *lyhwh*, for Yahweh; and for him are *tôṣā'ôṯ*, goings out, *lammāweṯ*, to death, i.e. for execution. It may be that the 'goings out' are from prison at the beginning of the procession, and that we should render, 'and for Yahweh the Lord are men led forth to execution'; or perhaps more likely they 'go out' from the sanctuary to the place of execution at the end of the victory march. Benaiah wanted Joab to be killed outside the altar precinct in 1 Kgs 2.30, and Jehoiada had Athaliah brought out of the Temple to be put to death in 2 Kgs 11.15: of course these are not sacrifices, but there are decencies which must be observed, and the place of death for animal sacrifices was away from the place of divine presence in Lev. 16.15 ('. . . and brings his blood within the veil').

tôṣā'ôṯ is mainly used elsewhere for the 'goings out', i.e. the limits, boundaries, of the land. The usual translation, 'escapes', does not go easily with *lammāweṯ* (we should expect from death, not to death), and ignores the contrast, 'unto us. . . unto Yahweh'.[12] The exegesis above not only provides a smooth rendering of the Hebrew, with a happily concrete meaning for *tôṣa̱'ôṯ*, but also a continuity with the human sacrifices of v. 18 and the executions of vv. 21.23.

68.21ff. The meaning runs straight on: there is no change of direction (*'aḵ* means 'Yea', or 'verily', not 'But' with RV), and the imperfect *yimḥaṣ* is not a prophecy but a continued description like the other imperfects in the psalm. God smashes in the head of his enemies, their scalp: the execution is done by beating in the brains with a mace or axe. No doubt he normally deputed the duty: perhaps to a prophet, for Samuel hewed Agag in pieces before the Lord (1 Sam. 15.33), or Benaiah the son of Jehoiada seems to have been experienced in such matters. The scalp is hairy, *śē'ār*, because the rebels also grew their hair long to consecrate themselves for battle; and the long hair makes them look like demons (*śā'îr*, a hairy one), and so suited to extermination for the public good.

God said he would bring David back from Mahanaim in Bashan; no doubt the royal prophets felt that such a prediction was a corollary of his more general covenant to David in 2 Samuel 7. He would bring him back from the deep places of the sea: the Dead Sea is indeed a deep place, 3,870 ft. below Jerusalem, and as the psalmist waded through Jordan on the way east, up to his waist and more, a few miles from the sea, he may well have thought, 'Save me, O God; I sink in deep mire' (*yᵉwēn mᵉṣûlâ*, 69.1f.). Here, it seemed, was the low point of the royal fortunes. God promised that he would bring David back that he might wash his feet in blood: the singer addresses the king, 'thou... thy foot... thy dogs'. The MT says 'that thou mayest smash (*timḥaṣ*) thy foot in blood'; but this can hardly be right. The righteous was to wash (*yirḥaṣ*) his feet in blood in 58.10, so a single letter would be involved; the copyist's mind could have been distracted by *yimḥaṣ* two verses up, and the Greek has βαφῃ, So the victors ceremonially dip their feet in the blood of the vanquished traitors; and the ill-kept dogs get their share, as with Ahab at the pool of Samaria.

It may be that my gentle reader, who is studying the psalms for edification, is estranged by this grisly scene, and at the barbarity of early times. But I think that even here we can empathize with the psalmist. The rebel leaders were traitors to their king, and the British executed the leaders of the Dublin Rising as traitors as recently as 1916. The notion that the land is polluted by death, and that God will therefore withdraw his presence and blessing, is an idle superstition; but the allied superstition, that without shedding of blood is no remission of sin, is preached annually (and even weekly) in churches today. The death of Jesus is in fact a good parallel. The execution of the prisoners marked the climax of the day's celebrations, as the people stood in massed silence to watch outside the sanctuary. The atmosphere combined the joy of VE Day with the blood-lust of a public hanging and the religious catharsis of Good Friday.

68.24 They have seen thy procession (*hᵃlîḵôṯeîḵā*), O God,
Even the procession (*hᵃlîḵôṯ*) of my God, my king, into the sanctuary (RV text).
25 The singers went before, the minstrels followed after,
In the midst of the damsels playing with timbrels.
26 Bless ye God in the congregations,
Even the LORD (BHS), *ye that are* of the fountain of Israel.

27 There is little Benjamin their ruler,
The princes of Judah, their company,
The princes of Zebulun, the princes of Naphtali.

The psalm began with God's arising, and the procession beginning, and the whole of the first twenty-three verses has been given to God—his rendering of justice to the faithful deprived, his leading of the march in the storm, his putting of the enemy to flight, his ascent of Zion, his acceptance of the rebel leaders as sacrifice. His 'goings' (*h^{a}lîḵôṯ*) were in Hab. 3.6 his war-march through the heavens; but here what has been 'seen' is his going in procession. God has led the column up the hill in person of his Ark, drawn no doubt on an ancient cart by oxen exactly as in 2 Samuel 6, and only so made visible on rare occasions. 'They' is the people, who have lined the route cheering, and fallen in behind. The goal of the procession has been the sanctuary, the ark's abode; and now that the progress of the psalm has brought it thither, with the slaughter of the prisoners, we hear how the rest of the procession was composed. The singers went before the ark, chanting words even older than our psalm. The minstrels came behind it with their harps and their lyres: they are *nōg^{e}nîm*, players on strings. Alongside it are the (younger) women, beating their tambourines and hand-drums, as they did with Miriam in the legendary days of old. The psalm was first sung in the evening, at the end of the jubilation: it was addressed to the king (vv. 23, 28) (and sometimes to God, the kingdoms of the earth, etc.), and the people's action is in the third person, and the perfect tense in vv. 24f. But the singer turns in imagination in v. 26 to bid the people cry their Hallelujahs, as he pictures the royal cortege following on in v. 27. They are standing in massed groups according to their tribes and clans (*maqhēlôṯ*): all stem (so they believe) from one fountain-forefather, Israel.

68.27. This verse has been the rock of stumbling upon which many expositions have fallen. It is usually argued: (1) *rōḏēm* is the participle of *rdh*, having dominion over, with suffix *-m*, them = the congregations of Israel in v. 26; (2) such a verb is suited to the king; and we should expect to find the king in a prominent place such as this behind the ark; (3) since David and his successors all stemmed from the tribe of Judah, the 'ruler' must be Saul, who was a Benjaminite. Hence the psalm contains elements going back to Saul's time, which have been included in a Jerusalem psalm (v. 29). The first two steps are correct: the fallacy lies in point (3).

There are two traditions of David's provenance. In 1 Sam. 16.1, and in most of the Samuel texts thereafter, his father is referred to as 'Jesse the Bethlehemite'. Bethlehem is a town securely in Judah, five miles south of Jerusalem, and this fact is made clear in passages such as Mic. 5.1, 'but thou, Bethlehem Ephrathah, which art little to be among the families of Judah...', or Ruth 4.11. David and his descendants are listed among the Judahites in 1 Chronicles 2, and this line of descent is then accepted in the opening verses of Matthew 1; Heb. 7.14, etc.

There is however a second tradition which we find in 1 Sam. 17.12 MT: 'Now David was the son of that Ephrathite of Bethlehem-judah, whose name was Jesse'. The writer wishes to stress the Judahite origin still ('Bethlehem-*judah*'), but Jesse is now stated to be an Ephrathite. Now Ephrathah is a town in Benjamin. Rachel died near there, giving birth to Benjamin: 'And they journeyed from Bethel; and there was still some way to come to Ephrath: and Rachel travailed... And Rachel died, and was buried in the way to Ephrath' (Gen. 35.16, 19). Bethel is on the border between Ephraim and Benjamin, and Jacob is travelling south; so Benjamin is born in Benjaminite territory. 1 Sam. 10.2 tells us specifically that Rachel was buried in Benjamin, 'thou shalt find two men by Rachel's sepulchre, in the border of Benjamin at Zelzah'.

Perhaps we should reconcile the two traditions by thinking that Jesse was a Benjaminite from Ephrathah who settled at Bethlehem. But it is clear that the biblical tradition has sought another method of reconciliation, by positing that Jesse's town of origin had *two names*, Bethlehem and Ephrathah. Hence the glosses (BDB): Gen. 35.19, 'in the way to Ephrath (the same is Beth-lehem)'; 'I buried her there in the way to Ephrath (the same is Beth-lehem)' (Gen. 48.7). The dual name is accepted by Micah, 'but thou, Bethlehem Ephrathah' (5.2), and Ruth 4.11, 'get thee wealth in Ephrathah, and be famous in Bethlehem'. People and places with two names are justly causes of suspicion, and a motive for this doubtful assimilation lies to hand: the family of David were kings of Judah, and it was therefore appropriate for David to have been a Judahite. He could be supposed to be such on the basis of the family having lived in Bethlehem (whether they did or not), and of his having sought refuge in Judah during Saul's persecution; and the Ephrathah tradition could be either forgotten, or else assimilated in the way we have seen.

The likelihood that David came from Ephrathah and not Bethlehem is enhanced by the ancient text, 'Lo, we heard of it in Ephrathah: we found it in the field of Jaar/the wood' (Ps. 132.6). This text is also a nest of obscurities. A natural understanding might be: 'we heard at Ephrathah (where, as David's men, we were living) of a 'place' for the ark; we found it in the wood-country, *biś^e ḏê-ya'ar'* (by Jerusalem)'. If so, the event took place in Benjamin. There is no trace of Ephrathah in the Samuel story. There the ark arrives without a driver at Kiriath-Jearim ('the town of the woods'), and in 1 Sam. 7.1 the townsmen 'brought it to the house of Abinadab on the hill'—so RV text, Heb. *baggiḇ'â*, RVmg Gibeah. Gibeah is on the road from Bethel to Jerusalem, and cannot be far from Ephrathah. Abinadab is the name of a brother of David (1 Sam. 16.8). In 2 Sam. 6.1ff. David, with thirty thousand men, 'went from Baale Judah to bring up from thence the ark of God... and brought it out of the house of Abinadab that was in the hill/Gibeah'. Baale Judah is also called Baala in Josh. 15.9f., where it is said, 'the border was drawn to Baalah (the same is Kiriath-Jearim)'. So it looks as if Baala (of Judah) also had a second name, Kiriath-Jearim; and Kiriath-Jearim has the virtue of being in Judah. It does look as if a loyal Judahite editor has been at work.

So it is probable that David's family hailed from Ephrathah, and so were Benjaminites; and the psalmist will have moved naturally from God's cortege escorting the ark, to the king, 'little Benjamin, their ruler' following next behind. The name of the tribe is used for the man, as in 60.7 'Judah is my commander' refers to Joab, and 'Ephraim is the defence of my head' refers to Benaiah. Benjamin is little, as being the smallest tribe (1 Sam. 9.21), and traditionally the youngest. Behind David come 'the princes of Judah, their company'—*rigmāṯām* only occurs here, and means 'their heap' or 'crowd' by derivation. Most of David's 'Thirty' came from Judah, and Joab and Abishai are reckoned as Judahites, no doubt because their father was such. Ps. 60.7 speaks of Joab as 'Judah'—they are always spoken of as the sons of David's sister Zeruiah (1 Chron. 2.16) and their father's name and tribe are never given. It is natural that they should follow David in a group.

Last among the nobility are 'the princes of Zebulun, the princes of Naphtali'. Here are the loyal and formidable northerners, whose fathers Sisera learned to fear (Judg. 5.18), and to whom David now owed his throne and his life. I have suggested above that the drought may not have been quite so severe in their well-watered lands, and so the superstition less prevalent that the king's sin was the nation's ruin (p. 175); but there may have been personal loyalties, or rivalries with the thrustful Joseph tribes. Mowinckel asks[13] (*68.Ps.*, p. 54) where were the princes of Ephraim and Manasseh. He thinks they were still under Philistine domination; but to my mind they are lying in the Forest of Ephraim, having paid the price that rebels pay in defeat. Some of them may be mentioned in vv. 18, 21.

Verse 27 presents severe difficulties. The idea that all Israel is intended but only four tribes are mentioned, two from the south and two from the north (Gunkel, Eaton, Anderson), is not very convincing—why these two northern tribes? Why is Benjamin their ruler? (Dahood's 'leader' is hard to justify). If the psalm is early, why is there no mention of the king? Mowinckel and Kraus think in terms of early Tabor traditions which have been taken over by Jerusalem, and this would link with the Song of Deborah echoes. But Tabor was in the territory of Issachar (Judg. 5.15) and Issachar should surely then have a mention; nor was Judah part of the amphictyony at the time, as Mowinckel well knows. Jacquet has the northerners give the key: the psalm covers Hezekiah's great Passover of 2 Chronicles 30f.—but the crowd attending are said to come from Ephraim, Manasseh, Issachar and Zebulun (30.18), and Naphtali is not mentioned. Rogerson and McKay have a visionary procession going from the Red Sea to Zion, with Saul as the first king of Israel for some reason in a prominent position.

68.28 Thy God hath commanded thy strength:
Show thyself strong (*'ûzzâ*), O God, thou that hast wrought for us (RV text).
29 Because of thy temple at Jerusalem
Kings shall bring presents unto thee.
30 Rebuke the wild beast of the reeds,
The multitude of the bulls with the calves of the peoples,
Every one submitting himself with pieces of silver;
He hath scattered the peoples that delight in war.
31 Princes shall come out of Egypt;
Cush shall hasten to stretch out her hands unto God.

The psalmist now turns to the future. The Lord gave the word in the battle, commanding strength for the king's army. He is now prayed to extend his work (*'ûzzâ*, *plene* impv. *'zz* intransitive—the translation is König's, cited by Delitzsch) in further victories. For the king has plans for a great new Temple at Jerusalem, and God will be pleased to see some generous contributions of tribute (*šāî*) from neighbouring kings. We have no reason to be sceptical about the traditions of David intending the building of a new temple. 2 Samuel 24 describes his purchase of the site of the Temple, and 1 Chronicles 22–29 give a much inflated picture of his preparations; but we have contemporary evidence both here and at 69.9, 'For the zeal of thine house...' Temples were status symbols in the ancient world, and no king of an empire like David could afford to be without one; besides he had to do more than keep up with the Jones's at Shechem and Dan.

68.30f. David's armies had now defeated the forces of almost all the small nations in a wide arc around Israel, culminating in the present campaign, which has been constantly felt as against 'strangers', 'the nations', 'the peoples', 'kings', invaders from the south. National confidence is at a high point, and God is prayed to 'rebuke', that is, thunder against, Egypt, the wild beast of the reeds. Reeds are a symbol of the Nile (Isa. 19.6; 36.6), and the monster of the Nile will later be called Rahab. But the singer knows that this will mean a new dimension of war. The large and well-armed Egyptian forces are 'a herd of bulls', a formidable sight to see charging one, compared with 'the calves of the peoples'. 'Calf' is often used as a pejorative or contemptuous diminutive, as when the bull figures on cult-objects are referred to as golden calves. The royal armies have now defeated these light-armed desert auxiliaries of Egypt, the Ishmaelite frontier tribesmen: God has scattered these 'people that delight in war'. The time is coming when they will take on Pharaoh's own forces, who should yield some worthy tribute; they will come abasing themselves (*miṯrappēs*) with bars of silver. Yes, princes will come out of Egypt, and even the Ethiopians beyond. 'Cush will make their hands to tun to God' perhaps echoes recent history in which a Cushite ran to bring the news of the victory to David (2 Sam. 18.21-33); at all events prompt abasement, worship and tribute are intended.

The verses are not easy, and are commonly heavily emended: I have followed MT and RV, and they yield good sense in the Davidic context. But there are many doubtful points. *mēhêḵāleḵā* more naturally means 'out of thy temple', and can be so rendered and taken with v. 28 (Kirkpatrick); but this leaves v. 29 in difficulties, and BDB give sufficient instances of *min* = on account of, under 2f. Gunkel's objection that the tribute should be for God, not his temple, is bypassed if the expenses of building such an edifice are in mind. Foreigners 'bring tribute' in Ps. 76.11; Isa. 18.7. The pointing of the verbs in v. 30 should not be changed. God is urged to 'rebuke' (*g^{ec}ar*) Egypt, i.e. to open hostilities, in continuance of his being asked to 'show his strength' in v. 28; but he has already scattered (*bizzar*) the arrow-happy peoples as kings of armies fled in v. 12. Delitzsch defends rendering the hithpael of *rps* 'cast oneself violently to the ground', and this seems to be the meaning at Prov. 6.3; better sense is given than 'trampling' followed by *b^e*. *ḥašmannîm* is a hapax, and the translation 'princes' a guess from the context: Anderson prefers 'bronze' (= *ḥašmāl*), Dahood 'blue cloth', either of which would be useful for temple furnishings. The syntax is obscure in the Cush hemistich: Cush should be masculine, which makes *tārîṣ* difficult, especially when followed by 'their hands'—but the general meaning is not in dispute.

68.32 Sing unto God, ye kingdoms of the earth;
O sing praises unto the Lord: (Selah
33 To him that rideth upon the heavens of heavens which are of old;
Lo, he uttereth his voice, *and that* a mighty voice.
34 Ascribe ye strength unto God:
His excellency is over Israel,
And his strength is in the skies.
35 Terrible is God out of thy holy places:
The God of Israel, he giveth strength and power unto *his* people.
Blessed be God.

The noble victory hymn moves to its climax. God has now put to flight all Israel's neighbours—Hamath, Zobah, Aram, Ammon, Moab, Edom, Ishmael and Philistia: they, and all those nations beyond them, are called upon to join in God's praises. The defeat of the Negeb tribesmen on the Egyptian frontier—maybe hired with Egyptian money—has raised the thought that God will thunder against Egypt next (*g^{ec}ar*, v. 30). Egypt is a land where thunder is unknown, where the gods have no voice; but Israel's God rides the heavens from creation, and when his voice is heard, it shakes the cedars of Libanus. This is the God whom all nations should honour, whose power is audible in the thunder, and visible in the Israelite army. He is awesome (*nôrā'* again, 65.5; 66.3, 5; cf. 68.7f.) as he issues from his sanctuary (plural of extension, Ezek. 21.7), whether for storm or for war; with him as God, his nation is invincible. We can hear the same confidence, only a little secularized, in the voice of

Mr Perez: the Entebbe raid was a demonstration to the world that the Israeli army had the power, and the Israeli government had the will, to protect its citizens anywhere.

Psalm 68 has three Selahs: one after v. 7, probably describing the storm; one after v. 19 ('God who is our salvation'), no doubt describing the battle; one after v. 32, perhaps listing tribes who promised to pay tribute after their defeat ('Sing unto God, ye kingdoms of the earth').

Most commentaries begin with a warning that the psalm is very difficult, its text corrupt and its thought episodic. In a famous article, W.F. Albright[14] resigned the attempt to interpret the psalm as a whole, and viewed it as a catalogue of opening lines ('Incipit's). But such a draconian solution has had little appeal, and almost all modern commentaries take the psalm as a reflection of the Exodus-Desert-Conquest-Zion epic. This interpretation goes back to Ewald, and it is confessed by Gunkel to be obscure. He supposes that the author has taken over elements of earlier poetry; the references in these were familiar to his 'readers', and the result is a 'learned composition' as in the Alexandrine period. Gunkel himself dates the psalm soon after 400, when Israel was under pressure from Egypt, so the Egyptian motifs at the end, and with the Exodus, arise from current troubles: the psalm is an eschatological hymn, in which the future is seen as a replay of the *Urzeit*, with Yahweh leading the ultimate victory march to Zion, and the destruction of his enemies.

With his fragments of older poetry, his audience of 'insiders' and his 'very numerous' emendations, Gunkel has made his hypothesis secure; but it feels far-fetched. 'He is a father of the fatherless...' seems too general to recall the Exodus, and his parallels with II-Isaiah are unconvincing: the exiles were literally afflicted, prisoners, etc., and knew that they were being addressed by the prophet, whereas in fourth century Israel there will have been too many widows, orphans and prisoners to evoke thought of Egypt. Similarly the rebels in the desert did not 'dwell' there: the account of the rain does not make one think of manna or quails; and the mountains of Hauran (Bashan) have a part in the psalm which is remote from that in the book of Numbers. The *Heilsgeschichte* hypothesis is weak at almost every point.

Mowinckel's *Der Achtundsechzigste Psalm* is in two ways an improvement on Gunkel. First, he sees much more clearly than Gunkel the liturgical setting of the Psalm. Gunkel has choirs of people chanting, but Mowinckel sees that the whole thing is a procession at the autumn festival, with Yahweh carried on a cart with his ark and two cherubim; and the opening words a signal for the procession to begin, and applied only later to the legend of the ark in the desert in Numbers 10. Secondly, Mowinckel has a broader base of exegesis. To him the psalm is basically the dramatization of God's victory over the demonic powers in Creation, which is also God's victory over the Egyptians, etc., and so the means to an annual renewal of life. This breadth enables Mowinckel to escape some of Gunkel's more doubtful claims with the *Heilsgeschichte*: so that the rain in vv. 7-10 is real rain refreshing the land, not quails. Also Mowinckel pushes the date back into the royal period, which accords with the feeling of many that the psalm is a genuinely early document, from the same world as Judges 5, and not just borrowing snippets from it.

However, Mowinckel retains Gunkel's stress on the futurity of God's victory in that no real battle is being celebrated, but all is in the imagination; indeed there is even less historical setting provided for it—it is annual and ideal. The concrete details are in part whittled away by emendation: thus the actuality of snow on Zalmon in the text becomes 'Like (white) snow on the Black Mountain'. Also Ugaritic roots are exploited. Bashan is related to *bṯn*, a snake: Mowinckel thinks the mountain of Bashan (of the Snake) *was* God's Mountain in earlier times, and a general name like Zaphon—in fact Mt Tabor. Earlier times are also called on for little Benjamin as Saul. The reader begins to feel that with *Heilsgeschichte*, so many amendments to the text, *and* earlier ideas being imported, Mowinckel would have no difficulty in explaining anything.

Most modern commentaries offer variations on either Gunkel or Mowinckel. A dissident is André Caquot,[15] in that he does not draw on the *Heilsgeschichte*, and is to that degree more convincing. He dates the psalm in Hezekiah's reign, partly on the strength of the mention of Ethiopia, but more because of the limited participation of northern tribes in the liturgy, which might be expected after 722. He has a New Year Enthronement festival like Mowinckel, with some additional ritual: the wax in v. 2 recalls Canaanite curses with wax, and the *kôšārôṯ* are Canaanite-type wise women. Many of the cruces are resolved with symbolism. The dove is a symbol of Israel, based on the birds which were symbols for Anat; Bashan with its rich cows is a symbol of human pride; 'I will bring back from Bashan/the sea' means that God will bring his victorious army back from any heights and depths.

The prejudice against a Davidic setting arises mainly from the large number of nineteenth-century commentators who accepted it from adherence to tradition and then guessed—and to these must be added twentieth-century critics like H. Herkenne (1937), H. Weil (1938) and B.D. Eerdmans (1947). Kirkpatrick lists the variety of historical settings from Joshua to the Maccabees and concludes: 'The obvious inference is that the data are insufficient' (II, 375). Kraus disallows the historical victory-hymn hypothesis on the ground that only part of the text is so explicable (he is thinking of the rain in vv. 7-10, for example). But in fact the Davidic setting explains many details which appeal to us as concrete, once the sequential theory is seen to give a setting after Absalom's rebellion. This is particularly the case with the two mentions of the rebels, with God's promise to bring back from Bashan

(Mahanaim), with 'little Benjamin their ruler' which could only refer to an early king, with Zebulun and Naphtali when most of Israel had sided with Absalom, and with Zalmon which corresponds with the site of the battle in 2 Samuel as in the forest of Ephraim. It also corresponds with the sense of immediacy and joy in the text, which answers so much better to a real situation of deliverance than to an imaginary and theological victory in eternity.

If eloquence is the communication of emotion, then Psalm 68 is the most eloquent among the Prayers, and perhaps in the Psalter. We should not leave it without a thought for the central figure, 'little Benjamin their ruler', the aged, gaunt, indomitable David. Here is his moment of triumph. He had risen to be the late king's royal champion, and his son-in-law, and had survived years of hounding, outlawdom and treachery. He had overthrown the house of Saul, and had made himself by skill and leadership the king of a united Israel and the master of a large empire. He had been driven from his capital and had endured in his sixties a hard and costly retreat, forced marches, and a siege that was nearly his end. Now, through his resilience, the loyalty of his troops and the generalship of his commanders, he goes up the path of victory, his God before him, his army behind, the cheers of his people resounding by the hour. Yet it is not joy which fills the old man's heart, but the thought of his wayward, too well-beloved son. He is draining the bitters of victory.

Chapter 9

THE UNDEPARTING SWORD (69–72)

Nathan prophesied, 'Now therefore, the sword shall never depart from thine house' (2 Sam. 12.10); and we may be sure that such a prophecy, whether historical or (as we may think) ex-post-facto, corresponded with history. David had to contend with the great rebellion under Absalom (Pss. 52–68), and when that was over with the rebellion of Sheba ben Bichri (Ps. 69); and when that was over, his troubles were not finished yet (Pss. 70–71). Our main difficulty with 69 is that the historical element in 2 Samuel 20 is so sketchy, being heavily overwritten by the Succession Narrator; and the latter is concerned with concubines and with personal matters like Joab's feud with Amasa, or with a wise woman helping Joab (2 Sam. 20; cf. 14.1-20). We have no option but to seek for a plausible basis for Sheba's rebellion, with the help of hints from 69: we have enough support for the sequential hypothesis from the earlier psalms not to be liable to charges of circular arguing.

69 For the Chief Musician. At (*'al*) Lilies. For (*l*^{e}) David.
1 Save me, O God;
For the waters are come in unto my soul.
2 I sink in deep mire, where there is no standing:
I am come into deep waters where the floods overflow me.
3 I am weary with my crying; my throat is dried:
Mine eyes fail while I wait upon my God.
4 They that hate me without a cause are more than the hairs of mine head:
They that would cut me off, being mine enemies falsely, are mighty:
Then would I have restored (*'āšîḇ*) that which I did not extort (*lō'-gāzaltî*).

5 O God, thou knowest my foolishness;
And my guiltinesses are not hid from thee.
6 Let not them that wait on thee be ashamed through
me, O Lord GOD of hosts:
Let not those that seek thee be brought to dishonour
through me, O God of Israel.
7 Because for thy sake have I borne reproach;
Shame hath covered my face.
8 I am become a stranger unto my brethren,
And an alien unto my mother's children.
9 For zeal for (*qin'aṯ*) thine house hath eaten me up;
And the reproaches of them that reproach thee are
fallen upon me.
10 When I wept with the fasting (*baṣṣôm*) of my soul,
That was to my reproach.
11 When I made sackcloth my clothing,
I became a proverb unto them.
12 They that sit in the gate talk of me,
And *I am* the song of the drunkards.

With 68, the processional route had been completed: from the Temple (51, 52) to Mahalat on Olivet (53–55); to *Yônaṯ-'ēlîm-rᵉḥōqîm* by Bahurim (56–59); to *Šûšan-'ēḏûṯ* on Mt Scopus (60–67); and finally thence to the Temple with 68. Psalm 69 has a new site, in the court of the palace. Lilies were the royal insignia, in Israel as in France, and these emblems were chiselled on the ashlars of the king's court (p. 142). This is the last direction of location (*'al-*), and the remaining psalms will have been chanted at the palace.

Superstition was rife in monarchic Israel, and it was often felt that if national affairs were going badly, the best thing was to kill the king, who had forfeited God's blessing, and start again. David is wise enough to let God kill Saul off himself;[1] but after Jehoash had yielded all the Temple gold to Hazael, he was killed (2 Kgs 12.18-21), and the loss of the northern provinces to Assyria in 732 similarly brought about the murder of Pekah (2 Kgs 15.29f.). Hence Israelite kings lived in a kind of Golden Bough atmosphere: they might or might not have come to power through the violent death of their predecessor, but if they were not successful they would go the same way themselves. We feel this atmosphere of panic strongly in 69: David's reign has not been going well, and he is desperate about what he can do to regain the divine blessing.

The sense of beleaguered fear is everywhere in the psalm, reminding us of the last months of President Nixon in the White House. The king is hated, for no reason, by innumerable enemies who speak to him falsely, and would like to cut him off (v. 4). He is constantly under 'reproach' (vv. 7, 9, 10, 19, 20, 26), and his religious activities are part of what is spoken against (vv. 10, 11). The murmuring goes on openly in public, in the *r^eḥôḇ* by the gate of Jerusalem, where people sit and do business, or gossip (v. 12). His name is a byword (v. 11), and a topic for drinking songs (v. 12). His subjects are disaffected, and there is but a step between him and death (v. 4b). He is glad however to be able to count upon some loyalists: 'them that wait on thee', 'those that seek thee' (v. 6). But the hostile faction has come to include members of his own family, 'my brethren', 'my mother's children'. We may think that the atmosphere is not dissimilar to that in David's court at the time of Sheba's rebellion: scarcely has one major uprising been put down than another begins, and 'all the men of Israel went up from following David, and followed Sheba, the son of Bichri' (2 Sam. 20.2). Only the Judahites remained loyal, and 'clave unto their king, from Jordan even to Jerusalem' (*ibid.*)—precisely the places which God will save and build in 69.35. It is they who could so suitably be those that wait on/seek God, i.e. act as if his covenant with David were a fact; and they are related to 'the Lord Yahweh of hosts'/'the God of Israel' (v. 6), titles suited to those who were going to war for their faith. We are not told of any of David's blood-brothers who were implicated in the rising, but the leader is again a Benjaminite, and the palace was a hotbed of family intrigue in 1 Kings 1. The seriousness of the situation with Sheba is revealed by David's comment, 'Now shall Sheba the son of Bichri do us more harm than did Absalom' (2 Sam. 20.6): the country is divided on exactly the Israel/Judah line that was to be permanent after Solomon's death, and only Joab's generalship and the divisions of the northern tribes were able to postpone the evil day.[2]

The normal response of a psalmist under pressure from his enemies is to plead his innocence, but this is not what is done by the speaker of 69; nor would David have been able to take such a line. His sins were notorious, including the killing of Uriah; and in face of a second national disintegration (and very likely other troubles—see below), all he could do was to confess his sins afresh. Hence v. 5, 'O God, thou knowest my foolishness: And my guiltinesses are not hid from thee': his *'ašmôṯ* recall the trespasses and sins of 51.3, and the *dāmîm* of 51.14. But he expressed his penitence in deed as well as in word. He wept (*bkh*, often used of formal mourning), and fasted, even his soul (if that is how we should take the difficult Hebrew of v. 10); he wore sackcloth (vv. 11); he called on God till he was hoarse (v. 3); he 'awaited' God's response till his eyes were sore from weeping (ibid.). Naturally, these sacramental actions have only served to intensify the derision of his enemies. The fasting and the sackcloth are to them a confirmation of God's having deserted him, and cause them to 'reproach' him as a *māšāl* all the more.

A problem arises over the waters, mire, flood, pit, etc. of vv. 1f., which recur in vv. 14f. It is normal to see these as an image for the close approach of death, water being a standard symbol of Sheol (Gunkel, Eaton, Anderson, etc.), and there certainly are passages where water is used in this straightforwardly symbolic way (Ps. 124.4). But Delitzsch (who thought the psalm was about Jeremiah) took the pit, water, mire, etc. to be intended literally (Jer. 38.6-13), and although Kraus accepts the metaphorical exegesis, he also is attracted to the literal view. If the crying, weeping, fasting, sackcloth, reproaches, songs, byword, etc., are all intended literally, there is an uncomfortableness over taking the water, etc. symbolically; and this is felt especially with the recurrence of the same ideas in vv. 14f. We might have expected 'Sheol', 'death', 'the dead', etc. as the real counterparts of water and mire if the symbolic view were correct, but they do not appear.

The Israelites certainly did have cisterns (*b^{e}'ērôṯ*, Jer. 2.13) in whose bottoms there was 'mire' (*ṭîṭ*) with or without water (Jer. 38.6); and on occasion they would throw a man in and he would sink (*ṭb'*, *ibid.*). In the sixth century this might be a particularly unpleasant form of imprisonment: but we have what seems to be a liturgical use of the same action soon afterwards:

> They have chased me sore like a bird, that are mine enemies without cause.
> They have cut off my life in the dungeon (*bōr*), and have closed it over me with a stone (NEB).
> Waters flowed over my head; I said, I am cut off.
> I called upon thy name, O LORD, out of the lowest dungeon. (Lam. 3.53-56)

So much of Lamentations 3 seems to be liturgical that it is difficult to read this part otherwise: the speaker seems to have been whipped (v. 1), shut in the dark (v. 2), chained (v. 7), taunted (v. 14), made to consume bitter substances (v. 15), covered with ashes (v. 16), chased (v. 52), etc. It is easy to think that he is a priest or similar person who is acting as the community's scapegoat in a liturgy of expiation after the fall of Jerusalem.

In *PSK*, pp. 201-10, I have argued that a similar ritual was practised towards the end of the autumn festival at Dan, and that this is reflected in the Korah Psalm 88. We have the speaker crying day and night, his eye wasting away, he is shut up, cast off, etc.; and there is a sustained description of him among the dead, near the grave, in the lowest pit, in the deeps, etc. As there is a reference to waves, I suggested that the afflicted man was shut in an underground stream, such as there are at Dan. The experience was plainly very terrifying for him, whatever it was, but at least he was confident that his prayer would come before God in the morning (v. 13). In 69 the fear of the ghosts is less, but the cry for salvation is just as insistent. It is, it seems, a more primitive age, in which a king, and not just a national representative, is in dire trouble, and is prepared to undergo humiliating and frightening rites, to do anything to move the heart of God. It would not be surprising if with time such barbarous rituals fell into desuetude, and became either symbols of affliction, as in Psalm 124, or punishments for the dissident, as in Jeremiah 38.

There is one further feature of 69 which is, as Gunkel says, atypical, the 'zeal for thine house', of v. 9. I commented above that we have a trustworthy tradition that David planned the building of a national Temple at Jerusalem, to replace the local shrine served by Zadok (p. 216). We have the legends of his planning such in 2 Samuel 7, and of his buying the site for it in 2 Samuel 24; the highly embellished account of his preparations in 1 Chronicles 22–29 is not conjured from nothing, for such a Temple was necessary to outshine the long-established Israelite cultic centres, especially those at Shechem, Bethel and Dan. It would be a means to national cohesion (1 Kgs 12.27), and the overawing of visiting foreign notables (cf. 2 Kgs 16.10). Our psalmist looked forward at 68.29 to the coming of kings with tribute for it, so it is clearly envisaged at the time of the Great Rebellion; indeed, while he was vowing thank-offerings to God on the altars at Zion, it may be that David himself was vowing the Temple building.

The trouble with large buildings is that they cost a lot of money, and as David could no longer depend on the spoils of war for much, he could only raise money by taxation, or rather, since taxes were not yet invented, by forced levies of money. Such impositions caused trouble in the days of Charles I, and in America under George III, and it would be surprising if they were popular under David. His grandson Rehoboam unwisely refused to reduce his father's levies, and provoked the cry, 'What portion have we in David? neither have we inheritance in the son of Jesse: to your tents, Israel: now see to thine own house, David' (1 Kgs 12.16). The Succession Narrator does not know precisely what underlay the revolt of Sheba, but he makes the latter say, 'We have no portion in David, neither have we inheritance in the son of Jesse: every man to his tents, Israel' (2 Sam. 20.1). Both Sheba's and Jeroboam's revolts arose from the same cause, royal demands for money; and in both cases the money was going to the same main expense, the enormous cost of the Temple. We have this sad fact expressed in a more sympathetic and one-sided manner in 69.9: 'For zeal for thine house hath eaten me up; And the reproaches of them that reproach thee are fallen upon me'. People said, 'Five shekels of silver to pay for a temple at Jerusalem!', and the psalmist can represent this as a reproach of God, in whose honour the temple was planned, which has fallen on the king for planning it. In 69 he is the king's spokesman throughout.

69.4. This then gives us a credible basis for interpreting v. 4, which speaks of repaying 'what I did not extort'. *gzl* means to take by force (e.g. Gen. 21.25; Job 20.19), and there is clearly a difference between the complainants who allege that the speaker has taken their property by force, and the speaker who denies this. The situation would be easy to understand if the king has 'invited' a contribution for the Temple which has appeared as an imposition. This was a total, and deliberate, misunderstanding, says his spokesman. They have become the king's enemies 'for nothing' (*ḥinnām*), 'fraudulently' (*šeqer*). (If they had only been straightforward), then (*'āz*) would I have repaid (*'āšîḇ*) what I never extorted. *'āz* with impf. makes no sense without a suppressed protasis, and such a construction is found elsewhere: 'Why did the knees receive me? or why the breasts that I should suck? For now I should have lien down and been quiet; I should have slept; then had I been at rest (*'āz yānûaḥ lî*)' (Job 3.12f.). Here 'for if they had refused me' is to be supplied: *'āz* recurs with an implied protasis (with perfect where required) at Josh. 22.31; 2 Kgs 13.19; Eccl. 2.15.

We have the familiar differences between critics over the setting of 69. Delitzsch, Kirkpatrick, and even Rogerson and McKay take the speaker to be Jeremiah, so much of the language being in common with Jeremiah 38, etc. To Gunkel, Kraus, Schmidt, Weiser, Anderson, Dahood and Jacquet, we have an Individual Lament followed by an Individual Thanksgiving in vv. 30-36: often an oracle is taken to have been given between the two parts, and thus to explain the change of mood. Kraus follows Schmidt in thinking the speaker to have been falsely accused of theft (v. 4c); he is usually thought to be ill (vv. 20, 26). There is some tension between his innocence in not having robbed his accusers (v. 4) and his having sinned (vv. 5, etc.). His zeal for the Temple suggests a date around 500 when the Temple was being rebuilt, and also Zion and the cities of Judah (v. 35)—only Jacquet denies the unity of the psalm, with three original poems combined, plus two appendices. To Birkeland,[3] Mowinckel and Eaton, however, the speaker is the king who is undergoing rites of humiliation after a military defeat. Eaton[4] gives what seem convincing reasons of thinking the speaker to be a national leader: the dependence of the faithful followers of Yahweh on him (v. 6), his numerous enemies (v. 4), the public nature of the obloquy heaped on him, his concern for the Temple and the cities of Judah, 'my God' and the confidence which the speaker has in his *ḥesed̲*. But the national defeat hypothesis seems to leave some problems: why should the king's family turn against him, or how is his zeal for the temple involved?

69.13 But as for me, my prayer is unto thee, O LORD, in an acceptable time:
O God, in the multitude of thy mercy,
Answer me in the truth of thy salvation.
14 Deliver me out of the mire, and let me not sink:
Let me be delivered from them that hate me, and out of the deep waters.
15 Let not the waterflood overwhelm me,
Neither let the deep swallow me up;
And let not the pit shut her mouth upon me.
16 Answer me, O LORD, for thy lovingkindness is good:
According to the multitude of thy tender mercies, turn thou unto me.

17 And hide not thy face from thy servant:
I am in distress; answer me speedily.
18 Draw nigh unto my soul, and redeem it:
Ransom me because of mine enemies.
19 Thou knowest my reproach, and my shame, and my dishonour:
Mine adversaries are all before thee.
20 Reproach hath broken my heart, and I am sore sick;
And I looked for some to take pity, but there was none;
And for comforters, but I found none.
21 They gave me also gall for my meat;
And in my thirst they gave me bitters (*ḥōmeṣ*) to drink.

The king is praying at the optimum time, the time of prayer (Kraus suggests the morning), and he is depending on God's covenanted love, *rob̲-ḥasdek̲ā*, the sure mercies of David, for a favourable answer, *viz.* the news that the new rebels ('them that hate me') have been defeated. Perhaps the renewed water language is nothing but imagery; but it may be that we should rather think of the wretched old man driven to desperation, trying what means he may to move the heart of his inscrutable God. If so, we should think of him as let down into the spring (*b*ᵉ*'ēr*) of Gihon, scrabbling to find a footing in the mud (*ṭîṭ*), conscious of the unplumbed waters beneath (*ma'amaqqê-māyim, m*ᵉ*ṣûlâ*), fearful lest their welling force (*šibbōlet̲ mayim*) should take away his breath—they have come to his *nepeš* (v. 1), he may sink in them so that they swallow him and shut their mouth over him. Well might such a spectacle stir the compassion (*raḥ*ᵃ*meîk̲ā*) of his heavenly liege-lord.

69.17-21. David—so often 'thy servant' in scripture—is indeed in distress (*ṣar-lî*), with enemies/adversaries taking the field against him, reproach, shame and dishonour on every side in his capital, and very likely the physical trials of his ritual prayers from the water. His life (*napšî*) is in peril from such enemies, and he asks God to save it, using the images of the *gō'ēl* and of the payment of ransom in war (*pdh*). It is small wonder if after all this he does not feel too good; if indeed that is how we should render *'ānûšâ. nûš* is a hapax, and is usually connected with *'nš*, to be ill (cf. Jer. 17.9, *'ānuš*; cf. 8.15): BHS follow Duhm and Gunkel in transferring 'my shame and my dishonour' from v. 19, which are then said to be 'unhealable'. But with or without the transfer, it is difficult to think that sickness is the underlying anxiety of the psalm, as is often claimed: there is no amplification of the word, and the concern before and after is on public opinion—reproach, shame, dishonour and the absence of supporters. It is this lack of support from his own which is especially bitter to him, from his 'brethren' (v. 8) of the tribe of Benjamin, from his own family, his mother's children: he looked for a wave (*nûḏ*) from them, but there was not a movement, for those who might sympathize (*m*^{e}*naḥ*^{a}*mîm*) but there was none to be found.

69.21 brings us again to the question of literal or metaphorical interpretation. Almost all commentators take the 'gall' and 'vinegar' as metaphors: the heartlessness of so many enemies was bitterness to the psalmist's soul. But there seemed to be good reasons for thinking that David attempted to purge his sins literally with hyssop (and other means) in 51.7, that he might be true in the inward parts; and the weeping, fasting and sackcloth of 69.10f. must be similarly liturgical means to move heaven by the sincere expiation of his sins (v. 5). So it seems likely that the *rō'š* and the *ḥōmeṣ* of v. 21 are sacramental too: the redoubled trouble of Sheba's revolt shows that God is still angry over Uriah, and the king is driven by his Temple supporters (to whom he looked for 'pity' and 'comfort', v. 20) to take a second dose of the bitter medicine of the soul. *rō'š* is a bitter herb, often paired with *la'anâ*, wormwood, *artemisia absinthium*; *ḥōmeṣ* is normally wine-vinegar, proverbially undrinkable (Prov. 10.26), but perhaps mixed in this case to a still nastier potion. 'They gave me for my food... they gave me to drink...' certainly give the impression of literal eating and drinking; and there is something similar again in Lamentations 3, 'Remember... the wormwood and the gall...' (v. 19), a passage which seemed to be liturgical in other ways.

69.22 Let their table before them become a snare;
And when they are in peace, *let it become* a trap.
23 Let their eyes be darkened, that they see not;
And make their loins continually to shake.
24 Pour out thine indignation upon them,
And let the fierceness of thine anger overtake them.

25 Let their encampment be desolate;
Let none dwell in their tents.
26 For they persecute him who thou hast smitten;
And they tell of the pain of those whom thou hast wounded.
27 Add iniquity unto their iniquity:
And let them not come into thy righteousness.
28 Let them be blotted out of the book of the living,
And not be written with the righteous.

The king and his psalmist have been through some dire times since they heard of Absalom's raising his standard in 52; and they have said (52; 58) and done (68) some hard things. But they have never been as desperate as this before, and it is the first time that we have had such bitter curses: 'Now', said the king in the story, 'shall Sheba the son of Bichri do us more harm than did Absalom' (2 Sam. 20.6). As so often with curses, they arise from present experience. The thought that his fellow-tribesmen (v. 8) have so treated him leads naturally to the thought that their meals (their 'table') should be ruined; that they should sit down for refreshment and in fellowship, and find their food interfered with, and their guests their secret enemies. Perhaps v. 23 also reflects the plight of the old king, his eyes dimmed like the darkened windows of Eccl. 12.3, his frame shivering with fever from the impact of his troubles, or from the hours that he has spent in the cold spring. God seemed to be angry with David; let his wrath descend rather in earnest on his godless enemies. As Jerusalem is half-deserted by their defection, so let their encampment (*ṭîrāṯām*), their tents be empty. Verse 25 reveals the present situation clearly. The enemy are not wealthy accusers (Kraus), magicians (early Mowinckel), or godless oppressors (Gunkel). They are an army on campaign, living in tents, in an encampment, like the nomad tribes of Gen. 25.16; Num. 3.10.

69.26ff. David's enemies have not, of course, forgotten the episode of Uriah and Nathan. David did his best then to expiate his sin by accepting a whipping ('the bones which thou hast bruised', 51.8); but now they are still persecuting 'him whom *thou* hast smitten'—God is thought of as administering the sentences which he has decreed, as at 68.21, 'God smites through the hairy scalp. . . ', and *'attâ* is here in the emphatic position. But what is so odious is that they gloat over the memory of his humiliation; 'they recount of the pains of those whom thou hast wounded'. The plural is the vague generalizing plural of Lk. 24.24, τινες = Peter of 24.12, or of Acts 17.28, where 'some of your own poets' means Aratus. The wounds are the weals made by the whip. *sippēr 'el* means to speak about as a thing of significance, as at Ps. 2.7; the point has been missed by G, which has supplied προσέθηκαν.

The thought now runs on naturally to the question of forgiveness. David's guilt was so serious that he could say, 'Behold, I was shapen in iniquity (*'āwôn*)' (51.5), but he looked forward ultimately to offering sacrifices of righteousness (51.19), and to singing of God's righteousness soon (51.14). Since his enemies have not only taken delight in the anguish of his expiation, but have also hounded him, they deserve no forgiveness; rather they should have their *'āwōn* multiplied, and never enter God's *ṣᵉḏāqâ*. Permanent exclusion from the sphere of divine righteousness is in fact the sentence of death: they are to be blotted from God's register of the living, where at present their names are recorded alongside those of the faithful.

69.29 But I am wretched (*'ānî*) and in pain:
Let thy salvation, O God, set me up on high.
30 I will praise the name of God with a song,
And will magnify him with thanksgiving.
31 And it shall please the LORD better than an ox,
Or a bullock that hath horns and hoofs.
32 The meek have seen it, and are glad:
Ye that seek after God, let your heart live.
33 For the LORD heareth the needy,
And despiseth not his prisoners.
34 Let heaven and earth praise him,
The seas, and every thing that moveth therein.
35 For God will save Zion, and build the cities of Judah;
And they shall abide there, and have it in possession.
36 The seed also of his servants shall inherit it,
And they that love his name shall dwell therein.

With the many trials adumbrated in the psalm, David may well speak of himself as wretched and in pain.[5] He is hoping that his army may still win the battle against the rebels; so will God's 'salvation' put him on top once more. The turn from cursing to prayer brings with it an increase of hopefulness, and so a higher note on which (as so often) to end the psalm. It is a mistake to look for oracles to explain such a change of mood; anyhow there is no sign of such. The king has a covenant with God, a promise of his favour, and that is all the oracle we need. The psalm was probably originally written to be spoken in the evening hour of prayer (55.17; 'in an acceptable time', v. 13), and any ritual humiliations, with prolongued crying will be over for the day.

*69.30*f. Nathan prophesied that David's sin would cast a shadow over the rest of his life; and we may take it that the return of the sword with Sheba will have been a clear sign to David too that his guilt (v. 5) is remembered before God. That being the case, sacrifice is out of the question; only the sacrifices of righteousness are acceptable (51.19), and God delights not in the sacrifice of a sinner (51.16). But as in 51 the praise of the penitent and his contrite heart are not despised by God (51.15ff.), so here it can be said for the king's reassurance that God is better pleased with thanksgiving than he would be with a mature, clean animal offering.

69.32-36. The *'anāwîm*, who seek after God, his servants, are those who have been loyal to the king (cf. v. 6), and are present at the royal worship. They have seen the beginning of the return of hope (vv. 29ff.), and their spirits rise. For—and this is the first time that we have heard of them—those who have been taken prisoner (*'ᵃsîrāîw*), and who are in desperate want (*'eḇyônîm*), will have been praying, and their prayer will not be despised by God: they are *his* prisoners. The whole universe should join in the loyalists' praise, for God is with them. He will surely act, and Jerusalem and Judah will enjoy a time of prosperity, both in this generation and in those to come. It is a measure of the low point to which court expectations have dropped that so defensive a position is taken: the reconquest of the north is for the moment out of mind—all that is hoped for is the safety of Jerusalem and the prosperity of Judah. But perhaps the psalmist has an eye to those present, who are virtually all Judahites (2 Sam. 20.2). We are not told who the prisoners were, but it would have been politic for Sheba to have arrested the Zebulon and Naphtali leaders who had stood by David against Absalom.

The mention of prisoners, as well as of the enemies' encampment and tents, is decisive that Birkeland is right: the situation is a national one, and all

Eaton's points tend to the conclusion that it is spoken in the name of the national leader. But the defection of his 'brethren' and close family, and the accusations of extortion do not accord with Birkeland's hypothesis of a *foreign* war. These details suggest rather a civil war. The zeal for the temple is naturally set in one of three periods: the Maccabaean time, when Duhm and others set it, and which is now seen to be too late for the Psalter; the Haggai-Ezra period, adopted by most critics today; and the time of its original building in the tenth century. We do not have the detail in the psalm, as we had in 68, nor in 2 Samuel 20 as we had in 2 Samuel 18, to settle the matter conclusively for David; but we can say that even without the sequential theory, a Davidic dating is the most plausible.

L.C. Allen[6] sees a strong rhetorical structure to the psalm, with many key terms recurring in the same order in vv. 2-14a/14b-30 (Hebrew numbering) and in vv. 31, 34/35f., chiasmus, etc. The duplication of the water theme certainly is striking, but the claim of two sequences, and of a break in mid-verse, are hardly satisfying: 'rhetoric' sounds too self-conscious for a psalmist whose mind is obsessed with his predicament.

Many MSS take 70 and 71 as a single psalm; 71 is unnumbered in L, and has no heading in the Hebrew, a feature which is unique in the Prayers. Psalm 71 is also unique in having Yahweh in the opening phrase, 'In thee, Yahweh, do I put my trust': elsewhere the Prayers always begin by addressing *ᵉlōhîm*, though Yahweh may come in later (including 70.5, from which it might follow on). But the principal reason for seeing the two psalms as intimately linked is the common language. Both psalms open with the plea to 'deliver me', and 70.1 goes on, 'Make haste to help me, O LORD'. Ps. 70.2 continues, 'Let them be ashamed and confounded That seek after my soul: Let them be turned backward and brought to dishonour that delight in my hurt'. Ps. 71.1 has 'Let me never be ashamed'; 71.12f. run, 'O my God, make haste to help me. Let them be ashamed *and* consumed that are adversaries to my soul; Let them be covered with reproach and dishonour that seek my hurt'; the psalm ends with 71.24, 'For they are ashamed, for they are confounded, that seek my hurt'. It seems clear that there is the closest relation between the two psalms: even the hostile words of the enemy, and the praise of God by the righteous, which fill the rest of 70, are found in extenso in 71. The two psalms must be taken as a unity, like 42–43.

Psalm 70 has a near-duplicate in 40.13-17: earlier commentators, Delitzsch, Kirkpatrick, took 40 to be the earlier form, but most moderns, including Gunkel, Weiser and Kraus, argue that 70 is the original.

(1) The verbal differences can be seen as made deliberately by 40. Our psalmist prefers *ʾ^{e}lōhîm*, but varies it with a parallel Yahweh in 70.1, 5 (cf. 69.30f., 32f.): 40 falls in a strictly Yahwist Book I, and substitutes Yahweh in 40.13, 16 (with two Yahweh's in the former), and a variation in 40.17 (*ʾ^{a}dōnāî*/*ʾ^{e}lōhaî*). 70 opens with a breathless, 'O God, to deliver me, O Yahweh, to my help make haste', and we have the similar 71.12, 'my God, to my help make haste'; 40.13 smoothes with an opening 'Be pleased. . . '; 40.14 achieves the regular 3 + 3 by adding 'Let them be ashamed and confounded *together* That seek after my soul *to destroy it*'. Ps. 70.3 has *yāšûḇū* (as at 56.9) in parallel with *yissōgû*, two words for 'be defeated'; 40 embellishes by substituting *yāšōmmû*, be desolate, and by adding *lî*. In 70.4 our psalmist's normal form *y^{e}šû ʿāṯeḵā* becomes *t^{e}šû ʿaṯeḵā* (? from 71.15); in 70.5 the normal concrete *ʿezrî*, my helper, becomes *ʿezrāṯî*, my help, following 40.13. In 70.5 the good parallel 'Make haste (= 70.1). . . make no tarrying' becomes the pious 'The Lord thinks on me', *yaḥ^{a}šāḇ* coming in for *ḥûšâ*.

(2) Gunkel says that 40 has mixed the *Gattungen*; but it is a mixture in other ways too. Ps. 40.8, 'I delight to do thy will, O my God; Yea, thy law is within my heart': 40.12, 'Mine iniquities have overtaken me. . . ' 40.2, 'He brought me up also out of a pit of destruction': 40.13, 'make haste to help me'. Ps. 40 gives the impression of being a compound of 69 and 70, and even 71. The crying, the pit and the mire of 40.1f. recur in 69.1ff.; the new praise of God which many shall see in 40.3 is like the renewed praise of God which the meek have seen in 69.30ff.: God's preference of obedience to sacrifice comes in 40.6ff. and in 69.31; the iniquities which are 'more than the hairs of my head' in 40.12 are like the enemies of 69.4 who were 'more than the hairs of my head'. The declaration of God's righteousness before the great congregation in 40.9ff. echoes much of 71. 40 is the penultimate psalm of the David collection in Book I, and it looks as if the author is drawing together the thoughts of the next-but-last psalms of the David sequence in Book II.

70 For the Chief Musician. For (*l^{e}*) David; to make memorial.

1 O God, to deliver me (*ʾ^{e}lōhîm l^{e}haṣṣîlēnî*);
O LORD, to my help make haste (*Yhwh l^{e}ʿezrāṯî ḥûšâ*).

2 Let them be ashamed and confounded
That seek after my soul:
Let them be turned backward and brought to dishonour
That delight in my hurt.

3 Let them be turned back by reason of their shame (RV text)
That say, Aha, Aha.
4 Let all those that seek thee rejoice and be glad in thee;
And let such as love thy salvation say continually,
Let God be magnified.
5 But I am wretched and in want (*'ānî w^e'eḇyôn*);
Make haste unto me, O God:
Thou art my help and my deliverer;
O LORD, make no tarrying.

Nathan said that the sword should never depart from David's house: Absalom was to rebel, Sheba was to rebel, and still his sin was not expiated. Even in his old age, indeed, because of his old age, when his potency was at an end, his own son Adonijah, with the support of his nephews Joab and Abishai and his old priest Abiathar, would rise against him to usurp the crown. This was to be his last crisis, and God, faithful to the end, would not be deaf to his urgent pleas. Psalms 70 and 71 are our psalmist's words for David's thoughts in this final hour of need.

The urgency of the king's peril is admirably expressed by the defective opening line: 'O God, to deliver me; O Yahweh, to my help make haste'. We have a similarly effective staccato opening to 69: 'Save me, O God'. Anderson thinks that an opening verb is required at least for metrical reasons (*ad* 40.13), but Dahood justifies MT on an 8.8 syllable count, and by comparing Isa. 38.20, 'Yahweh, to save me!'. Matters were indeed urgent when Bathsheba, and then Nathan, came to warn David that Adonijah was being made king at En-rogel. The urgent note concludes 70, when Yahweh is also bidden not to tarry, and is present at 71.12, but less pressingly.

70.2f. There is a crisis: but it is nowhere near so serious as in 69, as we may tell from the restraint of the prayers, which are not really curses at all. In 69 the enemies were to be poisoned (v. 22), blinded and given St Vitus' Dance (v. 23), killed (v. 28) and their families annihilated (v. 25): here they are merely to be ashamed and confounded, turned backward and brought to dishonour. In other words the psalmist is praying for their defeat, as was often done in respectable European churches on both sides in the War. The singer is nervous because a coup is being attempted; but he puts his trust in the Cherethites and Pelethites as well as in God, and he will not fear. It may be noted too that the enemy are also seen as less vicious. In 69 God was prayed to redeem and ransom the king's soul (life). Here they are said to 'seek after my soul' also in v. 2a, but in v. 2b they merely 'delight in my hurt', and in 71.13 and 24 they 'seek my hurt'. The stress seems to be on *rā'āṯî*, the king's ill—in fact the frustration of his plans for the succession. Their gloating cries of *he'â he'â* are similarly lacking in lethal menace.

70.4f. The king has supporters as well as enemies, those who 'seek' God as opposed to those who 'seek' his life (v. 2, *m^e^ḇaqq^e^šeî/ḵā*); for those who are not against David are with him. As in 69.6, 32 the hope is that these loyalists will not be ashamed by the coup's success, but full of happiness at 'thy salvation', the victory of God's nominee, David. The prayer for God to be magnified (*yigdal*) recurs in the Psalter only in Pss. 35.27; 40.16, which are related to 70, and may perhaps be in contrast to Adonijah who 'exalted himself' (*miṯnaśśē'*). It is God (and his chosen one) and no usurper who should be great in Israel. As at 69.29, the singer tries to move God by the pathos of the king's condition. As BDB comment, *'eḇyôn* in parallel with *'ānî*, should be rendered here 'needing help, deliverance from trouble': in similar parallel usages, Pss. 9.19; 74.21, Isa. 29.19; 41.17, etc., the reference is to the Israelite people as a whole, and the translation 'poor and needy' is quite unsuitable. The king is not short of money, but his need is extreme.

The note *l^e^hazkîr*, to bring to remembrance, in the Heading, has been a puzzle: RVmg renders 'to make memorial', and this is usually explained by the hypothesis that the Psalm was used to accompany incense-offerings (cf. Isa. 66.3, 'he that maketh a memorial of frankincense'; Lev. 24.7). But there is no echo of incense offering in the psalm itself, and the idea looks like the guess of the Targumist, from whom Kirkpatrick and others have taken it. A better explanation would be in line with the long series of recitals which I have supposed to underlie the Selahs from 52.3 to 68.32. These were brief excerpts from the overall story of the Great Rebellion, which I have called the Passion of David: it began at our 2 Sam. 15.7, 'And it came to pass at the end of forty years. . . ', and we have seen its traces as far as 2 Sam. 20.3, where 'David' returns to Jerusalem. But with time more than this was felt to be needed: and especially there was needed a detailed and persuasive account of the succession, justifying (as Wellhausen correctly said) the accession of Solomon. Now from David's time on (2 Sam. 8.16; 20.24) there was an officer in the royal cabinet called the recorder, *mazkîr*; the same man, Jehoshaphat the son of Ahilud, held the post under Solomon (1 Kgs 4.3). So it would seem likely that the author of the Passion narrative, written in the last years of David's life, was this Jehoshaphat: his work, divided into short episodes, was used year by year to provide the historical setting for Psalms 52-68. Half a century later his replacement, perhaps his grandson, composed the first two chapters of 1 Kings as a record of how God put the house of Solomon on the throne at David's death; and this more leisured account was then recited each year before the chanting of 70-71, in one piece, so as to 'remind' the people of how their king, and not Jeroboam, was David's lawful successor. In this way an explanation can be offered for the note in line with the theory I have been offering throughout the Prayers, of a 'history' recital in exposition of the psalmody: the purpose expressed in the word *hazkîr* would agree with that supposed to lie behind the Narrative, and with the title of a contemporary officer, the *mazkîr*. The note comes again in the heading of Psalm 38 only, that is (once more) in one of the last psalms in the David collection in Book I: I have drawn attention above to the similarities of Psalms 35 and 40 to 69-71—see also pp. 84f., *ad* Pss. 53/14.

71.1 In thee, O LORD, do I put my trust:
Let me never be ashamed.
2 Deliver me in thy righteousness, and rescue me:
Bow down thine ear unto me, and save me.
3 Be thou to me a rock of habitation (RV text), whereunto I may continually resort:
Thou hast given commandment to save me;
For thou art my rock and my fortress.
4 Rescue me, O my God, out of the hand of the wicked,
Out of the hand of the unrighteous and cruel man.
5 For thou art my hope, O LORD GOD:
Thou art my trust from my youth.
6 By thee have I been holden up from the womb:
Thou art he that took me out of my mother's bowels (RV text):
My praise shall be continually of thee.

7 I am as a wonder unto many;
But thou art my strong refuge.
8 My mouth shall be filled with thy praise,
And with thy honour all the day.

David has sought refuge (*hāsîṯî*) in Yahweh, and trusts that he will never be defeated ('shamed'). He has God's promise in the royal covenant, and can expect that He will save him 'in his righteousness', and hear his prayer. God was a 'high tower', *miśgāḇ*, to him Mahanaim (59.9, 16f., etc.), and he is prayed to be a rock of habitation (*ma'ôn*) now: the rock above the City of David, now crowned with the Dome, was already set aside by the king as a site for the Temple (2 Sam. 24)—here was to be Yahweh's inexpugnable abode, where his chosen one might always find access and safety. God's covenant assures him that He will have given commandment to his angels to keep him—now is the hour for those commands to be put into action. We learn a little more of 'those that seek after my soul' (70.2). There is a particular 'wicked' and 'unrighteous' man: as the psalmist was so tactful in scarcely referring to Absalom, we may think that he has Joab in mind, for Joab had fallen from David's favour (2 Sam. 19.5ff., 13), and was a born plotter and potential kingmaker. The wicked man of v. 4 is described as *ḥômeṣ*, ruthless, and there are few adjectives that would fit Joab's character better.

71.5f. The distinctive thing about the speaker of 71 is that he is old: a feature found elsewhere in the Psalter only in 37.25, and perhaps in 39.13 and 41.5, all psalms at the end of the first David collection. Yahweh has been his trust from his youth (v. 5); he was supported (*nismaḵtī*) by God at birth in token that he was his son (Eaton, v. 6); it was God who acted as midwife at his birth, severing (*gôzî*) the cord for him (v. 6b). Now he is 'in the time of age'. and his 'strength is failing' (v. 9); God 'taught him from his youth' (v. 17), and he prays to be preserved 'unto old age and gray hairs' (v. 18). Such language suits the aged king David of 1 Kings 1. Already in Absalom's time he had let affairs slip, and he could be persuaded to stay safe in Mahanaim and let his nephews command the army in battle: now human frailty has brought him yet lower—he has lost his sexual powers and cannot keep warm (1 Kgs 1.1-4). *kôaḥ*, the failing 'strength' of 71.9 is used of sexual virility in Gen. 49.3.

Rogerson and McKay doubt whether the speaker is old, and the Hebrew permits the reading that he is still in middle years and hopes to live on till he is old in God's blessing. But Gunkel and most critics take him to be old (Delitzsch, not *very* old), and he certainly seems to have the span of life on his mind. Verse 9 is hard to understand without this supposition: why should a middle-aged man pray not to be cast off in the time of old age? The repeated phrases, 'Cast me not off... forsake me not...' sound like the negatives of 'Deliver me... rescue me...' There are also two views about *gôzî*, for which G reads σκεπαστής, with a likely Hebrew *'uzzî*; preferred by RVmg. But this looks like an easier reading, and Delitzsch declares the MT to be unassailable.

71.7f. Delitzsch thought the speaker a wonder because he had been so often delivered, Kirkpatrick because he had been so often chastised; Eaton translates *môpēṯ* a portent, neutral, but a sign from God, as in Isa. 8.18; Zech. 3.8. The dilemma arises from the lack of focus. But if the psalm is spoken in David's name, it is easier to see what is meant. He is a divine symbol because despite his sin (adversative w^e, v. 7b) God has stood by him and been true to his covenant; and for this he will give praise continually. For the negative aspects of a wonder, cf. Isa. 52.14; Deut. 28.46. The public position of the speaker comes through in that he is a wonder to *many*, as in the access which he has to 'my God' in his 'rock of habitation'.

71.9 Cast me not off in the time of old age;
Forsake me not when my strength faileth.
10 For mine enemies speak concerning me;
And they that watch for my soul take counsel together,
11 Saying, God hath forsaken him:
Pursue and take him; for there is none to deliver.
12 O God, be not far from me:
O my God, make haste to help me.
13 Let them be ashamed *and* consumed that are adversaries to my soul;
Let them be covered with reproach and dishonour that seek my hurt
14 But I will hope continually,
And will praise thee yet more and more.
15 My mouth shall tell of thy righteousness,
And of thy salvation all the day;

For I know not the numbers *thereof*.
16 I will come in the strength of the LORD GOD:
I will make mention of thy righteousness, even of thine only.

God has been David's help through his long life, and he trusts that he will not be rejected now. The psalm is somewhat repetitive (as old men are?): each of the eight-verse strophes follows the pattern Save me—I am old—I will praise you for it. If we may trust the account in 1 Kgs 1.1-5, the psalmist has exactly understood the mind of his enemies. The very fair damsel Abishag was brought to the king, 'but the king knew her not. Then (*w*^{e}) Adonijah the son of Haggith exalted himself'. When Joab and Abishai realised that David's 'strength failed', they conspired to put Adonijah on the throne, with the support of most of his brothers, and of Abiathar. Such enterprises are not put into action without the principals 'taking counsel together'; the failure of David's powers must have seemed a sign that 'God hath forsaken him'; and now that there was 'none to deliver', they were free to go after him and seize (*tpś*) him. Long acquaintance with Joab, and especially in his dealings with Abner and Amasa, left little doubt of what would happen after that: hence the phrases 'watch for my soul (life)', 'adversaries (*śōṭ*^{e}*nē*) to my soul'. RV has correctly rendered (*śṭ*^{e}*nē*); as a noun *śāṭān* usually means an adversary (e.g. Num. 22.22; 1 Sam. 29.4), and the denominative verb plainly has this meaning in Ps. 38.21. The translation 'accuse' is not suitable with 'my soul', and is introduced to support the view that the enemy were private accusers. They were adversaries to David's soul because they meant to kill him.

71.12-16. The thought of the enemies' intentions brings back the appeal of 70.1: only now that they are seen as planning the king's death, it is suitable for them to be 'consumed' in their turn. As the psalm advances, the urgency seems to diminish: perhaps 70 was composed when word of the conspiracy reached the palace, and it was extended into 71 as the day passed, and rumours arrived of the panic at En-rogel. In any case there is continual hope from v. 14, and the promise of praise for God's righteousness (in keeping the royal covenant) and his salvation (of the king's life, and his retinue's). David will come (v. 16) into the Temple, supported by the divine strength (*g*^{e}*ḇûrôṯ*), now he has so little of his own. He will cause Yahweh's righteousness to be remembered, 'even his alone', for he has not much of that either. Perhaps this 'causing to remember' (*'azkîr*) prompted the idea of having the *mazkîr* to cause the people remember in later times.

Verse 15c has been a puzle, 'For I know not *sᵉpōrôṯ*': *sᵉpōrâ* is a hapax, and could mean 'numbers', *viz.* of times my life has been saved ('thy salvation', v. 15b). This is not only the understanding of the Targum, and of Symmachus, but also, it seems, of the earliest commentator on Psalms 70–71, the author of Psalm 40—'the wonderful works which thou hast done... are more than can be numbered (*missappēr*)'; cf. above p. 230.

71.17 O God, thou hast taught me from my youth;
And hitherto have I declared thy wondrous works.
18 Yea, even unto old age and gray hairs, O God, forsake me not;
Until I have declared thine arm unto *the next* generation,
Thy might to everyone who comes (*yāḇô*).
19 Thy righteousness, O God, is very high;
Thou who hast done great things,
O God, who is like unto thee?
20 Thou, which hast shewed us many and sore troubles,
Shalt quicken us again,
And shall bring us up again from the depths of the earth.
21 Increase thou my greatness,
And turn again and comfort me.
22 I will also praise thee with the psaltery,
Even thy truth, O my God:
Unto thee will I sing praises with the harp,
O thou Holy One of Israel.
23 My lips shall greatly rejoice when I sing praises unto thee;
And my soul, which thou hast redeemed.
24 My tongue also shall talk of thy righteousness all the day long
For they are ashamed, for they are confounded, that seek my hurt.

The speaker is 'fairly clearly the king' (Eaton). He prays for his 'greatness' (*gᵉḏullāṯî*) to be increased: the word is normally used of God, or in Esther of the king and Mordecai—it is not suitable for the honour of a pious layman. He is in a position to address what seems to be the general public for protracted periods in the Temple, both in word and in music. His mouth will tell of God's righteousness 'all the day' (v. 15), and we have nearly the same phrase in v. 24. 'I will come' (v. 16) most naturally means 'to the Temple', and there he will make God's righteousness to be remembered, presumably by a public gathering there. These are specified in v. 18 as 'a generation', 'everyone that will come'. Although these expressions are not entirely clear, and the text has been doubted, RV's interpretation, 'the next generation', seems probable. Their translation, 'everyone that is to come', is more doubtful, since the aged speaker is asking to be spared to address them personally, and he cannot be expecting to live for ever. 'Everyone who shall come', sc. to the service, makes better sense. In v. 20 the written MT lapses into the plural, 'us', three times; the read version (Q) has the singular 'me' each time, which is likely to be the easier reading, assimilated to the singular of the rest of the psalm. So the speaker will be seeing his experiences as one with those of his hearers; just as David might do, since his 'sore troubles' and recovery from 'the depths of the earth' to 'life' once more would indeed be felt by his loyal followers as their escape from death also.

It is sometimes suggested that God 'taught' the speaker the great events of the national history from his youth; but the context seems rather to suggest that God taught him by experience. His soul, 'which thou hast redeemed', will greatly rejoice (v. 23); i.e. his own life has been saved, and he will sing praise to God for that. He asks God to 'turn again and comfort me' (v. 21): he and his hearers have been through many crises and close to death (v. 20), and he is looking for an easier time in the future. He has himself been a portent to many (v. 7), and his praises are for God's help in face of those conspiring against his life (vv. 10-15). Surely it is his own experiences which he wishes to tell the congregation, and which inspire such personal joy. Once more the wording suits David well. Few people had had so many and such sore troubles, and had been delivered times without number. In Adonijah's coup he had been to 'the depths of the earth', but had been restored to life. He had no doubt publicly related God's works 'hitherto', i.e. before the attempted revolution; now there would be yet more to tell and to sing of his 'truth' to his promise. He is the Holy One of Israel, whose word is his bond—the first time we meet the phrase of which Isaiah was to make such powerful use.

Older commentators, Delitzsch and (hesitantly) Kirkpatrick, thought of the speaker as Jeremiah; and at least he had a recognized position in the Temple, and was able to address crowds. But the dominant position, taken by Duhm, Gunkel, Kraus, Anderson and others, has been that the speaker is a private individual, sick and close to death, beset by enemies who accuse him of things he has not done; he is a religious man, and has sought refuge in the Temple, where he prays for God to take action on his behalf. Doubts do arise about this picture, which is offered by Kraus to explain many of the psalms. Could private individuals really have been permitted to address gatherings of their supporters in the Temple *all day*? And with music? How many such people are thought of as giving their personal witness at any one time? The only biblical parallel for such activities is the rather distant one of the prophetess Anna in Lk. 2.38; but Luke clearly sees this as something unique. The royal model proposed by Birkeland[7] and Mowinckel[8] and defended by Eaton[9] is far more persuasive, with a national gathering; and, once the sequential hypothesis is accepted, the detail can be seen to fit David closely. His day-long calling of his troubles to remembrance then easily becomes the annual festal procession with the chanting of the Prayers which I have spent this book proposing.

I have noted that vv. 12f., 24 are close to 70.1f.; and that the whole of 70 is nearly reproduced in 40.13-17. In addition to this 71.1-3 are almost the same wording as 31.1-3, and there are (less strong) links with 22. This has caused Kirkpatrick to speak of 71 as a mosaic, and critics tend either to think of our psalmist as copying pieces out of Book I (so Delitzsch), or as drawing on a common stock of phrasing. Both theories arise from the unfortunate idea of an 'Elohistic editor' going through Books II and III changing Yahweh to *ᵉlōhîm*: the uses of 'God' in 71 then become evidence of its secondariness. But in fact the secondariness of 40 should be seen as a strong pointer in the opposite direction, and the differences with 31 and 22 suggest the same conclusion. Thus 71's imperfects, *taṣṣîlēnî* and *tᵉpallᵉṭēnî* become the easier imperatives, *pallᵉṭēnî* and *haṣṣîlēnî* in 31.1f.; 71's 'rock of habitation' (*mā'ôn*) becomes the more usual 'rock of strength' (*mā'ôz*) in 31.3; and 71's 'to come to continually: thou hast commanded to save me', which Gunkel declares to be senseless, becomes 'for a house of defence' in 31.3, with many of the same consonants. Similarly 71's 'thou art he that severed me' (*gôzî*) at birth becomes 22.9's 'thou art he that brought me forth' (*gōḥî*). The original poem is 71.

David's life did not end in one more crisis: it ended with his abdication in favour of his son Solomon, and with the enthronement of the latter under his blessing (1 Kgs 1.48). Nathan had not only foretold bloodshed as the expiation of David's sin, but also that he would be succeeded by a permanent dynasty (2 Sam. 7.12ff.). So year by year the Israelite people did not close their autumn festival with a recollection of their founder-king's sufferings: they completed the cycle with the great hopes and aspirations of the new reign, expressed in the triumphalist Psalm 72.

72 For (*li-*) Solomon.
1 Give the king thy judgments, O God,
And thy righteousness unto the king's son.
2 He shall judge thy people with righteousness,
And thy poor with judgment.
3 The mountains shall bring peace to the people,
And the hills, in righteousness.
4 He shall judge the poor of the people,
He shall save the children of the needy,
And shall break in pieces the oppressor.
5 They shall fear thee while the sun endureth,
And before the moon, throughout all generations.
6 He shall come down like rain upon the mown meadow (*gēz*):
As showers that water the earth.
7 In his days shall the righteous flourish;
And abundance of peace, till the moon be no more.

As the preceding series of psalms has been composed 'for David', so has this final member of the sequence (72.20) been written 'for Solomon'. It is, like the others, an *^{e}lōhîm* psalm (v. 1); like 61, 62, 63, 64, 65, it is a prayer for the king; like some of the other Prayers, and especially 71, it lays great stress on *ṣ^{e}đāqâ*, God's righteousness in which the king is to share. Its theological basis is the link between this royal righteousness and the divine blessing on the produce of the fields; a theme which was also insistent in 65 and 67. It expects that in consequence of the new king's administration of divine justice (*kî*, v. 12), he will preside over a world empire in which the kings of the nations will lay their tribute at his feet—the same expectation which was in evidence in 67, and more specifically in 68.28-35. The 'heavy' style of 72 (Delitzsch) is to be accounted for by the grandiloquent mode suited to its topic. The Prayers have been mainly Laments: here they end with a royal intercession of high expectation.

72.1-7. 'The king' and 'the king's son' are the same person: that is, the Prayer is for the acceding crown prince, whose legitimacy is being stressed. It was perhaps felt proper to present him with a scroll inscribed with the divine law, in the same way as Hammurabi was presented with the Babylonian law by Shamash, the sun-god;[10] hence 'give the king *mišpāṭeîḵā*'—but he will also need God's own just heart if he is to do the work. The poor are especially God's concern, for there is no one to care for them but him (cf. 68.5f.); and by the same token he will hammer their oppressors (v. 4). With this firmness from the throne will come a wholesome fear of God from rich and poor alike; and this habit of godfearing virtue will be a permanency 'with the sun', 'before the moon', not just the passing way of a single generation (v. 5). The king's fair-minded administration will issue in untold prosperity (v. 7): good men will see the reward of their work in his lifetime, and the land will flourish in plenty under his successors, for ever. The link is made in v. 3: it is by the king's righteousness (*biṣᵉḏāqâ*) that the mountains and hills—the least rich land—will bring plenty (*šālôm*) to the people. When God purged away the old king's transgressions in 65.3, he visited the earth and blessed it in the rain (65.9): his son is to be just and attuned to God's rulings, and through his righteousness will come much blessing. He will bring wealth to his subjects as the rain does when the grass is mown and the shorn fields thirst for the means to their second crop (Amos 7.1); as in David's Last Words (2 Sam. 23.4).

gēz (from *gzz* to cut) is normally the mown grass (or cut fleece); it can hardly be either of these since rain does not improve them. Some scholars therefore take it to be the mown meadow (Kirkpatrick), in the moment when the latter rain will bring on more grass, as Amos mentions; others that it is the field with its burden of grass awaiting the scythe.[11] The distinction is not significant for our psalm; nor is the possibility of translating RV's futures ('He shall judge', etc.) as optatives ('May he judge'). Mowinckel wrote: 'In Israelite opinion intercessory prayer had the same creating might as the blessing and oracle... there may be cases where it is difficult to decide whether we have a word of blessing, an intercessory prayer, or a prophecy, and therefore we are uncertain how to translate. A psalm like 72 may easily be read as a prophecy of the ideal king'.[12]

72.8 He shall have dominion also from sea to sea,
And from the River unto the ends of the earth.
9 They that dwell in the wilderness shall bow before him;
And his enemies shall lick the dust.
10 The kings of Tarshish and of the isles shall render tribute:

The kings of Sheba and Seba shall offer gifts.
11 Yea, all kings shall fall down before him:
All nations shall serve him.
12 For he shall deliver the needy when he crieth;
And the poor, and him that hath no helper.
13 He shall have pity on the weak and needy,
And the souls of the needy shall he save.
14 He shall redeem their soul from fraud and violence;
And precious shall their blood be in his sight.

The thought of the psalm does not wander: the theme of the king's universal dominion (vv. 8-11) rests upon the presupposition of his righteous rule ('For he shall deliver the needy...', v. 12), and is resumed in v. 15 ('to him shall be given of the gold of Sheba') after the second statement (vv. 12-14) of his just reign. With righteousness comes God's blessing (Lev. 26.3-13), and so national prosperity, prestige and power. The singer's hopes are extensive: with such a God, and with such a king, the sky is the limit. 'From sea to sea' probably means the cosmos: the western ocean and the Arabian Gulf were the tale of foreign sailors, known in Israel as Pishon, a river from Eden girdling the earth.[13] The River is likely to be Euphrates, *hannāhār* of 1 Kgs 5.5 (EV 4.24), another of the rivers of Eden (Gen. 2.14), and a natural frontier of civilisation. The desert-dwellers were proverbially untameable; they delighted in war (68.30), and were like the wild ass (Gen. 16.12). Tarshish in Spain, and the isles of the Western Mediterranean, were the source of silver, iron, and other metals: Sheba in Arabia Felix and Seba, near Ethiopia (Isa. 43.3), were in the area famous for gold (Gen. 2.12; 10.28f.). The gold of Sheba comes again in v. 15, so the places are named both for their distance and for their wealth. The tribute is not exacted: the kings will 'return' it (*yāšîbû*) in gratitude for the peace which they now enjoy.

The perils from which the poor suffer are unclear, but include oppressors (*'ôšēq*, v. 4) and capital cases (v. 14).

72.15 And he shall live; and to him shall be given of the gold of Sheba:
And men shall pray for him continually;
They (RV text) shall bless him all the day long.
16 He shall be a strip of open country (*yᵉhî pissaṯ-bar*) in the land upon the tops of the mountains;

His fruit (*piryô*) shall shake like Lebanon:
And from (*mē-*) the city shall flourish like grass of the earth.
17 His name shall endure for ever;
His name shall have issue as long as the sun (RV text):
And men shall bless themselves in him;
All nations shall call him happy.
18 Blessed be the LORD God, the God of Israel,
Who only doeth wondrous things:
19 And blessed be his glorious name for ever;
And let the whole earth be filled with his glory.
Amen and Amen.
20 The Prayers of David the son of Jesse are ended.

As in Psalm 45, the thought turns finally from the king's just reign and foreign conquests to his numerous progeny; v. 16 is not a repetition of the prophecy of corn in plenty (RV and most commentators) but of his own fruitfulness.[14] He (the king) will live (long, cf. 1 Kgs 1.34, 39, '*yᵉhî* King Solomon'), and (one) will give him gold, etc., and bless him all day: cf. 1 Kgs 8.66, 'Solomon sent the people away, and they blessed the king'. In v. 16 *yᵉhî* must also refer to the king, as *pissaṯ* would be naturally followed by a fem. verb. *pissâ* is a hapax, but *pss* in later Hebrew means to cut into strips, cf. *pss* a strip of the sea in Gen. R. 84, ad 37.3. *bar* means open land, cf. Job 39.4, '(The young deer) grow up in the open field'. So the king is to be like a stretch of land on the hilltops, like Mt Lebanon; as the mighty cedars wave there (*r'š* in its normal sense, to shake, rather than G.R. Driver's postulated second verb, to abound,[15]) so will his offspring be (*pᵉrî*, descendants, as in Deut. 7.13 and often). But they will spread, not of course from the mountain-valleys but from the city (*mē'îr*), and flourish like grass. Caquot's view of the king's personal fruitfulness resolves the problems of v. 16; cf. Anderson's citing of Job 5.25, 'your descendants shall be many, and your offspring as the grass of the earth'. This then leads naturally into v. 17: the king's name will 'send forth shoots' (K)/'receive shoots' (Q), and people will say, 'May thy house be like the house of Solomon'. So would his dynasty be a permanency, for ever.

72.18f. It has been normal to regard vv. 18f. as a blessing closing Book II, and thus a later addition: there are similar, but shorter blessings at the end of 41 (Book I) and 106 (Book IV); a much shorter blessing at the end of 89 (Book III); and 150 is a doxology to end Book V and the whole Psalter. In recent times doubts have been expressed about this by Weiser, and by Rogerson and McKay, on the grounds that the blessing must have been in place by the time that v. 20 came to be added. Such doubts are surely justified. (1) 51–72 are indeed a collection, the Prayers of David, which come to a triumphant conclusion in 72, and a blessing of God to end the collection must have seemed natural to the author. He has been witness of so many crises into which God brought the errant David, and of deliverances without number, and of the consummation of his hopes in the accession of Solomon. He has closed every other psalm from 51 to 71 with the thought of God's goodness, and sometimes even with the promise of 'thanks because thou hast done it' (52.9; cf. 54.6f.; 56.12f.; 57.9ff.; 59.17; 61.8; 64.10). It is not likely that he would fail to keep his word now. (2) Two of the other Prayers actually close with a blessing: 66.20, '*Blessed be God*, Which hath not turned away my prayer, nor his mercy from me'; 68.35, 'Terrible is God out of thy holy places, *The God of Israel*... *Blessed be God*'. (3) The blessings at the end of 41 and 106 use the form, 'Blessed be Yahweh, the God of Israel'; 89.52 has simply 'Blessed be Yahweh'. Our psalm has 'Blessed be Yahweh *ᵉlōhîm*, the God of Israel'. It is noticeable that whoever wrote the final verses to 41, 89 and 106 did not include the 'clumsy' *ᵉlōhîm*, and an editor would have been likely to leave it out here too (as do some modern editors, with G and S). But our psalmist wrote *ᵉlōhîm ᵉlōhê yiśrā'ēl* at 68.8 and 68.35, and *yhwh ᵉlōhîm ṣᵉḇâ'ôṯ ᵉlōhê yiśrā'ēl* at 59.5, and the sequence of piled up divine names, including the *ᵉlōhîm* which has been his first preference throughout the Prayers, seems natural to his way of writing. (4) We may note also the mention of *nip̱lā'ôṯ* in this doxology only, which are done by God *lᵉḇaddô*, alone: God's *nip̱lā'ôṯ*, the acts of 'thy righteousness *lᵉḇaddeḵā*' also occurred in 71.16f. The concluding prayer, that the whole earth be filled with God's glory, is particularly suitable, too, for a psalm which anticipates a golden age encompassing all nations.

For a change (as Eaton observes wryly), 'peace reigns also among the commentators'. Only Delitzsch and Dahood, and (hesitantly) Rogerson and McKay, ascribe the psalm to Solomon. It is rather a prayer of blessing on the Davidic king, either at his accession or at an annual renewal of his kingship, whether at some annual enthronement liturgy (Mowinckel, Anderson, etc.) or less specifically on the king's (?birth)day (Gunkel). As such it was a word of power looking forward to a golden age from the coming year on, with just government, prosperity and worldwide prestige. Earlier suggestions of a provenance from Persian or Greek times are refused: the psalm is for an Israelite king, pre-exilic, perhaps Hezekiah (Kirkpatrick), relatively early (Kraus).

Even without the sequential hypothesis we may think this consensus a good example of scholarly timidity. When nineteenth-century critics from Hitzig to Duhm had popularized a radical, post-exilic date, it seemed bold enough to carry the composition back into the monarchic period. The Solomon tradition was as easily written off as the Davidic tradition for 51-70: it could be lightly explained as the later editor's inference from similarity to the traditions of Solomon's reign of peace, the visit of the Queen of Sheba, etc. To accept such a tradition would be to court suspicions of naivety if not of fundamentalism. But in fact the case for an original association with Solomon is strong.

The Deuteronomists were suspicious of Solomon. He loved many foreign women who turned away his heart so that he went after Ashtoreth and Milcom; he built high places for Chemosh and Molech. So Yahweh was angry with Solomon because his heart had turned away: 1 Kings 11 is appended to the traditions friendly to Solomon in 1 Kings 1-10, because Solomon was seen as starting Israel on the downward path. Similarly in Deut. 17.14-20, a king is permitted in Israel: 'only he must not multiply horses for himself. . . and he shall not multiply wives to himself, lest his heart turn away; nor shall he greatly multiply for himself silver and gold' (vv. 16f.). These are the very things which Solomon did: 666 talents of gold (1 Kgs 10.14), fourteen hundred chariots and horses (10.26), and seven hundred wives (11.3). So the traditions friendly to Solomon are pre-Deuteronomic.

But these traditions are in part factual—his administration, and the building of the palace and Temple—and in part legendary; and the legends cover the same matters as Psalm 72. 1 Kings 3 describes Solomon's prayer for wisdom and his marvellous *judgment* for the two harlots (v. 28). Solomon had *peace* on all sides round about him, and Israel and Judah dwelt in safety, from Dan even to Beersheba, every man under his vine and under his fig tree (5.4f. Heb.). He *had dominion over all* on this side *the River*, over *all the kings* on this side the River; they brought *presents* and *served* Solomon all his days (5.1, 4). Output was legendary and the population multiplied: Judah and Israel were as many as the sand by the sea, and they ate and drank and were happy (4.20). The queen of *Sheba* came bearing very much *gold* (10.1f.). It is obvious that this happy picture derives from Psalm 72. Not only is it at variance with reality, the series of revolts described in 1 Kgs 11.14-40, but the sober outline of the psalm has been clothed with the colourful garments of the imagination. The tale of the baby and the sword gives life to the dry picture of the good king giving justice to the poor; and the humble kings of Sheba, the fabled land of gold, kneeling with their tribute, have become a Queen, more suited to Solomon's taste, with a very great retinue and precious stones and camels, enquiring of the great king's wisdom.

Kraus is right that the psalm is relatively early. The worldwide empire and the boundless fruitfulness of the land are not the literal expectation of the singer, but they are the extrapolation of real hopes: better times, peace and plenty, hegemony and prestige. But after Solomon hopes of hegemony and prestige were gone: Judah was a little place, dominated for two centuries by her northern neighbour, and after that by the great Near Eastern Empires. The prophets often uttered visions of God's dealings with these 'nations', but it is striking how rarely Judah is thought of as 'having dominion over them'. One might cite Mic. 7.12 or Zech. 9.9; but people are comforted by believable prognostications, not wild dreams, and the prophets generally limit themselves to the destruction of Judah's enemies. In the Psalter similarly the king is expected to defeat neighbouring countries in battle (Pss. 20, 21, 45), but worldwide dominion is not much spoken of. It comes in Ps. 2.8, but Psalm 2 may be a very early psalm also. It forms the basis of the long reproach in 89; but here it is not a hope at all, but a long-remembered tradition from Solomon's days, at wide variance with present reality.

It is the sequence revealed in the Prayers which settles the matter. Our psalmist put into David's mouth suitable words of penitence for his ill deeds in 51; he expressed the king's anguish through the hard days of the retreat, and his triumph after the battle, in 52–68; he wrote two long laments for the revolts of Sheba (69) and Adonijah (70–71); and here is his paean of hope for the young Solomon, *spes tanta futuri*. The reader may think that so close a fit with the traditions behind 2 Samuel 12–20, 1 Kings 1, and the other Old Testament data we have examined, is not likely to be a coincidence.

A HISTORICAL POSTSCRIPT

Commentaries normally provide an exegesis of the text of the psalms: I have tried to expound the text of the Psalter—that is, I have regarded the technical notes (Selah, Michtam, etc.), the topographical notes ('At the Dove of the Distant Terebinths', etc.), the musical notes ('On a stringed instrument', etc.), the order in which the psalms stand, and above all the terminal note ('The Prayers of David. . . ') as integral and indispensable to the understanding of the psalms themselves. Only the historical notes have I in general treated as later and mistaken comments; and even there I have thought that the historical notes to 51 and 72 were either faint traditions or accurate guesses. I should like to conclude with a brief account of the steps which I see as leading from the composition of the Prayers to the formation of Book II of the Psalter. In part this must be based on my earlier book, *The Psalms of the Sons of Korah*; and in part it must be speculation, like so much else in Old Testament study.

In 71.17 David says, 'hitherto have I declared thy wondrous works': that is, even before Adonijah's rising, David had been used to addressing his people, giving an account of his deliverances from peril and death.He speaks of declaring God's arm to a generation (to come, v. 18), and of his praise lasting 'all the day long' (vv. 15, 24); partly he will tell the story (*yesappēr* v. 15, *'azkîr*, v. 16; *'aggîḏ*, v. 18), and partly he will sing God's praise to music (vv. 22f.). Processions were a normal part of celebration in ancient Israel (2 Sam. 6; Neh. 12; Ps. 48), and it is not easy to see how the people could participate much without them. The first step, then, in the liturgical use of the Prayers, is likely to have been a procession taking a full day during the autumn Festival in David's lifetime. The procession went from the Temple, up Olivet, past Bahurim to the Terebinths, down and over to Mt Scopus, and back via the Temple area to the palace. It included stops at the places mentioned in 2 Samuel 15–16. David himself told of the events at each point, and led the choral singing of Psalms 51–68. Perhaps he survived to do the same with Psalms 69–

72 after the troubles with Sheba and Adonijah; but we may hardly think his health up to it.

After David's death, this liturgy will have been maintained. It 'caused to remember' effectively: that is, it brought home to people from all over Israel God's faithfulness to his covenant with David, and with Solomon his son now reigning in his stead, with so much wisdom, prosperity, and international prestige. The liturgy did something vital: it weaned 'the men of Israel' away from the fact that they and their fathers had fought for Absalom and Sheba, and would have fought for Adonijah, and subtly assimilated them with the 'righteous' and the *ḥ^{a}sîḏîm* who had stood by the king. This alchemy worked for the whole of Solomon's reign, and might have fused a united nation permanently but for the folly of Rehoboam. All the Prayers were now used, with a magnificent climax in 72. As David was there no more, Jehoshaphat the *mazkîr*, or some such person, stood in with his own account of the Great Rebellion, which I have called the Passion of David. The number of halts on the procession was cut to the three (Mahalath, the Terebinths, the Lily of Testimony) mentioned in the Headings, and the narrative was recited in short sections where indicated by the Selahs (which run from 52.3 to 68.32). Solomon had an account of his Accession prefaced to 70–71 'to bring to remembrance'.

With time the memories of the setting of these things faded; and after Solomon's death the need was felt the more acutely for a justification of the status quo, now rejected by the northern tribes. There were still hazy memories of the upheavals of the 970s, and the Passion narrative could be incorporated into a longer, continuous tale, beginning with David's adultery with Bathsheba, and ending with a full and detailed account of the events surrounding his death. It included a much fuller account of Absalom's rise (2 Sam. 13.1–15.6), and it painted Sheba's rebellion in the colours of Jeroboam's. The result was the Succession Narrative, a brilliant piece of story-telling, charged with personal interest, obsequious to 'the king', sexy, dramatized, pathetic, and triumphally pro-Solomon. Much of the old Passion Narrative was now cut—the detail of the Mahanaim siege, and of the Zalmon campaign: probably the whole new story was recited in the Temple area, with the psalms appended as may be. We cannot tell how long the procession lasted.

It takes a major religious crisis to change a liturgy (as we have witnessed in our own time), and something along these lines probably continued for two centuries. But in 732, or soon after, the Assyrians took Dan, and the Korahite priesthood over the next decade took refuge in Jerusalem (*PSK*, 71f.). These men were priests of genuine Levitical descent, and they had presided over the annual celebrations of a considerable empire within living memory. Their traditions, and their psalmody, were received with acclaim in Jerusalem, a provincial centre and easily impressed (2 Kgs 16). Furthermore their psalms (which went back at least to the 9th century), had recently been adapted with eloquent laments calling on God to save their country from the Assyrians (42–44; 48–49), and threats from the same quarter now seemed an urgent peril in Jerusalem, and were to become so in the next two decades. It came therefore to seem an attractive option to adapt the old Korahite psalmody for worship at Jerusalem; so should the dew of Hermon fall on the hill of Zion.

The Korah psalms had, in their final form from the 730s, provided a sequence of psalmody for the autumn festival at Dan. Each day had its own theme and liturgy, and a psalm was sung in the evening: Yahweh would command his lovingkindness in the day, and in the night his song would be sung (42.8). The sequence ran as follows:

Bul	*Theme/Liturgy*	*Psalm*
10th	Pilgrimage march arrives at Dan	42
11th	Sacrifice the following morning	43
14th	Eve of Festival Lament	44
15th	Blessing of King: Procession, Enthronement, Marriage	45
16th	Victory over Waters: Procession to Jordan-source, Fire	46
17th	God's Kingship: Procession with Ephod to Temple	47
18th	God's City: Procession round walls	48
19th	God's enemies warned	49
20th	Expiation rites: priest in underground stream	88
21st	Creation: Triumphal March past Ephod	89.1f., 5-18

Earlier, more serene, Korahite psalms, 84, 85, 87, had been ousted by the more anxious and therefore more needful 42–43, 44, 48, but the former were still remembered.

The Korahites were willing enough to adapt their well-loved psalms to their new home: one or two references to mount Zion were substituted for Dan (48.2,11f.), and the mention of Hermon, the Jordan (42.6) and the northern frontier (48.2) escaped notice. But the Judahites were attached to their Davidic traditions, and it was agreed to retain the Jerusalem liturgy for the last period of the week. The themes were closely similar, for David's troubles were the expiation for his sin just as the Korahite priest's day of terror among the ghosts was in expiation for the nation's sins; indeed the imagery of the water in 69 was very close to that of 88. So 51-71 took over from 88 as the psalmody for 20th (Ethanim now, the seventh month); and 72 was the prayer for a coming golden age in place of 89A on 21st. 88 and 89 joined 84, 85 and 87 in a Korahite appendix. In the course of time an eighth day was added the feast (Lev. 23.36; Num. 29. 35-38), and an extra psalm was needed: it was inserted suitably between the Korah and the David sequences, and 50 was chosen from the Asaph group as being close in theme to 51—obedience rather than sacrifice. So was Book II formed.

NOTES

Notes to Chapter 1

1. The idea that the rubric in 72.20 refers to all the foregoing David psalms recurs occasionally in more modern literature, e.g. Gerald Wilson, 'The Use of Royal Psalms at the "Seams" of the Hebrew Psalter', *JSOT* 35 (1986), pp. 85-94. But Wilson's royal psalms are really limited to 2, 72 and 89: as 2 marks the beginning of a sequence, we might have expected 41, 42 and 73 to be royal psalms, and indeed 90, 106, 107 and 150, if the theory is to carry conviction.
2. So K. Rupprecht, *Der Tempel von Jerusalem*. Gründung Salomos oder jebusitisches Erbe? (BZAW 144, Berlin/New York, 1977), passim.
3. *Der Tempel*.
4. *Commentar über die Psalmen* (Heidelberg, 1811), pp. 3ff.
5. *Das Ich der Psalmen* (FRLANT 16, Göttingen, 1912).
6. Denzinger, 2132-35.
7. I, p. 524.
8. *Das Buch der Psalmen* (Bonn, 1936), p. 192.
9. W. Grossouw, in a preface to Pius Drijvers, *Les Psaumes* (Paris, 1958).
10. *Les Psaumes* (1950), p. 16; cited by Drijvers, pp. 29f.
11. *The Book of Psalms* I (Dublin, 1953), p. xxx.
12. Honourable exceptions would include Aubrey Johnson, who is open to early dates for a number of psalms; cf. for Ps. 51, *The Cultic Prophet and Israel's Psalmody*, (Cardiff, 1979), pp. 412-31; and more generally, John Eaton, *The Psalms Come Alive*, (London/Oxford, 1984) pp. 39-42.
13. Gunkel, *Einleitung in die Psalmen* (Göttingen, 1933), p. 451.
14. Cf. J. Wilkinson, *Egeria's Travels* (London, 1971), pp. 253-77.
15. JSOT Suppl., 1982. (*PSK*).
16. *ANET*, pp. 331-34; cf. Eaton, *Kingship and the Psalms* (2nd edn, Sheffield, 1986), pp. 87-101. (*KP*).
17. *The Logic of Scientific Discovery* (expanded edn, London, 1959); a series of papers collected as *Conjectures and Refutations* (London, 1963).

Notes to Chapter 2

1. The idea is also occasionally canvassed that such an independent narrative is a scholars' fiction, e.g. Peter Ackroyd, 'The Succession Narrative (so-called)', *Int* 35 (1981), pp. 383-96. Ackroyd makes some valid points, which I should echo; but he concedes that 'there has come to be a strong consensus that (2 Sam. 9–20, 1 Kgs 1–2) do form a unit', and there are good reasons for this, set out below.

2. 4th edn, Berlin, 1878.

3. *BWANT* 3.6 = 42, Stuttgart, 1926. Rost's book is conveniently available in an English translation by M.D. Rutter and D.M. Gunn (Sheffield, 1982), with an Introduction by Edward Ball, to which I am indebted.

4. Eissfeldt, in *Orientalische Literaturzeitung* 31 (1928), cols. 801-12, sees weaknesses in Rost which are now widely accepted, e.g. the absence of a clear beginning, or the novelistic, non-eyewitness nature of the 'history'; but despite his (rather unfair) accusation that Rost's claim of an independent Narrative depends on content and not style, he does finally allow its unity, as part of J; cf. *The Old Testament, An Introduction* (ET, Oxford, 1966), p. 276.

5. *Die Ewige Dynastie* (Helsinki, 1975).

6. *Die Erzählung von der Thronfolge Davids* (*TS* 115, Zürich, 1974); *Der Erste Buch der Könige, Kapitel 1–16* (ATD 11/1, Göttingen, 1977).

7. Mostly in *Revue Biblique*, 1976.

8. *The Story of King David* (Sheffield, 1978).

9. 'The So-Called "Biography of David" in the Books of Samuel and Kings', *HTR* 44 (1951), pp. 167-69.

10. *The Succession Narrative* (London, 1968).

11. Crenshaw's original critque was 'Method in Determining Wisdom Influence upon "Historical" Literature', *JBL* 88 (1969), pp. 129-42. Whybray had in part depended on G. von Rad's analysis of the Joseph story in 'The Beginnings of Historical Writing in Ancient Israel', *The Problem of the Hexateuch and other essays* (ET, New York, 1966), pp. 166-204; Crenshaw was effective in calling into question the 'Solomonic Enlightenment'; cf. his *Old Testament Wisdom* (Atlanta, 1981/London, 1982), pp. 40, 53.

12. *The Story of King David*.

13. The widespread interest in narrative as a profound literary art has called forth a number of studies in the Succession Narrative as a story since Gunn's book. Charles Conroy's *Absalom Absalom!* (Rome, 1978) has some interesting passages, noting for example how the narrator moves from sympathy for Absalom to antipathy, while the feeling for David is greater when he is called 'David', and is distanced in ch. 19 (pp. 111-20). J.P. Fokkelman's *King David* (Assen, 1981) is a long and detailed study, with many chiastic analyses. But the very detail raises doubts, from the first

study, that on the Ziba-Mephibosheth passages. If the narrative is to be treated as a whole, then the critic has to decide who was telling the truth, and Fokkelman opts for Mephibosheth; and this leaves David 'demeaning himself' in ch. 19, 'putting on a very brave show underneath which lies fear' (p. 39). Did the narrator really intend to give us such an image of David? It seems better to see him as faced himself with two opposed traditions, and endeavouring to leave the impression of a king administering as much justice as was practicable, to the satisfaction of all.

There is a series of essays on the topic in *Interpretation* (Oct. 1981), of which James Wharton's 'A Plausible Tale' helpfully stresses the strong providentialism underlying the story: but an overview of the recent discussion of the Succession Narrative lies beyond the purview of this book.

14. *The Story of King David*, pp. 32f.

15. Such fatigue is a common feature of Matthew and Luke, who may begin a Marcan pericope by making some improvements, but later slip back into their *Vorlage*'s wording; e.g. Mt. 14.1 'Herod the tetrarch', slipping back at 14.9 to Mark's 'the king'.

16. Julian Morgenstern, 'The Cultic Setting of the "Enthronement Psalms"' *HUCA* 35 (1964), pp. 1-42, suggested that David's ascent of Olivet was similarly liturgical; but he thought the liturgical procession was part of David's historical escape from Absalom. The article is massively speculative: a pentecontad and a solar calendar, the king enacting the ritual death of Tammuz, a temple of Tammuz on the peak of Olivet, a spring New Year, a sizeable reconstruction of the events as described in 2 Samuel. The liturgical procession which I am supposing is solely in remembrance of David's sufferings.

17. At this stage I am merely following the suggestion of the 2 Samuel text: where a place is given and a event described, I am inferring a 'station' in the supposed procession. As will become clear, this suggestion can be checked against the Selahs in the Prayers, which provide a context coinciding closely with the 2 Samuel stations.

18. *Egeria's Travels*, trans. John Wilkinson (London, 1971), 35.2-36.3.

Notes to Chapter 3

1. *Psalmen* I (BKAT 15, 5th edn, Neukirchen-Vluyn, 1978), p.384.

2. *Psalm Fifty-One in the Light of Ancient Near Eastern Patternism* (Leiden, 1962), p. 227.

3. *Plants of the Bible* (Cambridge, 1982), pp. 96f.

4. *Interpreter's Dictionary of the Bible* II (Nashville, 1976), pp. 669f.

5. *Sumerische und akkadische Hymnen und Gebete*, p. 306.

6. *KP*, pp. 178f.

7. *Rediscovery*, p. 154, cited by Anderson.
8. *Scrolls*, p. 150.
9. *The Cultic Prophet in Israel's Psalmody*; pp. 412-31.
10. *From Moses to Qumran* (London, 1963), p. 96.
11. 'The Meaning of Sacrifice in the Old Testament' in *From Moses to Qumran*, pp. 67-107.
12. P.K. McCarter Jr, *II Samuel* (AB 9, New York, 1984), p. 141.
13. *Le Psautier selon Jérémie* (Paris, 1960), p. 115.

Notes to Chapter 4

1. De Vaux, *Ancient Israel*, p. 13, says how commonly 'tents' was used for homes which were in fact houses. Judg. 19.9 is an instance of this (cf. Judg. 19.29), but Judg. 20.8 shows that people were thought of as living in both houses and tents. The Deuteronomic historian imagines this situation as continuing till Solomon's death or so (1 Sam. 13.2; 4.10; 2 Sam. 18.17; 20.1; 1 Kgs 8.66; 12.16); but he knows that they lived in houses (1 Kgs 22.17) and towns (1 Kgs 22.36) by Ahab's time.
2. *PSK*, pp. 181-95.
3. *PSK*, pp. 102-106.
4. *Der 52. Psalm* (Stuttgart, 1980).
5. Cf. my *PSK*, pp. 183.
6. 'Notes on the Composition of 2 Samuel', *AJSL* 16 (1900), p. 161.
7. *II Samuel*, p. 358.
8. Against Langlamet, 'Pour ou contre Salomon?', *RB* (1976), p. 351, though Langlamet is right that 2 Sam. 13f. did not belong with the original story of the Revolt.
9. 'Notes', pp. 153, 160.
10. McCarter, *II Samuel*, p. 357.
11. *Die Erzählung. . .* , p. 40.
12. 'Pour on contre. . . ', p. 352; 'Absalom et les concubines de son père', *RB* (1977), pp. 161-209.
13. *Die Erzählung. . .* , p. 43.
14. 'Pour on contre. . . ', p. 352.
15. *Die ewige Dynastie* (Helsinki, 1975), p. 46.
16. *PSK*, pp. 123f.
17. *PSK*, pp. 139f.
18. The cave on Olivet is first referred to in the apocryphal Acts of John, 97: John has fled to the Mount of Olives on Good Friday and the Lord comes to him, lightening *the cave*. Constantine built churches over three such caves, the Holy Sepulchre, Bethlehem and Eleona.
19. In 2 Sam. 8.18 it is said that 'David's sons were priests', a statement accepted by most critics, even the reluctant McCarter (p. 255). This might

account for the otherwise surprising 'my people'; but cf. Hos. 4.6, 'my people are destroyed for lack of knowledge'; 4.12, 'My people ask counsel at their stock', etc.

20. *The Text of the Revised Psalter* (London, 1963), p. 5.

21. 'Two Little-Understood Amarna Letters from the Middle Jordan Valley', *BASOR* 89 (1943), p. 30, n. 13.

22. For the meaning of *zārîm*, cf. L.A. Snijders, 'The Meaning of *zr* in the OT', *OTS* 10 (1954), pp. 1-154.

23. *The Psalms in Israel's Worship* (Oxford, 1962), I, p. 217. (*PIW*).

24. G. Dalman, *Arbeit und Sitte in Palästina*, VII (Gütersloh, 1928-42), pp. 273ff. The *keeping* of doves cannot be proved for so early a date, but *awareness* of doves goes back deep into OT times, cf. Ps. 74.19, or 68.13 from the Prayers. There were doves on the Mount of Olives in Josephus' time; BJ 5.12.2, περιστερέων καλουμένη πέτρα.

25. McCarter, *II Samuel*, pp. 371f.

26. *II Samuel*, p. 371.

27. *The Holy Land*, (Oxford, 1980), p. 85.

28. 'Pour on contre...', pp. 352f.; 'Ahitofel et Houshaï', in Y. Avishur *et al.* ed., *Studies in the Bible and the Near East Presented to Samuel E. Loewenstamm* (Jerusalem, 1978), pp. 59ff.

29. *Die Erzählung...*, pp. 33-42.

30. The traditional (LXX) understanding is that Meribaal was son of Jonathan and grandson of Saul; but Timo Veijola argues that he was in fact Saul's son, 'David and Meribaal', *RB* 85 (1978), pp. 338-61. Fokkelman, *King David*, p. 33, calls his article 'a stunning example of diachronic hair-splitting'.

31. 'Notes', pp. 169f.

32. 'Pour on contre...', p. 353; *RB* 86 (1979), pp. 481f.

Notes to Chapter 5

1. *II Samuel*, p. 374.

2. *Biblical Commentary on the Psalms* I (ET, London, 1887), pp. 273ff.

3. *PIW*, I, p. 226.

4. 2 Sam. 7 in its present form is no doubt the composition of the D-historian, and it is a matter of debate what history may underlie the tradition of God's promise of a dynasty to David. The earliest text is (probably) 2 Sam. 23.5, 'He hath made with me an everlasting covenant'; but Mowinckel ascribed this to the religious liturgical ceremonial of the kingdom, 'Die letzten Worte Davids', *ZAW* (1927). H. Kruse, 'David's Covenant', *VT* (1985) maintains that a historical core underlies 2 Sam. 7, though most of his texts are late (e.g. those from the expansion of Ps. 89, vv. 3f., 19-52). But even if Mowinckel is right, it is surely likely that David himself would have

buttressed his claim to the kingdom with all resources he could, especially prophecy and 'liturgical ceremonial'.

5. *Contra* McCarter, *II Samuel*, p. 374.
6. 'Notes', pp. 162ff.
7. *Die Erzählung...*, pp. 34-40.
8. 'Ahitofel at Houshaï', pp. 69-73.
9. *The Story of King David*, pp. 115f.
10. *PIW*, I, p. 148f.
11. 'Studies in the Vocabulary of the OT' V, *JTS* 34 (1933), pp. 40-44.
12. M. Zohary, *Plants of the Bible*, p. 154, 'extremely common' near Jerusalem.
13. *PIW*, I, p. 213.
14. 'Psalm 58: Ein Lösungsversuch', *VT* 30 (1980), pp. 53-66.
15. *KP*, p. 47.
16. 'Notes', pp. 162ff.
17. Cf. Gunn. *The Story of King David.*
18. *PIW*, I, p. 266.
19. *KP*, p. 47.
20. Eaton, *KP*, p. 47.

Notes to Chapter 6

1. See also W.B. Dinsmoor, *The Architecture of Ancient Greece* (London, 1950), pp. 59ff.; illustration Y. Yadin, 'Excavations at Hazor', *IEJ* 9 (1959), pl.9B.
2. At Dan: cf. *PSK*, pp. 121-37.
3. 'Tel-Dan' in M. Avi-Yonah, ed., *Encyclopaedia of Archaeological Excavations in the Holy Land*, pp. 313-20.
4. For an ingenious but unconvincing theory that Abigal was Abigail, David's wife, see J.D. Levenson and B. Halpern, 'The Political Import of David's Marriages', *JBL* 99 (1980), pp. 507-18.
5. Cp. Langlamet, 'Pour ou contre...', p. 355.
6. *Ps. st.* III, pp. 65-69; IV, pp. 29-33.
7. IV, p. 33.
8. Cf. Y. Aharoni, *The Land of the Bible*, pp. 34f.
9. *PIW*, p. 59.
10. *Psalmenstudien* III (Kristiania, 1921-24), pp. 65-69.
11. Cf. K. Rupprecht, *Der Tempel von Jerusalem* : see above p. 000.
12. Z.b.S. Halevi, *The Way of Kabbalah* (London, 1976), p. 29 and *passim.*
13. Cf. T.N.D. Mettinger, *The Dethronement of Sabaoth* (Lund, 1982).
14. *PIW*, p. 266.
15. *KP*, pp. 47ff.

16. Cf. J.J. Stamm, *The Ten Commandments in Recent Research* (SBT 2.2, London, 1967), p. 99.
17. B. Gemser *et al.* ed., *Studies on Psalms*, (OTS, Leiden, 1963), p. 141f.
18. *PIW*, I, pp. 219ff.
19. *KP*, p. 49.
20. H. May & J. Day, *Oxford Bible Atlas* (3rd edn, Oxford, 1984), p. 51.
21. *PSK*, pp. 23-50.
22. *KP*, pp. 5, 10ff.
23. *KP*, pp. 50ff.
24. *Ps.*, pp. 160ff.
25. *PIW*, I, p. 219.

Notes to Chapter 7

1. G. Dalman, *Arbeit* II, pp. 179ff.
2. The Gezer calendar is usually dated around 1000 BC and is therefore our closest to a contemporary agricultural comment on 65. But it knows only eight 'months', and is therefore not too exact a comment. De Vaux, p. 184, renders 'Two months: *'sp* = Ingathering, Two months: *zr'* = Seedtime, Two months, *lqsh* = Late Seedtime. . . ' Sowing would thus be envisaged as going on from November to February, with flax-gathering and barley harvest to follow in March and April. Kraus, *Worship*, p. 38, is more vague with 'One month' for each activity.
3. *Ps. st.* II, pp. 137-40; *PIW* I, pp. 162ff.; *PIW* II, pp. 29f.
4. May & Day, *Oxford Bible Atlas*, p. 51.
5. *PSK*, pp. 144-47.
6. *The Historical Geography of the Holy Land* (25th edn, London, 1931), p. 485.
7. London, 1952
8. Cf. H.-P. Müller, 'Die Wurzeln *'iq*, *y'q* und *'uq*', *VT* 21 (1971).
9. *The Evildoers in the Book of Psalms* (Oslo, 1955), p. 14.
10. *PIW* II, pp. 27f.
11. *PIW* II, p. 28.
12. *KP*, p. 51.
13. Cf. his *WI*, pp. 152-65.
14. *Evildoers*, p. 57.
15. *PIW* II, p. 30.
16. 'The Date of Ps. 67', *VT* 12 (1962), pp. 201-205.

Notes to Chapter 8

1. *Der achtundsechzigste Psalm* (Oslo, 1953), p. 24.
2. *Der 68. Ps.*, p. 30
3. *The Problem of the Hexateuch*, pp. 79-93.
4. *Shechem* (Copenhagen, 1955), p. 166.
5. 'Yahweh and the God of the Patriarchs', *HTS* (1962), pp. 244-50.
6. Pp. 365, 370, ed. Wilberg.
7. *68. Ps.*, pp. 39f.
8. *PSK*, pp. 59-71.
9. For such questions see Albrecht Alt, 'Die Wallfahrt von Sichem nach Bethel', *Kleine Schriften* I, (Munich, 1953), pp. 81-92.
10. *PSK*, pp. 65-71.
11. *Sacral Kingship in Ancient Israel* (Cardiff, 1955), p. 73.
12. Cf. M.R. Hauge, 'Some Aspects of the Motif "The City Facing Death" of Ps. 68.21', *SJOT* 1 (1988), pp. 1-29.
13. *68. Ps.*, p. 54.
14. 'A Catalogue of Early Hebrew Lyric Poems (Psalm LXVIII) ', *HUCA* 23 (1950).
15. 'Le Psaume LXVIII', *RHR* 177 (1970), pp. 147-82.

Notes to Chapter 9

1. Cf. J. Pedersen, *Israel* (London/Oxford, 1940), *passim*.
2. There is no Selah in 69. When discussing the Passion of David in Ch. 2, I gave reasons for including elements from 2 Sam. 20, even though other interests—the concubines, Joab's treacherous murder of Amasa, Joab and the wise woman of Abel—belonged with the Succession Narrative. Perhaps a Selah has dropped out of 69; or perhaps the Passion Narrative originally covered the Absalom rebellion only, and the extension in 2 Sam. 20 did not receive liturgical recognition till the Succession Narrative took over.
3. *Die Feinde des Individuums in der israelitischen Psalmenliteratur* (Oslo, 1933), pp. 209-15.
4. *KP*, pp. 51f.
5. For a recent comment on *'ānî*, see Susan Gillingham, 'The Poor in the Psalms', *ExpT* 100 (1988), pp. 15-19.
6. 'The Value of Rhetorical Criticism in Psalm 69', *JBL* 105 (1986), pp. 577-98.
7. *Feinde*, pp. 230ff.
8. *PIW* I, p. 220.
9. *KP*, p. 54f.
10. Cf. D.W. Thomas, *Documents from Old Testament Times* (London, 1958), p. 28.

11. Johnson, *Kingship*, p. 8, followed by Anderson.
12. *PIW* II, pp. 62ff.
13. Cf. Johnson, *Kingship*, p. 9; Anderson.
14. A. Caquot, 'Psaume 72.16', *VT* 38 (1988).
15. 'Vocabulary', p. 43.

BIBLIOGRAPHY

Ackroyd, P.R., 'The Succession Narrative (so-called)', *Interpretation* 35 (1981), pp. 383-96.

Aharoni, Y., *The Land of the Bible* (2nd edn, London, 1979).

Albright, W.F., 'Two Little-Understood Amarna Letters from the Middle Jordan Valley', *BASOR* 89 (1943), pp. 29ff.

—'A Catalogue of Early Hebrew Lyric Poems (Psalm LXVIII)', *HUCA* 23 (1950), pp. 1-39.

Allen, L.C., 'The Value of Rhetorical Criticism in Psalm 69', *JBL* 105 (1986), pp. 577-98.

Alt, A., 'Die Wallfahrt von Sichem nach Bethel', *Kleine Schriften I* (Munich, 1953), pp. 81-92.

Anderson, A.A., *The Book of Psalms I-II* (New Century Bible, London, 1972).

Ball, E., 'Introduction to Rost's Work', in L. Rost, *The Succession to the Throne of David* (ET, Sheffield, 1982), pp. xv-l.

Balla, E., *Das Ich der Psalmen* (FRLANT 16, Göttingen, 1912).

Beyerlin, *Der 52. Psalm* (Stuttgart, 1980).

Biran, A., 'Tel-Dan', in M. Avi-Yonah, ed., *Encyclopedia of Archaeological Excavations in the Holy Land* I (Oxford, 1975), pp. 313-20.

Birkeland, H., *Die Feinde des Individuums in der israelitischen Psalmenliteratur* (Oslo, 1922).—*The Evildoers in the Book of Psalms* (Oslo, 1955).

Bonnard, P.E., *Le Psautier selon Jérémie* (Paris, 1960).

Brown, F., Driver, S.R., and Briggs, C.A., *A Hebrew and English Lexicon of the Old Testament* (Oxford, 1907) = BDB

Calés, J., *Le Livre des Psaumes* (Paris, 1936).

Caquot, A., 'Le Psaume LXVIII', *RHR* 177 (1970), pp. 147-82.

—'Psaume 72.16', *VT* 38 (1988), pp. 214-20.

Caspari, W., *Die Samuelbücher* (KAT 7, Leipzig, 1926).

Conroy, C.C., *Absalom Absalom!* (AB 81, Rome, 1978).

Cook, S.A., 'Notes on the Composition of 2 Samuel', *American Journal of Semitic Languages* 16 (1900), pp. 145-77.

Crenshaw, J.L., *Old Testament Wisdom* (Atlanta, 1981/London, 1982).

—'Method in determining Wisdom Influence upon "Historical" Literature', *JBL* 88 (1969), pp. 129-42.

Cross, F.M., 'Yahweh and the God of the Patriarchs', *HTR* 55 (1962), pp. 225-60.

Dahood, M., *Psalms I-III* (AB 16-17A, New York, 1965-1970).

Dalglish, E., *Psalm Fifty-One in the Light of Ancient Near Eastern Patternism* (Leiden, 1962).

Dalman, G., *Arbeit und Sitte in Palästina* I-VII (Gütersloh, 1928-1942).

Delitzsch, F., *Biblical Commentary on the Psalms* I-III (ET, London, 1887 = 4th German edn, Leipzig, 1883).

Dinsmoor, W.B., *The Architecture of Ancient Greece* (London, 1950).

Drijvers, P., *Les Psaumes* (French translation from Dutch, Paris, 1958).
Driver, G.R., 'Studies in the Vocabulary of the O.T.—V', *JTS* 34 (1933), pp. 40-44.
Duhm, B., *Die Psalmen* (HKAT, Tübingen, 1899).
Eaton, J.H., *Psalms* (Torch, London, 1967).
—*Kingship and the Psalms* (2nd edn, Sheffield, 1986).
—*The Psalms Come Alive* (London/Oxford, 1984).
Eerdmans, B.D., *The Hebrew Book of Psalms* (Leiden, 1947).
Eissfeldt, O., Review of Rost, *Thronnachfolge*, in *Orientalische Literaturzeitung* 31 (1928), cols. 801-12.
—*The Old Testament. An Introduction* (ET, Oxford, 1966 = 3rd German edn 1964).
Ewald, H., *Die Dichter des Alten Bundes* (Göttingen, 1835/40).
Fokkelman, J.P., *Narrative Art and Poetry in the Books of Samuel. I King David* (Assen, 1981).
Gillingham, S., 'The Poor in the Psalms', *ExpT* 100 (1988), pp. 15-19.
Goulder, M.D., *The Psalms of the Sons of Korah* (JSOT Suppl. 20, Sheffield, 1982).
Gressmann, H., *Die älteste Geschichtsschreibung und Prophetie Israels* (2nd edn, Göttingen, 1921).
Grossouw, W., Preface to P. Drijvers, *Les Psaumes* (Paris, 1958).
Gunkel, H., *Ausgewählte Psalmen* (Göttingen, 1904).—*Die Psalmen* (HKAT, Göttingen, 1929).
—completed by J. Begrich, *Einleitung in die Psalmen* (Göttingen, 1933).
Gunn, D.M., *The Story of King David* (JSOT Suppl. 6, Sheffield, 1978).
Halevi, Z. b.S., *The Way of Kabbalah* (London, 1976).
Hauge, M.R., 'Some Aspects of the Motif "The City Facing Death" of Ps. 68.21', *Scandinavian Journal of the OT* 1 (1988), pp. 1-29.
Hengstenberg, E.W., *Commentar über die Psalmen* (Berlin, 1842-47).
Herkenne, H., *Das Buch der Psalmen* (Bonn, 1936).
Hitzig, F., *Die Psalmen* (Leipzig, 1863-65).
Hupfeld, H., *Die Psalmen* (Halle, 1855-62).
Jacquet, L., *Les Psaumes et le coeur de l'Homme* I-III (Gembloux, 1975-79).
Jastrow, M., *A Dictionary of the Targumim, the Talmud . . . and the Midrashic Literature* (New York, 1971).
Jefferson, 'The Date of Ps. 67', *VT* 12 (1962), pp. 201-205.
Johnson, A.R., *Sacral Kingship in Ancient Israel* (Cardiff, 1955).
—*The Cultic Prophet in Israel's Psalmody* (Cardiff, 1979).
Kidner, D., *Psalm 1-72, 73-150* (London, 1973-75).
Kirkpatrick, A.F., *The Book of Psalms, I-III* (Cambridge, 1891-1901).
Kissane, E.J., *The Book of Psalms I-II* (Dublin, 1953-54).
Köhler, L., and W. Baumgartner, *Lexicon in Veteris Testamenti Libros* (Leiden, 1953).
Kraus, H.-J., *Psalmen I-II* (BKAT 15, 5th edn, Neukirchen-Vluyn, 1978); *III Theologie der Psalmen* (1979).
Kruse, H., 'David's Covenant', *VT* 35 (1985), pp. 139-64.
Langlamet, F., 'Pour ou contre Salomon?', *RB* 83 (1976), pp. 321-79, 481-529.
—'Absalom et les concubines de son père', *RB* 84 (1977), pp. 161-209.
—'Ahitofel et Houshaï', in Y. Avishur *et al.* ed., *Studies in the Bible and the Near East Presented to Samuel E. Loewenstamm* (Jerusalem, 1978), pp. 57-90.
Levenson, J.D., and B. Halpern, 'The Political Import of David's Marriages', *JBL* 99 (1980), pp. 507-18.
McCarter, P.K., Jr, *II Samuel* (AB 9, New York, 1984).
May, H.G., revised by J. Day, *Oxford Bible Atlas* (3rd edn, Oxford, 1984).

Mettinger, T.N.D., *The Dethronement of Sabaoth* (Lund, 1982).
Morgenstern, J., 'The Cultic Setting of the Enthronement Psalms', *HUCA* 35 (1964), pp. 1-42.
Mowinckel, S., *Psalmenstudien I-VI* (Kristiania, 1921-24).
—'Die letzten Worte Davids', *ZAW* 45 (1927), pp. 30-58.
—*The Psalms in Israel's Worship* (Oxford, 1962).
—*Der achtundsechzigste Psalm* (Oslo, 1953).
Müller, H.-P., 'Die Wurzel *'iq, y'q* und *'uq*', *VT* 21 (1971), pp. 556-64.
Murphy-O'Connor, J., *The Holy Land* (Oxford, 1980).
Nielsen, E., *Shechem* (Copenhagen, 1955).
Olshausen, J., *Commentar zu den Psalmen* (Leipzig, 1853).
Pedersen, J.P.E., *Israel I-IV* (London/Oxford, 1940).
Ploeg, J. van der, 'Notes sur le Psaume LXIX', in B. Gemser *et al.*, eds. *Studies on Psalms* (OTS, Leiden, 1963).
Popper, K., *The Logic of Scientific Discovery* (London, 1934).
—*Conjectures and Refutations* (London, 1963).
Pritchard, J.B., ed., *Ancient Near Eastern Texts* (2nd edn, Princeton, 1955).
Rad, G. von, *The Problem of the Hexateuch and Other Essays* (ET, New York, 1966).
Rogerson, J.W., *Old Testament Criticism in the Nineteenth Century* (London, 1984).
Rogerson, J.W. and J.W. McKay, *Psalms 1-50, 51-100, 101-150* (Cambridge Bible Commentary, 1977).
Rost, L., *Die Überlieferung von der Thronnachfolge Davids* (BWANT 42, Stuttgart, 1926).
Rowley, H.H., *From Moses to Qumran* (London, 1963).
Rupprecht, K., *Der Tempel von Jerusalem* (BZAW 144, Berlin/New York, 1977).
Schmidt, H., *Die Psalmen* (HAT, Tübingen, 1934).
Seybold, K., 'Psalm 58: Ein Lösungsversuch', *VT* 30 (1980), pp. 53-66.
Smend, R., 'Ueber das Ich der Psalmen', *ZAW* 8 (1888), pp. 49-147.
Smith, G.A. *The Historical Geography of the Holy Land* (25th edn, London, 1931).
Smith, M., 'The So-Called "Biography of David" in the Books of Samuel and Kings', *HTR* 44 (1951), pp. 167-69.
Snilders, L.A., 'The Meaning of *zr* in the OT', *OTS* 10 (1954), pp. 1-154.
Stamm, J.J., and M.E. Andrew, *The Ten Commandments in Recent Research* (SBT 2.2, London, 1961).
Thomas, D. Winton, *The Text of the Revised Psalter* (London, 1963).
—ed., *Documents from Old Testament Times* (London, 1958).
Trever, J.C., *Interpreter's Dictionary of the Bible* II (Nashville, 1976), pp. 669f.
Vaux, R. de, *Ancient Israel, Its Life and Institutions* (2nd edn, ET, London, 1965).
Veijola, T., *Die ewige Dynastie* (Helsinki, 1975).
—'David und Meribaal', *RB* 85 (1978), pp. 338-61.
Weiser, A., *The Psalms* (ET, London, 1962 = ATD 5th edn, 1959).
Wellhausen, J., rev. F. Bleek, *Einleitung in das Alte Testament* (4th edn, Berlin, 1878).
Wette, W.M.L. de, *Beiträge zur Einleitung in das Alte Testament* I-II (Halle 1806-1807).
—*Commentar über die Psalmen* (Heidelberg, 1811).
Wharton, J.A., 'A Plausible Tale', *Interpretation* 35 (1981), pp. 341-54.
Whybray, R.N., *The Succession Narrative* (London, 1968).
Wilkinson, J., *Egeria's Travels* (London, 1971).

Würthwein, E., *Die Erzählung von der Thronfolge Davids* (TS 115, Zürich, 1974).
Yadin, Y., 'Excavations at Hazor', *IEJ* 9 (1959), pp. 79ff.
Zohary, M., *Plants of the Bible* (Cambridge, 1982).

INDEX OF AUTHORS

JOURNAL FOR THE STUDY OF THE OLD TESTAMENT

Supplement Series

1 I, HE, WE AND THEY:
A LITERARY APPROACH TO ISAIAH 53
D.J.A. Clines

*2 JEWISH EXEGESIS OF THE BOOK OF RUTH
D.R.G. Beattie

*3 THE LITERARY STRUCTURE OF PSALM 2
P. Auffret

4 THANKSGIVING FOR A LIBERATED PROPHET:
AN INTERPRETATION OF ISAIAH CHAPTER 53
R.N. Whybray

5 REDATING THE EXODUS AND CONQUEST
J.J. Bimson

6 THE STORY OF KING DAVID:
GENRE AND INTERPRETATION
D.M. Gunn

7 THE SENSE OF BIBLICAL NARRATIVE I:
STRUCTURAL ANALYSES IN THE HEBREW BIBLE (2nd edition)
D. Jobling

*8 GENESIS 1-11: STUDIES IN STRUCTURE AND THEME
P.D. Miller

*9 YAHWEH AS PROSECUTOR AND JUDGE:
AN INVESTIGATION OF THE PROPHETIC LAWSUIT (RIB PATTERN)
K. Nielsen

10 THE THEME OF THE PENTATEUCH
D.J.A. Clines

*11 STUDIA BIBLICA 1978 I:
PAPERS ON OLD TESTAMENT AND RELATED THEMES
Edited by E.A. Livingstone

12 THE JUST KING:
MONARCHICAL JUDICIAL AUTHORITY IN ANCIENT ISRAEL
K.W. Whitelam

13 ISAIAH AND THE DELIVERANCE OF JERUSALEM:
A STUDY OF THE INTERPRETATION OF PROPHECY
IN THE OLD TESTAMENT
R.E. Clements

14 THE FATE OF KING SAUL:
AN INTERPRETATION OF A BIBLICAL STORY
D.M. Gunn

15 THE DEUTERONOMISTIC HISTORY
M. Noth

16 PROPHECY AND ETHICS:
ISAIAH AND THE ETHICAL TRADITIONS OF ISRAEL
E.W. Davies

17 THE ROLES OF ISRAEL'S PROPHETS
D.L. Petersen

18 THE DOUBLE REDACTION OF THE DEUTERONOMISTIC HISTORY
R.D.Nelson

19 ART AND MEANING: RHETORIC IN BIBLICAL LITERATURE
Edited by D.J.A. Clines, D.M. Gunn, & A.J. Hauser

20 THE PSALMS OF THE SONS OF KORAH
M.D. Goulder

21 COLOUR TERMS IN THE OLD TESTAMENT
A. Brenner

22 AT THE MOUNTAIN OF GOD:
STORY AND THEOLOGY IN EXODUS 32-34
R.W.L. Moberly

23 THE GLORY OF ISRAEL:
THE THEOLOGY AND PROVENIENCE OF THE ISAIAH TARGUM
B.D. Chilton

24 MIDIAN, MOAB AND EDOM:
THE HISTORY AND ARCHAEOLOGY OF LATE BRONZE AND IRON AGE JORDAN AND NORTH-WEST ARABIA
Edited by J.F.A. Sawyer & D.J.A Clines

25 THE DAMASCUS COVENANT:
AN INTERPRETATION OF THE 'DAMASCUS DOCUMENT'
P.R. Davies

26 CLASSICAL HEBREW POETRY:
A GUIDE TO ITS TECHNIQUES
W.G.E. Watson

27 PSALMODY AND PROPHECY
W.H. Bellinger

28 HOSEA: AN ISRAELITE PROPHET IN JUDEAN PERSPECTIVE
G.I. Emmerson

29 EXEGESIS AT QUMRAN:
4QFLORILEGIUM IN ITS JEWISH CONTEXT
G.J. Brooke

30 THE ESTHER SCROLL: THE STORY OF THE STORY
D.J.A. Clines

31 IN THE SHELTER OF ELYON:
ESSAYS IN HONOR OF G.W. AHLSTRÖM
Edited by W.B. Barrick & J.R. Spencer

32 THE PROPHETIC PERSONA:
JEREMIAH AND THE LANGUAGE OF THE SELF
T. Polk

33 LAW AND THEOLOGY IN DEUTERONOMY
J.G. McConville

34 THE TEMPLE SCROLL:
AN INTRODUCTION, TRANSLATION AND COMMENTARY
J. Maier

35 SAGA, LEGEND, TALE, NOVELLA, FABLE:
NARRATIVE FORMS IN OLD TESTAMENT LITERATURE
Edited by G.W. Coats

36 THE SONG OF FOURTEEN SONGS
M.D. Goulder

37 UNDERSTANDING THE WORD:
ESSAYS IN HONOR OF BERNHARD W. ANDERSON
Edited by J.T. Butler, E.W. Conrad & B.C. Ollenburger

38 SLEEP, DIVINE AND HUMAN, IN THE OLD TESTAMENT
T.H. McAlpine

39 THE SENSE OF BIBLICAL NARRATIVE II:
STRUCTURAL ANALYSES IN THE HEBREW BIBLE
D. Jobling

40 DIRECTIONS IN BIBLICAL HEBREW POETRY
Edited by E.R. Follis

41 ZION, THE CITY OF THE GREAT KING:
A THEOLOGICAL SYMBOL OF THE JERUSALEM CULT
B.C. Ollenburger

42 A WORD IN SEASON: ESSAYS IN HONOUR OF WILLIAM McKANE
Edited by J.D. Martin & P.R. Davies

43 THE CULT OF MOLEK:
A REASSESSMENT
G.C. Heider

44 THE IDENTITY OF THE INDIVIDUAL IN THE PSALMS
S.J.L. Croft

45 THE CONFESSIONS OF JEREMIAH IN CONTEXT:
SCENES OF PROPHETIC DRAMA
A.R. Diamond

46 THE BOOK OF THE JUDGES: AN INTEGRATED READING
B.G. Webb

47 THE GREEK TEXT OF JEREMIAH:
A REVISED HYPOTHESIS
S. Soderlund

48 TEXT AND CONTEXT:
OLD TESTAMENT AND SEMITIC STUDIES FOR F.C. FENSHAM
Edited by W. Claassen

49 THEOPHORIC PERSONAL NAMES IN ANCIENT HEBREW
J.D. Fowler

50 THE CHRONICLER'S HISTORY
M. Noth

51 DIVINE INITIATIVE AND HUMAN RESPONSE IN EZEKIEL
P. Joyce

52 THE CONFLICT OF FAITH AND EXPERIENCE IN THE PSALMS:
A FORM-CRITICAL AND THEOLOGICAL STUDY
C.C. Broyles

53 THE MAKING OF THE PENTATEUCH:
A METHODOLOGICAL STUDY
R.N. Whybray

54 FROM REPENTANCE TO REDEMPTION:
JEREMIAH'S THOUGHT IN TRANSITION
J. Unterman

55 THE ORIGIN TRADITION OF ANCIENT ISRAEL:
THE LITERARY FORMATION OF GENESIS AND EXODUS 1-23
T.L. Thompson

56 THE PURIFICATION OFFERING IN THE PRIESTLY LITERATURE:
ITS MEANING AND FUNCTION
N. Kiuchi

57 MOSES: HEROIC MAN, MAN OF GOD
G.W. Coats

58 THE LISTENING HEART: ESSAYS IN WISDOM AND THE PSALMS
IN HONOR OF ROLAND E. MURPHY, O. CARM.
Edited by K.G. Hoglund

59 CREATIVE BIBLICAL EXEGESIS:
CHRISTIAN AND JEWISH HERMENEUTICS THROUGH THE CENTURIES
B. Uffenheimer & H.G. Reventlow

60 HER PRICE IS BEYOND RUBIES:
THE JEWISH WOMAN IN GRAECO-ROMAN PALESTINE
L.J. Archer

61 FROM CHAOS TO RESTORATION:
AN INTEGRATIVE READING OF ISAIAH 24-27
D.G. Johnson

62 THE OLD TESTAMENT AND FOLKLORE STUDY
P.G. Kirkpatrick

63 SHILOH: A BIBLICAL CITY IN TRADITION AND HISTORY
D.G. Schley

64 TO SEE AND NOT PERCEIVE:
ISAIAH 6.9-10 IN EARLY JEWISH AND CHRISTIAN INTERPRETATION
C.A. Evans

65 THERE IS HOPE FOR A TREE:
THE TREE AS METAPHOR IN ISAIAH
K. Nielsen

66 SECRETS OF THE TIMES:
MYTH AND HISTORY IN BIBLICAL CHRONOLOGY
J. Hughes

67 ASCRIBE TO THE LORD:
BIBLICAL AND OTHER ESSAYS IN MEMORY OF PETER C. CRAIGIE
Edited by L. Eslinger & G. Taylor

68 THE TRIUMPH OF IRONY IN THE BOOK OF JUDGES
L.R. Klein

69 ZEPHANIAH, A PROPHETIC DRAMA
P.R. House

70 NARRATIVE ART IN THE BIBLE
S. Bar-Efrat

71 QOHELET AND HIS CONTRADICTIONS
M.V. Fox

72 CIRCLE OF SOVEREIGNTY:
A STORY OF STORIES IN DANIEL 1-6
D.N. Fewell

73 DAVID'S SOCIAL DRAMA:
A HOLOGRAM OF THE EARLY IRON AGE
J.W. Flanagan

74 THE STRUCTURAL ANALYSIS OF BIBLICAL AND CANAANITE POETRY
W. v.d. Meer & J.C. de Moor

75 DAVID IN LOVE AND WAR:
THE PURSUIT OF POWER IN 2 SAMUEL 10-12
R.C. Bailey

76 GOD IS KING:
UNDERSTANDING AN ISRAELITE METAPHOR
M. Brettler

77 EDOM AND THE EDOMITES
J.R. Bartlett

78 SWALLOWING THE SCROLL:
TEXTUALITY AND THE DYNAMICS OF DISCOURSE
IN EZEKIEL'S PROPHECY
E.F. Davis

79 GIBEAH:
THE SEARCH FOR A BIBLICAL CITY
P.M. Arnold

80 THE NATHAN NARRATIVES
G.H. Jones

81 ANTI-COVENANT:
COUNTER-READING WOMEN'S LIVES IN THE HEBREW BIBLE
M. Bal

82 RHETORIC AND BIBLICAL INTERPRETATION
D. Patrick & A. Scult

83 THE EARTH AND THE WATERS IN GENESIS 1 AND 2
D.T. Tsumura

84 INTO THE HANDS OF THE LIVING GOD
L. Eslinger

85 FROM CARMEL TO HOREB:
ELIJAH IN CRISIS
A.J. Hauser & R. Gregory

86 THE SYNTAX OF THE VERB IN CLASSICAL HEBREW PROSE
A. Niccacci

87 THE BIBLE IN THREE DIMENSIONS
D.J.A. Clines, S.E. Fowl & S.E. Porter

88 THE PERSUASIVE APPEAL OF THE CHRONICLER:
A RHETORICAL ANALYSIS
R.K. Duke

89 THE PROBLEM OF THE PROCESS OF TRANSMISSION IN THE PENTATEUCH
R. Rendtorff

90 BIBLICAL HEBREW IN TRANSITION:
THE LANGUAGE OF THE BOOK OF EZEKIEL
M.F. Rooker

91 THE IDEOLOGY OF RITUAL:
SPACE, TIME, AND THE STATUS IN THE PRIESTLY THEOLOGY
F.H. Gorman

92 ON HUMOUR AND THE COMIC IN THE HEBREW BIBLE
Y.T. Radday & A. Brenner

93 JOSHUA 24 AS POETIC NARRATIVE
W.T. Koopmans

94 WHAT DOES EVE DO TO HELP? AND OTHER READERLY QUESTIONS TO THE OLD TESTAMENT
D.J.A. Clines

95 GOD SAVES: LESSONS FROM THE ELISHA STORIES
R.D. Moore

96 ANNOUNCEMENTS OF PLOT IN GENESIS
L.A. Turner

97 THE UNITY OF THE TWELVE
P.R. House

98 ANCIENT CONQUEST ACCOUNTS: A STUDY IN ANCIENT NEAR EASTERN AND BIBLICAL HISTORY WRITING
K. Lawson Younger, Jr

99 WEALTH AND POVERTY IN ANCIENT ISRAEL
R.N. Whybray

100 A TRIBUTE TO GEZA VERMES. ESSAYS ON JEWISH AND CHRISTIAN LITERATURE AND HISTORY
P.R. Davies & R.T. White

* (Out of Print)